W43 £2

IPTV Crash Course

Joseph Weber

Tom Newberry

New York   Chicago   San Francisco   Lisbon
London   Madrid   Mexico City   Milan
New Delhi   San Juan   Seoul   Singapore
Sydney   Toronto

The *McGraw·Hill* Companies

Cataloging-in-Publication data is on file with the Library of Congress.

McGraw-Hill books are available at special quantity discounts to use as premiums and sales promotions, or for use in corporate training programs. For more information, please write to the Director of Special Sales, Professional Publishing, McGraw-Hill, Two Penn Plaza, New York, NY 10121-2298. Or contact your local bookstore.

IPTV Crash Course

2 3 4 5 6 7 8 9 0   DOC DOC   0 1 9 8 7

ISBN-13: 978-0-07-226392-3

ISBN-10:   0-07-226392-X

Sponsoring Editor Jane Brownlow	**Indexer** Karin Arrigoni
Editorial Supervisor Jody McKenzie	**Production Supervisor** Jean Bodeaux
Project Manager Patricia Wallenburg	**Composition** TypeWriting
Acquisitions Coordinator Jennifer Housh	**Illustration** TypeWriting
Technical Editor James Alexander	**Art Director, Cover** Anthony Landi
Copy Editor Lisa Theobald	**Cover Designer** Anthony Landi
Proofreader Paul Tyler	

To my wife, Lucy, for her patience and support in this endeavor. And to my parents who always encouraged and supported me in any pursuit.

—Joseph Weber

To my wonderful wife, Karen; our three precious kids, Corey, Katie, and Olivia; my mother; my entire family; and to the memory of my late father (who provides me with inspiration).

—Tom Newberry

ABOUT THE AUTHORS

Joseph Weber, Ph. D., has more than a decade of experience in digital video and its application to television services. He is currently Director of Product Management at personal video recorder (PVR) pioneer TiVo, Inc. Previously, as Director for Digital Video Platforms in the Strategic Assessment department for Cable Television Laboratories, Inc., Dr. Weber participated in the department's analysis of new technologies and business models that affect the cable industry. His particular focus was on the next generation of digital video technology and the transition of cable services to digital technologies. Dr. Weber also served as a product marketing manager at C-Cube Microsystems and participated in the development of consumer MPEG-2 video encoding technology, including the first PVR devices.

Dr. Weber received his Ph.D. in Electrical Engineering and Computer Science from the University of California at Berkeley. His thesis was on the measurement and use of visual motion, in particular as applied to robotics. He also holds a Master of Arts in Physics from Berkeley, an MBA from the University of Colorado at Boulder, and a Bachelor of Science in Physics from the University of Notre Dame. After completing his Ph.D., he was a lecturer at the California Institute of Technology and then at Santa Clara University, where he taught classes on video compression, image processing, and computer vision.

Thomas (Tom) Newberry has more than 12 years of experience in digital video product development (consumer electronics) and more than 26 years of industry experience. He has worked on various facets of digital television, from its earliest days. His experience spans the digital end-to-end product value chain including content creation (with Technicolor in Los Angeles), network integration (including various headends), and client/end user devices including various digital set-top box architectures (IP STB, MMDS, cable, and so on). He contributed to the design and development of various set-top boxes for usage in consumers' homes, including MPEG-based decoders, media processors, and System on a Chip (SoC) solutions. His many contributions include participation in standards bodies such as the DVD forum. Mr. Newberry received his Bachelor of Science in Electrical Engineering from the University of Michigan. He is currently an advanced product development manager at Thomson, Inc.

About the Technical Editor
James Alexander, Ph.D., has developed software and technology for video services for more than 25 years. He has created interactive television services, Internet yellow pages, digital cable television systems, and supporting software tools. He participated in the development of software standards for cable television, including the Open Cable Application Platform (OCAP). He currently leads the development of back-end systems supporting interactive services delivered via satellite television for EchoStar's Dish Network.

CONTENTS

Acknowledgments   ix

Foreword   xi

Introduction   xiii

Chapter 1   How IPTV Changes the Business of Television   1

Internet-based Television Services	5
The Driving Forces Behind IPTV	6
"Over-the-Top" IPTV Services	11
New IPTV Distributors: Telco TV	18
New Sources of Content	23
Power Shifts in the Television Service Market	24
The Shift from Distributors to Content Providers	24
More Power to Consumers	26
New Advertising Models for IPTV	27
Operational Efficiency from IPTV	30
Lower Costs of IP Equipment	30
Switched Digital Broadcast	30
IPTV for Business	32

Chapter 2   The IPTV System Model   35

Broadcast Services, Unicast Services, and Switched Digital Video	36
Facilities-based IPTV System Architecture	38
Content/Headend	41
Core Network	44
Telco Access Network	47
Cable Access Network	49
Home Network	50

Content Security	50
Internet Television	56
Internet Television System Architecture	56
Additional Applications for IPTV	61
Digital Signage	61
Enterprise Video	65
Peer-To-Peer (P2P)	66

Chapter 3   The Technology of Internet Protocol Networks   69

The Internet Protocol Suite	70
The Layer Model	71
The OSI Reference Model	73
Unicast versus Multicast	81
Multimedia over IP	85
Video Streaming Protocols	87
Encapsulating Media Data into IP Packets	93
Channel Change Delay	94

Chapter 4   The Technology of Digital Television   99

Digital Images	100
Color	101
The Advantages of Digital over Analog	104
Analog Television	105
The NTSC Scan Line	108
The NTSC Frame	109
Color in the NTSC Signal	111
The Analog Audio Signal	113
Putting It All Together: The Composite NTSC Signal	113
The Digitization of Analog Television	113
Sampling and Quantization	114
CCIR 601 Digitization Standard	116
601 Color Sampling	118
Horizontal and Vertical Sampling	119
Quantization	120
Audio Digitization	121
Digital Video Compression	125
The Need for Compression	126
Video Compression Formats	127

Contents

The Key to Compression: Removing Redundancy 129
The MPEG-2 Video Compression Standard 130
The System Layer 144
Video Formats Based on MPEG-2 152
Other Video Compression Standards 155
Chapter Summary 159

Chapter 5   IPTV in the Home   161

Digital Home Networking (DHN) 162
   DHN Transmission Mediums 164
   Emerging Trends with Computers 173
IP Client Devices for the Home 174
   Routers/Gateways 175
   IP STB Hardware Architectures 175
   IP Set-top Software Architectures 188
   Personal Computers 200
   Advanced Features for Client Devices 201
Advanced Services 203
   Triple Play 203
   Mobility 204
   Network Gaming 204
   Video Conferencing 205
   Remote Control 206
   Remote Diagnostics 206

**Chapter 6   Copy Protection and Digital
Rights Management   207**

The Need for Security 208
A Layer Model for DRM 210
   Encryption 211
   Access Control 215
   Authentication 218
   Rights Management 224
DRM System Implementations 228
   Hardware, Software, and Renewability 229
   DRM Vendors 232
Protecting Analog and Digital Outputs 233
   Digital Output Copy Protection 235
   Analog Output Copy Protection 239

Chapter 7   IPTV Standardization Efforts   241

The Internet Streaming Media Alliance   243
The Digital Video Broadcasting Project   245
The Consumer Electronics Association   247
The Alliance for Telecommunications Industry Solutions   248
Digital Living Network Alliance   248
DSL Forum   251
Internet Standards Organizations   251

**Chapter 8   The End of TV as We Know It
               or Business as Usual?   253**

New Delivery Protocol, Same Old TV?   254
   Will the Telcos Succeed?   256
   Not Just for Telcos   257
   New Over-the-Top Approaches   258
   Content Is King   260
What the Future Holds for IPTV   260

Appendix A Further Details on Channel Change Delays   263

**Appendix B IPTV Company References and
            Information Sources   271**

Glossary   279

Index   321

ACKNOWLEDGMENTS

Like many other new technologies, IPTV is rapidly changing as it evolves from a technical proof of concept to a billion dollar industry delivering new services to millions of customers. No single person could keep pace with this rapidly developing technology and business phenomenon. Therefore, I wouldn't have been able to accomplish my dream of creating this book without the help and encouragement of many individuals. I would like to acknowledge Cable Television Laboratories and in particular David Reed for their support in the early stages of this book, and TiVo and David Sandford for their continuing understanding of the responsibilities of an author. Tim Elliott, Ralph Brown, Steve Saunders, Jiong Gong, Bob Lund, and many others I'm remiss in not naming taught me new concepts that were instrumental to understanding IPTV. And I'd like to thank my volunteer editors for their help and contribution—my sister, Barbara Oglesby; my office-mate, T. Kat; and especially my wife, Lucy.

Joseph Weber
San Francisco

A book about IPTV has to acknowledge the efforts of many fine technical professionals who have worked hard to advance and promote IP technology as it applies to television. Across the world, a significant amount of research and development is underway, with difficult deadlines and pressures and scores of critically important trials proving out IPTV. My hearty thanks go out to the engineers worldwide who have broken ground before me, and to the engineers who follow.

I can't thank enough the numerous people who have proofread numerous drafts and provided me with valuable input and constructive criticism, which will hopefully provide enjoyable reading. I know that many of the people who did help out were already tapped out or overworked with their own projects, and their efforts in assisting me are truly appreciated! I'd like especially to thank Karen (my first line of editing), who by far proofread the most (and to think, an artist proofreading a technical book); Dave Weaver; Ron Johnson; Bill Lagoni; Herman Haas; Barry Weber; Herb Jones; Keith Broerman; Keith Wehmeyer; Jason Shostrand; Ed Graczyk; and Kris Mohan. I would also like to thank the numerous professionals at Thomson who helped enable this project for me, worked with me on numerous IPTV-related projects, or who got me involved in IPTV—specifically, Bruce Tenerowicz, John Stewart, Kumar Ramaswamy, Mike Deiss, Andy Flickner, and the entire IP STB team.

Tom Newberry
Westfield, Indiana

We'd both like to thank Jane Brownlow, Jenni Housh, and the McGraw-Hill team for their help and dedication in creating this manuscript. Jenni and Jane were always there supporting us, leading us through the quagmire, pushing and prodding us to maintain schedule, and ensuring a successful project.

We also want to thank Enrique Rodriguez from Microsoft for providing a foreword for this book.

Joe and Tom
October 2006

FOREWORD

TV dramatically changed the way we live, work, and learn. Today, with the advent of Internet Protocol TV (IPTV), brought about by the combination of IP technology and two-way broadband networks, the TV experience is undergoing a fundamental shift that will drive even more exciting changes in the coming years.

A leading indicator of this transformation can be found by examining the evolution of the personal computer (PC). When PCs first found their way into our homes in the 1980s, they delivered value by helping us perform isolated tasks like games, word processing, and personal finance. Then in the 1990s with the proliferation of the Internet, the PC developed into a much more useful device that connected us to the world. It became part of a global computer network, but more importantly, it became a channel for social networking, new ways to communicate, and delivered new experiences that today we all take for granted. The PC not only became connected, it connected us.

In many ways, the TV today is like the PC 25 years ago; it is primarily a standalone device that certainly delivers a lot of entertainment value. We spend an extraordinary amount of time watching, flipping through channels, and discussing what's on with friends and family. Television today is still mostly a linear, one-dimensional, one size fits all experience. We are passive recipients of whatever is being delivered or pushed to us. Most of us still have limited choice of what we watch, when we watch it, and how we watch it.

Does TV have the potential to be far better? The answer is most certainly "yes". Progress in broadband adoption and advances in a range of important technologies are finally enabling the TV to become *connected*, *interactive,* and *personalized*. The 1.6 billion television sets in the world become not only "receivers" of programming signals, they become connected devices that give us more control over our entertainment and enable new connected entertainment experiences both inside and outside the home.

For consumers, IPTV means a better, more personalized TV experience with connected services tailored to their individual tastes. They can have access to virtually limitless content: from the local football game or soccer match, to Japanese news programming or their favorite telenovela; from personal video uploaded by friends and family, to easily finding and watching that special episode from their favorite TV show as a child. This programming won't be limited to viewing just on the TV but will be available on a range of devices that can be used in the home or on the go. To content providers and advertisers, IPTV enables new ways for storytelling, a deeper engagement with the viewer, and a platform for new forms of more valuable advertising. To network operators, IPTV is the cornerstone of a rich suite of services that will increase satisfaction and loyalty. People in the industry often refer to this suite as the "triple-" or "quadruple-play." Bundling multiple services over a single network certainly delivers a lot of value to operators and consumers alike, but that's just the beginning. The real transformation will come as video, voice, broadband, mobile, and other services are integrated to enable new services and consumer experiences that are not available today. This service-level integration—we call it the "single play"—will change the ground rules for everyone involved in the communications and entertainment industries.

While Telcos are the early movers today, IPTV is not just a telecommunications industry phenomenon. It represents the future of television for all service providers and the excitement it is generating in the industry is well deserved. Excitement is good, but hype is not, and we should all keep in mind that transformative technologies like this evolve over time. Historically our industry tends to overestimate the possibilities that new technologies can bring in the near term and underestimate them over the long term.

We are just beginning to scratch the surface of the impact IPTV will have on the telecommunications and entertainment industries. This book explores the steps toward making IPTV a reality and unleashing its potential and is a must-read for anyone involved in the IPTV industry. The next few years promise to be a fun ride with many unexpected twists and turns. Along the way, however, one thing is certain: the TV experience for many of us will change more in the next five years than it has in the past fifty.

—Enrique Rodriguez, Corporate Vice President
Microsoft TV Division, Microsoft Corporation

INTRODUCTION

We are in the midst of two technological revolutions that are having a profound impact on society. The first and more obvious one is the rapid increase in the use of the Internet for information, commerce, and entertainment. Through the Internet, people can now select news of interest to them and receive it whenever they request it. Personalization and on-demand are now common elements of information and news. The Internet has also opened up the truly global marketplace, allowing direct connections between consumers and retailers like never before, again by bringing more personalization and on-demand qualities to commerce.

The second, perhaps less conspicuous revolution is the digitization of television. While initially digital television allows for better picture quality and high definition images, ultimately the digitization of television will bring about the same changes that the Internet brought to information: on-demand service and personalization. The recent introduction of digital video recorders such as TiVo is made possible by the digitization of television. As the infrastructure for digital television grows, more and more people will be able to receive video content on-demand and personalized to their tastes.

Internet Protocol Television (IPTV), the convergence of these two technological revolutions, promises yet another revolution in how we find, select, and consume our digital entertainment. Both television and the Internet were the result of technological innovations that led to new products and services, which brought about major sociological and economic changes. Few could argue the significant impact on society caused by both technologies. Both have redefined how people get information and entertain themselves. Just as television (in the decades since its introduction) has brought about profound changes to our society (for better or for worse), the Internet has also made a huge impact on how people live. IPTV may yet again bring about profound changes to society.

Shortly after the rise in popular usage of the Internet and the wide recognition of its potential to change the human experience as television did, the concept of a "convergence" of the computer experience (or, more accurately, the Internet experience) with television was proposed. Because of the failure of earlier attempts to market the concept of a convergence of the two technologies, perhaps coincidental with the implosion of the Internet bubble, the commonly held belief seemed to be that the two technologies were destined to remain separate, at least for the short term.

But away from the distractions of IPOs and outlandish business models, the technology layers of the Internet and television have indeed been converging (as shown in the following illustration). While initially different and distinct, gradually the technology underlying both television and the Internet is coming together. As television services migrate toward digital technology and broadband Internet services become more pervasive, the opportunity for IPTV to emerge as a new business model is shaping and developing.

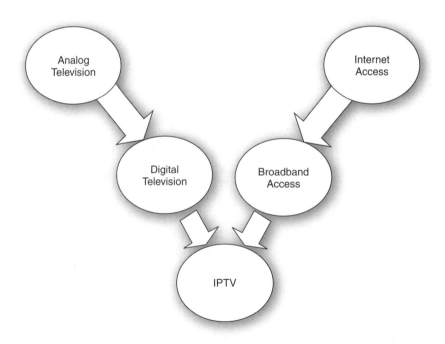

This convergence is perhaps nowhere more apparent than in the networks created by cable television and telephone operators, as they both continue to expand their telephone, television, and Internet service offerings. While initially creating separate networks for traditional telephony, television, and Internet services, network operators such as the cable companies and telephony companies quickly realized that certain elements of their system could be interoperable, therefore reducing the need and expense for separate equipment. In fact, many parts of a modern cable and telephone network are similar because digital data is handled in a manner that is agnostic to its ultimate service type. Digital data is handled like all Internet traffic, by utilizing Internet Protocol (IP) packets. Only as the data approaches the consumer's house, or in some cases when it reaches the final destination in the home—be it a telephone, computer, or television—does the data resolve itself into the telephony, Internet, or television service for which it was originated.

A lot of excitement today centers on the convergence of television and Internet services into IPTV. Major telephone companies around the world are investing billions of dollars to roll out IPTV services. Internet search companies such as Google and Yahoo! have deployed their own IPTV services, extending their businesses way beyond a search for websites on the Internet. New services and business models using IPTV are being developed even as you read this book.

The Internet Revolution

The Internet has come a long way from its modest beginnings connecting a few scientific and military laboratories. While initially providing a way for scientists to share correspondence (later called e-mail) and data, the World Wide Web built on the Internet grew rapidly and has become an influence on society, commerce, and even politics.

Today, people all over the world from all walks of life connect to and use the Internet. The number of people with fast (that is, broadband) Internet connections has grown phenomenally in just two decades and continues to grow at incredible rates. The following table (from eMarketer website, March 2004) shows the percentage of households in various countries around the world with broadband access. The number of households with any form of Internet access is even higher.

Country	Percentage of Households with Broadband Access to the Internet
South Korea	70.5
Hong Kong	50.3
United States	45.1
Taiwan	43.2
Canada	36.2

The growth of Internet services comes from both demand-side and supply-side forces. On the demand side is people's desire to connect, to receive and share information instantly among the growing number of people and companies connected via the Internet. On the supply side of the equation, companies have realized the enormous potential for reaching large, targeted audiences of customers. Amazon, eBay, and other online businesses developed rapidly to tap into this market. Online holiday shoppers spent more than $30 billion during the 2005 holiday season, up 30 percent from 2004. This was on top of the 28 percent increase in online sales that the year 2004 saw over 2003 (Goldman, Sachs & Co., Harris Interactive, and Nielsen//NetRatings' Holiday eSpending Report).

The Internet revolution was made possible only by the earlier revolution of the personal computer. Once a sufficient number of people had access to and used PCs, the Internet developed and emerged rapidly as a popular communications medium. Metcalf's Law states that the economic value of a network is proportional to the square of the number of people who are part of that network. Therefore, the value of the Internet really took off as PC usage moved out of the smaller scientific communities and into the mainstream. With the phenomenal growth in the number of people online, it is easy to understand how a company like Google can be valued at more than $100 billion after only a few short years.

As the capabilities of computers (the end devices of the World Wide Web providing the interface to consumers) advance, the type and volume of content shared on the Internet has changed from simple text and still pictures to multimedia entertainment. E-mail is quickly being replaced by audio and video content as the primary reason people use the Web. While still in the early stages, watching simple video on the Web forms the basis of the convergence between the Internet and television.

The Digital Television Revolution

The technology behind analog television, the National Television System Committee (NTSC) standard, is more than 50 years old and has changed little during that time. The last major technological innovation in television was the introduction of color TV in the 1950s. Digital television brings about a fundamental change in the way television is produced, edited, broadcast, and displayed. As such, it requires massive infrastructure changes for creating and transmitting digital signals, along with a replacement of analog television sets (more than 200 million in the US alone) with devices capable of receiving the digital signals. The transition from analog to digital television began in the 1990s and continues today. The Federal Communications Commission (FCC) has reaffirmed its commitment to end analog television broadcasts in the US by December 2008.

Digital television has a number of distinct advantages over analog television. Some of those advantages are directly apparent to the viewer, while others provide benefits to content producers, television broadcasters, and cable operators. Following are some of the perceived benefits of digital television to consumers:

- **Improved video quality.** Digital television has a number of features that can improve image quality over analog television. These include better color reproduction, higher pixel resolution, progressive image frames, and fewer transmission artifacts such as ghosting or snow. High Definition Television (HDTV) offers more than six times the image resolution of current standard definition analog television.

- **More audio options.** In addition to improved digital audio quality, digital television can also deliver multichannel audio such as surround sound, as well as multiple language options for each program.

- **Interoperability with PCs.** As part of the convergence with computer technology, digital television can be received, viewed, and manipulated not only on digital televisions but also on PCs and other digital consumer electronics devices.

- **Random access storage.** The compression of digital television data allows for storage of video programs on a digital storage medium such as hard disk drives. This has advantages over linear storage such as video tape because any portion of the program can be accessed instantly without the need for fast forwarding or rewinding.

- **Time shifting.** Just one of the new applications possible with digital television and random access storage is the ability to pause live broadcast television or perform your own instant replay at any time. TiVo pioneered the market for personal video recorders (PVRs) and introduced people to a whole new way of enjoying television.

As with the phenomenal growth of broadband adoption and other Internet access, consumer adoption of digital television is also dramatic. DVD players saw one of the fastest adoption rates of any new consumer electronics device. In only about five years, the percentage of homes in the US with DVD players went from zero to about 50 percent. HDTVs, although showing much slower growth rates than DVD players, are also being widely adopted by consumers. According to a 2005 report from In-Stat on the status of HDTV service, the end of 2005 saw more than 15 million homes worldwide with an HDTV, with projections of more than 50 million homes by 2009. (The statistics on DVD sales are from a Money/CNN online article from September 23, 2004: http://money.cnn.com/2004/09/15/news/fortune500/dvds/. The numbers on HDTV households data comes from the 2005 In-Stat publication "Got HD? High-Def TV Service Now in Over 10 Million Homes" [www.instat.com]).

It is not just the consumer who benefits from digital television technology. Content creators and distributors can also take advantage of the technology in the following ways:

- **More efficient use of bandwidth.** Television service providers can offer multiple digital channels within the same amount of bandwidth used by just one analog television channel. Alternatively, service providers can offer new services (such as video on demand) by using the freed bandwidth.

- **Less storage requirements.** Digital compression allows for storing more content with less space (or bits). This would enable service providers to amass large amounts of content and make it available on demand to consumers.

- **Easier, cleaner splicing.** Digital splicing allows content providers and advertisers to insert and combine program and advertising elements more easily. Customized and targeted advertisements are easier to create, with less expensive equipment and fewer artifacts than analog splicing equipment.

- **Archive management.** Content stored digitally is easier to manage than a physical library of tapes and catalogs. Digital content can be searched, cataloged, and indexed much easier than analog content.

- **Multi-use hardware.** The convergence of digital television with the Internet (the focus of this book) allows transport equipment to be multifunctional for both video and data services. This allows the service provider to offer expanded mixed services such as two-way interactive television using the same equipment, ultimately lowering the cost of deploying these new services.

DTV Applications

The technology behind digital television not only provides advantages to users and service providers, but it has also enabled new applications and delivery options. Earlier we mentioned the development of DVR devices from TiVo and other companies as an example of the new market opportunities that have developed because of the transition to digital television. Following are some of the new services developed because of the capabilities of digital television:

- **Digital cable.** Digital cable service takes advantage of digital television to offer better picture quality and many more channels over analog cable. Cable operators started offering this service in the 1990s, and it is currently available across the US.

- **Satellite broadcasters.** Digital television and the associated compression technologies enabled the development of digital broadcast satellite (DBS) services such as DirecTV and EchoStar (Dish Network). Both DBS and digital cable share the same MPEG-2 digital video compression standard for digital content.

- **DVD video.** DVDs are based on the same digital compression technology used by digital cable and DBS. DVDs have quickly replaced analog videotapes as the choice for consumer video. In fact, according to an A.G. Edwards report in 2002, the DVD has experienced the fastest adoption rate of any consumer electronics device to date. As mentioned, DVD and other random access storage formats can be used with digital media, as it allows for easier access to parts of the content.

- **Video CD.** While little known in the Western world, a lower cost alternative to DVD called Video CD was the leading playback format throughout Asia before DVDs were widely available in the West. In fact, many homes in China went directly to digital video and skipped the analog tape-based VCR altogether.

- **DV camcorders.** Digital video camcorders are smaller, lighter, and can store more content than analog camcorders. Also, the random access nature of the storage medium makes it possible to perform video editing with a PC. A number of successful television and movie products make use of PCs in production.

- **Digital video recorders.** Sometimes called a "VCR on steroids," digital video recorders (DVRs) take advantage of the nature of digital television not only to make it easier to record your favorite programs, but to perform other functions not previously possible with analog recording. One of those is the ability to "timeshift" live television—to pause or rewind not only a previously recorded program but also one that is being broadcast live. As you will see later in this book, digital television services include electronic program guides and metadata that make it easier to locate and select content of interest. This is one of the fundamental features of DVRs as well.

IPTV: The Convergence of Digital Television and the Internet

We define IPTV as the creation of a video service by means of serving digital audio and video over IP. With this broad definition, IPTV has many different flavors and applications. IPTV can be a consumer in his or her home, downloading content and streaming audio and video from one device to another within the home. IPTV can be a professional video service operator (such as a large telephone company), creating a multi-channel television service over a multibillion-dollar broadband network to compete with local cable or satellite companies. IPTV can be applied to a Business-to-Business (B2B) video application for training material, teleconferencing, or even in the content creation field where video content is streamed between the client and supplier. IPTV can be applied to the education, financial, and medical fields, streaming live classes or operations over a broadband connection. IPTV can be a Business-to-Consumer (B2C) application where video material can be copied over a broadband connection and stored on a hard drive for playback at a later time. These are just some of the applications to which IPTV can be applied. As IPTV evolves and the technical and business communities understand and embrace it, the possibilities are endless.

The technology behind IPTV is the blending of digital media and IP standards. Digital television services are based on the digitization of analog signals: the act of taking an analog video source (such as camera or film) and digitizing it into a (very long) string of 1s and 0s. This digital bitstream is then compressed with a compression algorithm to make it of manageable size. Existing digital television services broadcast these bitstreams to consumers using a number of (surprisingly) analog technologies, such as broadcasting from radio towers to roof antennas or sending down a coaxial cable to your home. IPTV uses the purely digital method of delivering data defined in IP for delivering digital television services. As you will see later, IP is far from ideal for this purpose and in fact was created for a completely different type of delivery service. However, the convergence of these two technologies leads to new service elements that make it worth overcoming the inherent limitations.

Of course, streaming video over the Internet to PCs has been going on for years. These early efforts typically involved content of a different nature than entertainment television and are displayed on devices (typically a PC) usually not found in a living room. IPTV is about streaming entertainment quality content to your primary viewing device—the TV—and not a computer monitor. Most consumers prefer to watch TV in their living room, in a laid-back experience on the sofa from 10 feet way. Typical computer usage is a "lean forward" experience from just a few feet away in your home office.

The Switch to Digital

There is no doubt that the introduction of digital TV technology affected the landscape of the TV service business. The satellite broadcast industry owes its existence to the technology, which makes it economically feasible to broadcast many high-value channels to consumers' homes from space. The cable industry also adopted the technology, to a lesser extent, and incorporated digital video into their commercial offerings. While having a tremendous impact on the service provider market by introducing competition via an alternative to cable in DBS, digital TV technology did not have as wide an impact on the industry as a whole that IPTV will. IPTV will affect not only distribution but also the creation and advertising markets as well. It will blur the hard distinction between content creators and distributors, introduce new entrants that are both, and change the flow of advertising dollars throughout.

New IPTV Services

The bidirectional nature of a cable network allows it to offer content on demand to the consumer, as with video on demand (VOD) services from cable operators today. IPTV (much like cable) relies on a bidirectional network. In this way, IPTV can offer television services that include the following:

- Traditional broadcast (linear) channels
- Video on demand
- Peer-to-peer (file sharing) services
- Interactive and personalized television
- Customized programming and advertising

Interactive television has been discussed for many years but its development has so far met with limited results. Many companies have invested millions more dollars than they have made on interactive services or other devices that offer interactive components to television. Many people believe that interactive TV will never be a successful business because TV is fundamentally a passive form of recreation. Active interactivity is anathema to the couch potato and passive appeal of TV. However, interactive TV may meet its success when it is used to create personalized TV. This form of interactive TV results in content and advertising tailored to the viewer. It uses interactivity to alter the content subtly and deliver it in a way that the user (or the advertiser) finds most effective. Through limited interaction with your TV, the experience will become customized. This goes beyond content on demand to personalized content, delivered on demand.

One goal of this book is to examine the various business models enabled by IPTV and how those business models will affect existing services. As consumers start receiving their TV entertainment over the Internet, will it fundamentally alter how we experience TV, or will it be the same 1950s experience with a new name? Will these new services generate additional revenue for entertainment services or will they simply shift from incumbent service providers to new ones? Will the investors who recently gave an IPTV startup called Sling Media $46.6 million see a return on their investment? Are the CEOs of AT&T and Verizon making a sure bet when they commit almost $10 billion to building an IPTV service to compete with cable and satellite? While this book cannot answer these questions directly, we hope to provide some insight into how they might be answered.

About This Book

IPTV Crash Course is an introduction and a reference for anyone who wants to understand how IPTV works and the underlining technology. This book also covers some of the business aspects of IPTV and discusses how IPTV may evolve to shape the future of the television industry.

Chapter 1, "How IPTV Changes the Business of Television," describes various IPTV business models and how they relate to current incumbent video services. This chapter explores the entrance of telephone companies into the video broadcast business, as well as new and revolutionary approaches that may challenge both incumbents and telephone companies (Telcos).

Chapter 2, "The IPTV System Model," breaks down the system components required for an IPTV system. This includes system elements from facilities-based broadcast systems such as Telcos, to "over-the-top" Internet-based video services.

Chapter 3, "The Technology of Internet Protocol Networks," covers the technology of Internet protocols and how they are utilized by IPTV networks and services. This chapter includes a discussion of multicast and unicast services and the Internet protocols that enable them.

Chapter 4, "The Technology of Digital Television," explains the technical details associated with digital audio and video. This includes a historical background of analog video, how it is converted into digital video, and the digital compression required for efficient transport of digital video signals.

Chapter 5, "IPTV in the Home," explores how IPTV can be utilized within consumers' homes. It details IP networking and how networked devices operate within the home, including a breakdown of popular home networking technologies. It also provides a thorough description of IP set-top boxes—the various hardware, software, and system architectures often utilized.

Chapter 6, "Copy Protection and Digital Rights Management," investigates the various components that protect valuable content within a networked environment. Several copy protection and digital rights management (DRM) approaches are discussed.

Chapter 7, "IPTV Standardization Efforts," provides an overview of how standards bodies worldwide are approaching IPTV and providing specifications that enable interoperability and eventually lower costs to network operators and consumers.

Chapter 8, "The End of TV as We Know it or Business as Usual?," is a peek into the future, with the authors' predictions of how IPTV may affect TV enjoyment in the years ahead.

Appendix A, "Further Details on Channel Change Delays," provides additional details into the critical aspect of channel change delay in IPTV systems.

Appendix B, "IPTV Company References and Information Sources," contains references to various companies and resources applicable to IPTV technology. This includes company websites where additional information can be found for their products and services.

The glossary provides definitions for many of the acronyms and terms used in this book and within the IPTV community.

How IPTV Changes the Business of Television

The delivery of television and movie services over the Internet promises to revolutionize almost every component of the television industry. It will change how content is created and distributed and how advertisers will use the medium to reach their intended audience. Just as the Internet has changed the way we shop, read the news, and personally interact, television services over the Internet will change how we integrate television entertainment into our daily lives. Decades-old business models will have to change as a result of the technological shift to IPTV.

There appear to be several different definitions of IPTV used in the press and by different industries. Definitions range from a single person using a webcam to produce a video blog to multibillion-dollar investments in new services by telephone operators. While fundamentally the technology behind IPTV is the distribution of digital television signals using Internet Protocols (IP), its application can IPTV greatly. We hope to help disambiguate the various uses of the term IPTV based on how the technology is applied by businesses and individuals.

For some, IPTV is a medium for self-publishing and a cultural shift to personalized content, while for others it is an opportunity to compete with incumbent pay-television service providers. While the technology is fundamentally the same, how it is applied, the business model behind the applications, and how they affect the current business of television varies greatly.

To understand how IPTV changes the business of television we need to first discuss the current business of television. The television service industry can be divided roughly into content owners and creators, content distributors, and advertisers, as represented in Figure 1-1. The owners and creators are the major networks (ABC, CBS, and so on), the cable networks (CNN, HBO, and so on), and the movie studios (otherwise known collectively as *Hollywood*). In general, the content owners do not sell their content directly to consumers. Instead, the content is aggregated, packaged and sold to consumers via content distributors or multichannel video program distribution (MVPD) services. Today these are primarily the local TV broadcast stations (who may be owned by the major networks), cable operators (who may own cable networks), and direct broadcast satellite (DBS) operators, namely DirecTV and EchoStar in North America. According to the J.D. Power and Associates 2006 Residential Cable/Satellite TV Satisfaction Study, 29% of US households receive their television service exclusively from a DBS and 58% exclusively from a cable operator. While the exact numbers seem to vary slightly, it is clear that a large majority of households in the US receive television services from a MVPD.

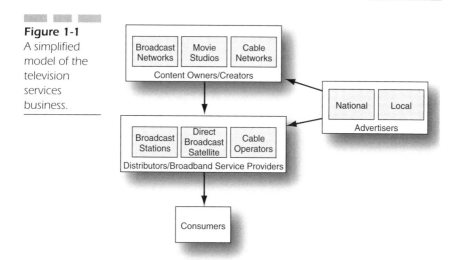

Figure 1-1
A simplified model of the television services business.

Note: While originally only distributed on cable, today cable networks are distributed on satellite, and soon IPTV networks will distribute programming as well. Despite this evolution away from exclusive cable distribution, the historical name *cable network* has remained.

Distributors make it possible for content creators to get their product to the consumer. It would not make economic sense for each content creator and each movie studio to create its own network to reach directly into millions of households; therefore they must rely on a few common distributor networks to deliver their product to the consumer. The owner-distributor relationship can be both adversarial and codependent as content owners depend on distributors to get their content to consumers and distributors depend on content owners to provide sufficient content to entice consumers to pay for the service. Until the introduction of DBS as a viable competitor, cable operators were virtual monopolies of distribution, sometimes holding the fate of a new network in their hands. A new network that hoped to reach the millions of households necessary for it to be economically viable was sometimes forced to give up significant percentages of the company and even executive control to the cable operators in exchange for the opportunity to reach an audience.

Of course, the model in Figure 1-1 is extremely simplified. Some content owners are also distributors, such as some cable operators who also hold majority ownership in cable networks. For example, the largest cable operator in the US, Comcast, owns a series of network channels including the Golf Channel and OLN (previously Outdoor Life Network). Comcast recently made a bid to purchase Disney, which would have made the corporation a major content owner indeed. NBC Universal is a content creator, broadcaster, and theme park operator as well. With IPTV, the lines might get even more blurred as the business model changes. With an Internet distribution model, content creators for the first time would have an economical delivery system that could offer content directly, bypassing the distributor.

Despite the competition between cable and DBS, television service offerings from both appear the same to the consumer. Cable and DBS offer basically the same channels in similar packages. However, a fundamental difference between cable and satellite networks is the fact that cable has a bidirectional network and satellite does not. Within the bidirectional cable network are two directions of communication: downstream and upstream. The downstream communication (or downstream traffic) consists of the typical broadcast video channels, which are transmitted to all of the customers on the common cable. For digital cable, this also includes digital bitstreams in the MPEG-2 format that are broadcast to cable set-top box (STB) devices. These devices convert the signals back to analog to display on the television.

Upstream communication is just the opposite of downstream communication. Upstream traffic occurs when the client STB needs to send data back to the network devices. The fact that the cable network is bidirectional will be a major advantage as television services become interactive as they are in IPTV. This allows cable operators to offer video on demand (VOD) and other interactive services. Because the cable client can send information back up the network, the user can control the content they watch instead of having to watch whatever is being broadcast at that time. With this capability, the cable operator can offer customers content beyond broadcast or linear channels. It can also add VCR functionality, allowing viewers to fast forward, pause, and rewind programs that they are watching. This bidirectional aspect of a network is fundamental to IPTV and forms the basis for many of its industry-changing attributes.

Another major component of the television industry is commercial advertising. Content creators, in particular the major networks, sell billions of dollars' worth of commercial advertising space. The distributors, both cable and satellite, also participate in selling commercial advertising space. Instead of paying for the content with all of the advertising space already filled, distributors barter with content creators for rights to sell some of the commercial spots. The content creator thus sells to the distributor both the rights to broadcast a program as well as the rights to sell some of the commercial spots within the program. These advertising slots made available to distributors are also called *avails*. Typically the content creators use the commercial slots they keep to sell national advertising that reaches millions of homes, while distributors will offer their avails to local advertisers to reach more targeted audiences. The interactive and digital nature of IPTV will make new advertising models possible.

Let's look at some of the ways IPTV is changing the business models—in particular, how the content creator–distributor model may be affected, how new entrants into the field will alter the business landscape, and finally how the advertising model will change as a result of IPTV.

Internet-based Television Services

As the Internet continues its phenomenal growth, it will increasingly become the source of digital television services. These offerings may take a familiar form such as that provided by cable and satellite operators today. Telephone operators have already started to deploy IP-based television services that are almost identical to existing pay-TV services. Subscribers will pay monthly fees for the ability to view a bundle of broadcast channels. Movielink, CinemaNow, and Starz have all launched Internet-based movies on-demand services that offer rental windows very similar to cable-based VOD services today.

On the other hand, IPTV services could look very different from the traditional models, offering per-program purchases or entirely non-broadcast on-demand programming. Until these new business models are proven, expect the large telephone operators and online movie services to continue to develop "me-too" IPTV services that look similar to existing cable and satellite offerings. Considering the billions of dollars that the major telephone network operators are expected to spend to provide television services, it is perhaps understandable that they would opt for a proven model, at least in the beginning.

We segment the market for Internet-distributed television services into three categories: over-the-top service providers, new distributors, and new content providers. An over-the-top service provider uses the existing broadband service of a distributor, either a cable operator or telephone operator, to provide a television service. The service rides on top of the broadband service with, or in most cases without, the broadband provider's involvement. Examples include the iTunes video service or Movielink movie download service. IPTV distributors set up their own IP-based broadband network and use it as a new distribution channel for television content. Traditional telephone operators such as Verizon and AT&T are currently deploying such networks as alternatives to cable and satellite. Finally, IPTV may provide an opportunity for a new breed of content providers. The personalized, on-demand nature of the Internet may extend to television services and therefore enable the proliferation of specific, niche content tailored to individual tastes. Google Video, for example, allows anyone to create video content and make it available to the broadband audience.

The various IPTV service models are summarized in Table 1-1.

Table 1-1 Various IPTV Service Models

IPTV Service Model	Proponents	Examples
New distributors	Telephone network operators	Verizon, AT&T/SBC
Personalized content	Web content aggregators	Google, Yahoo!, YouTube
Over-the-top services	Content owners and new video aggregators	iTunes, Movielink, ABC.com

The relationships among IPTV service models and existing television industry components are illustrated in Figure 1-2. New distributors will aggregate content from content owners and using their own networks deliver it directly to consumers, while over-the-top service providers will use existing broadband networks to deliver aggregated content. New personalized content providers aggregate niche and user-generated content and provide it over existing broadband networks. We will examine each of these new service models in more detail in this chapter.

The Driving Forces Behind IPTV

Regardless of the business model used, Internet-based services are feasible because of the confluence of a number of technical and other drivers.

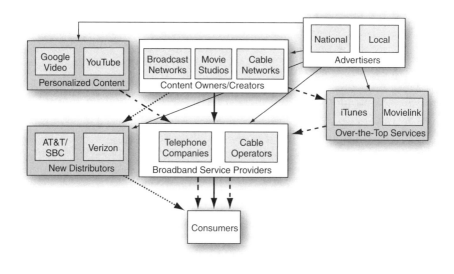

Figure 1-2

Relationships among different IPTV service models and existing television industry components.

Advances in technology have made it possible to use the Internet for distribution of television services, and growth in the broadband subscriber base has created a ready market of potential customers. Some of the trends that are enabling IPTV services are

- The growth of the broadband Internet subscriber base
- Ever increasing broadband speeds
- Continuing improvement in video compression efficiency
- Cost reductions in digital video equipment components

Broadband Subscriber Growth   The number of households with broadband Internet access, and therefore the number of potential IPTV services customers, continues to grow. According to Point Topic's World Broadband Statistics report for 2006 there were over 26 million broadband subscribers in North America, with about 54 percent of them getting service from their cable provider and the other 46 percent from DSL or other providers. Worldwide, almost 200 million broadband subscribers exist, with the majority of subscribers outside of the US receiving service from DSL and their local telephone operator.

Each broadband subscriber represents a potential customer for an IPTV service. IPTV deployments by telephone system operators will wire even more homes with high-speed broadband service. While some indications point to a slowing trend in broadband growth, from the phenomenal growth rates of 30 to 50 percent per year to more sustainable rates, it still represents a large and quickly expanding potential market for IPTV services.

Increasing Broadband Speeds   In addition to the number of broadband subscribers, the effective bitrates of their service continues to grow. Higher bitrates make it easier for IPTV service providers to deliver content quickly and with higher quality. The nature of digital video compression requires broadband throughput (bitrate) on the order of 1.5 to 8 million bits per second (Mbps) for a high quality standard definition program, and 5 to 19 Mbps for a high definition program. For an IPTV service to deliver content in real-time, the continuous broadband bandwidth must be higher than these values. Any real-time live broadcast television service requires at least this much bandwidth.

As the bitrate of the broadband service increases, more services can be delivered simultaneously. A broadcast television service, such as the one MVPDs currently provide, requires sufficient bandwidth to deliver multiple television programs at once to possibly multiple televisions within the home. Figure 1-3 shows that as the bitrate of a broadband service increases, it is able to deliver more television channels simultaneously. Initially the bitrate is sufficient to deliver only one or two standard definition programs in real-time, but as the bandwidth increases, high definition programs can also be delivered. If the broadband service's bitrate is lower than these numbers, the video content must be downloaded to the user's home at a slower than real-time rate. This delay would be acceptable only for on-demand movies and other services that don't require immediate viewing.

The technical distinction between real-time and non-real-time delivery has consequences to the two categories of IPTV services. Over-the-top services, which are dependent on the networks of broadband providers, may not get the bandwidth required for broadcast services. Without sufficient bandwidth, the video signal would be discontinuous and not play back in real-time. And when the bandwidth is only slightly larger than that required, the service provider has no control over the quality of the signal as it travels over someone else's network. Parts of the signal may get delayed or lost as it makes its way to the subscriber's home. Therefore, over-the-top IPTV service providers may be limited to

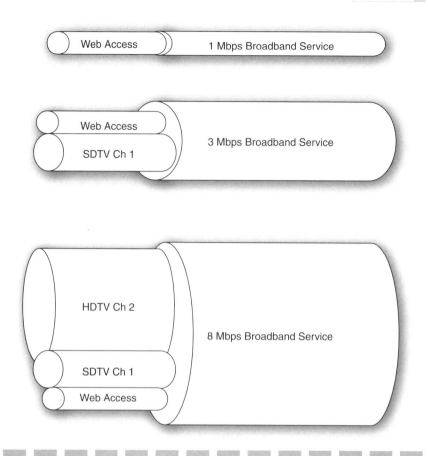

Figure 1-3

As the bitrate of a broadband service increases, more standard definition and high definition services can be delivered in real-time. If the bitrate is too low, only non-real-time services such as video on demand can be delivered.

on-demand models. The telephone operating companies (Telcos), as owners of the distribution network, are able to guarantee the bitrates necessary to deliver multiple digital television channels simultaneously over the broadband network and therefore can offer a broadcast service as well as an on-demand service. Facilities-based service providers such as the Telcos and cable operators will always have this advantage.

Continued Improvement in Video Compression   Digital television can produce a clearer, more vivid image than analog television. However, transmitting 30 high definition digital images per second to produce a television broadcast would require almost 1500 Mbps of bandwidth, far beyond the reaches of any existing consumer broadband service. By using compression algorithms such as MPEG-2 and MPEG-4, IPTV providers can reduce the required bitrates to the ranges mentioned above: 1.5 to 8 Mbps for a standard definition program, and 5 to 19 Mbps for a high definition program. As these algorithms improve over time, they continue to reduce the bandwidth required. At the same time, the effective bitrates of broadband services increase, making it possible to deliver digital video over the Internet, at first in a reasonable amount of time and eventually in real-time. These two trends, as show in Figure 1-4, will enable IPTV services over time.

Reducing Costs of Digital Video Equipment   An IPTV service provider needs to create an infrastructure for storing and serving large amounts of digital video. Server-grade computers are needed to send content when requested to subscribers of the service. Large arrays of hard drives are required to store many hours of video content on servers.

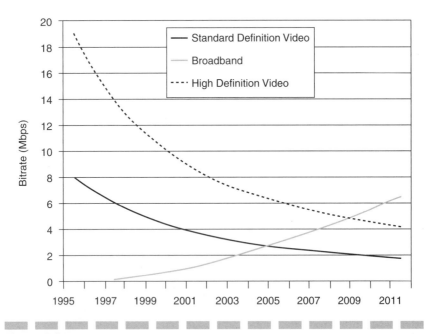

Figure 1-4
The compression efficiency of both standard and high definition video improves over time, while broadband services increase in bitrate, making it easier to deliver video over broadband. Source: Cable Television Laboratories.

Application-specific processors are required for compressing digital video via billions of operations per second to achieve the 100-fold compression in bitrate from raw (uncompressed) video. Only recently have the costs associated with these various components approached a level necessary to make an IPTV service economically viable.

As with any other Internet-based service, IPTV services benefit from the continuing decrease in the cost of computational power and storage over time. The processing power required to receive and view multiple video streams continues to improve every year, and digital video compression hardware will become less expensive and more efficient over time. But perhaps the biggest factor leading to favorable economics for an IPTV service is the dramatic decrease in the cost of digital storage in the form of hard drives. The cost per megabyte (million of bytes) of hard disk drive storage has continued to drop precipitously, with storage capacity more than doubling every year on average for the same unit cost.

A typical standard-definition digital video stream is produced at a bitrate of 6 Mbps, so one hour of video requires $6 \times 60 \times 60 = 21,600$ million bits, or 2.5 GB (gigabytes). An IPTV service may have thousands of hours of video content. It is not difficult to see how the cost of storage plays an important role in the economics of an IPTV service. Figure 1-5 shows the cost of storage per megabyte over time, and the corresponding cost to store one hour of video at 6 Mbps. Without this dramatic decrease in the cost of storage, IPTV services would not be economically viable.

"Over-the-Top" IPTV Services

A number of third-party service providers have emerged to deliver IPTV services to broadband subscribers. These "over-the-top" third-party providers of IPTV services often operate independently of the broadband service provider. Many over-the-top services are designed as software clients running on a home PC. For these software-based video services, content is hosted and served from the Internet and delivered over broadband connections to the software clients on media PCs. Examples of this type of service are Movielink and CinemaNow. Another group of over-the-top services do not use the PC but have special hardware connected to the broadband subscriber's home network. Hardware-based over-the-top services do not require a PC for receiving the service and instead use consumer premises equipment, typically an IP set-top box (IP STB) that bridges the home network directly to the television. Examples in this category include TiVo, Akimbo, and Sling Media. Hardware-based services

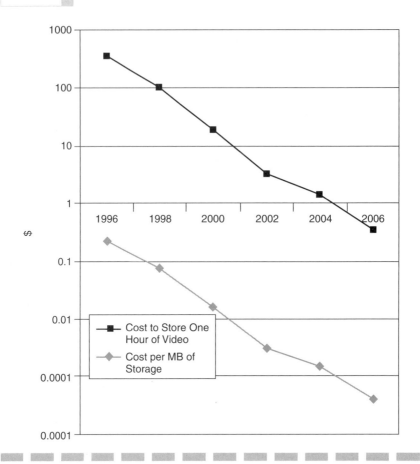

Figure 1-5
The cost per megabyte of disk drive storage has dropped dramatically over the past decade, resulting in a significantly lower cost to store one hour of compressed digital video. Source: "Historical Notes about the Cost of Hard Drive Storage Space," at http://www.alts.net/ns1625/winchest.html.

typically require a service commitment that subsidizes the hardware cost. So far, hardware-based over-the-top services have focused on the niche content market instead of mainstream movies or broadcast television.

Regardless of the approach, all of these services face the challenge of obtaining premium content. Movie studios and television producers are wary of making content available to a platform that has the potential of high-value content leaking onto the Internet where illegal copies can proliferate. To date, a limited amount of content is available to these services, typically late release movies (movies that have already been released to theaters, to DVD, to premium movie channels, and so on).

However, this could quickly change as Hollywood becomes more comfortable with the security systems deployed for PCs and IP STBs. And as the potential audience grows, the economics will become more attractive.

Ultimately, Internet delivery might be the next distribution channel for purchasing movies. Hackers will quickly learn how to rip DVDs (using a computer to take the content off the DVD and creating new copies). Ripping CDs led to Napster and the eventual shift of music sales from retail stores to the Internet. The movie studios may want to replace the currently lucrative retail DVD purchase channel with a new, more secure channel using the Internet, thus avoiding the establishment of a video Napster phenomenon. The Internet could provide a new retail channel for movie purchases, but questions remain. Will the purchase service be direct to the consumer from the studios, or will it be available through content aggregators such as cable and DBS service providers? Can the security system meet the studio's requirements for securing the content from unauthorized copies? Given the long history of cable operators being content aggregators, it may be important for cable networks to evolve to provide an attractive Internet-delivery channel.

PC/Software-Based Over-the-Top IPTV Services   Initially, PC-based IPTV services were limited to short-format, small screen video content from a number of news, sports, or adult websites. This has expanded into Internet video services offering full-length movies or television shows on demand. Examples of video on demand services include CinemaNow, iTunes, and Movielink. Subscribers to these services must have broadband Internet access and in most cases specific Microsoft software on their PC to provide the copy control security.

CinemaNow, Movielink, and Vongo began with a limited number of recent release and older movies available for viewing on home PCs for short rental periods, typically 24 hours. These services offer a subscription model, with unlimited downloads for a monthly fee. The major Internet movie services are backed by the major movie studios: Lions Gate backs CinemaNow; MGM, Paramount, Sony, Universal, and Warner Brothers back Movielink; and Starz backs Vongo. These studios supply the content and carefully control what they release through these services. By supporting these ventures, the studios are experimenting with the Internet as an alternate distribution path, possibly eliminating or reducing their dependency on third parties to distribute their content.

Apple's iTunes service offers a number of television shows and movies for download. TV shows can be downloaded from the service within 24 hours of their airing on broadcast TV. ABC, NBC, and CBS all sell content through the iTunes website. In early 2006, the television networks began offering their own content on the Web for free, becoming over-the-top service providers themselves. Disney/ABC offers episodes of hit TV shows on its website the day after they air on broadcast television. As with iTunes, users can fast-forward and rewind the content they have downloaded. But unlike the for-fee iTunes, content directly from the broadcasters contains commercials. By offering the content themselves, content owners will continue to be able to sell advertising space within the content. This free TV on the Web via IPTV has the potential to change the fundamental business of television distribution.

Initially the over-the-top services provided content in a limited resolution format with quality comparable only to VHS tape. They did not reach the full potential of digital video and were far from the quality possible with high definition digital television. The iTunes video service, for example, delivers content suitable for the smaller screen of a video iPod or desktop PC, but the picture may not look great on a big screen TV. This restriction in image quality on these services is probably the result of Hollywood studios not yet being ready to release full-resolution, high quality digital video to the Internet until the security and business models have been proven. As the distribution model proves itself, high definition quality video suitable for large screens will be made available.

While the technical restrictions are related to the network bandwidth necessary to support a quality viewing experience and the transfer of files to multiple viewing devices within the home, the security requirements cut to the core of the content business. Digital rights management (DRM) is necessary to ensure that content owner's copyrights are preserved and illegal copies are not made by consumers. CinemaNow, Vongo, and Movielink use the DRM provided in Microsoft Windows Media software to manage the licensing restrictions of their pay-for-view products. iTunes uses the Apple FairPlay DRM that was designed for purchasing content as opposed to renting it for a finite time.

While digital television offers many advantages in terms of image quality and efficient delivery, to content owners it also raises serious concerns. Copies of digital content are perfect copies and can be duplicated many times without loss of quality. Also, digital content can be sent instantaneously anywhere in the world via the World Wide Web. Questions and concerns about the ability of DRM software to prevent wide-scale distribution of content without the corresponding compensation to the content owner are being carefully scrutinized. Once content owners feel secure with DRM, HDTV and other high-value content will soon make its way to PCs and other IP-enabled devices within the home.

Hardware-based Over-the-Top IPTV Services   Hardware-based over-the-top IPTV services use a device other than the PC that bridges a user's broadband service (to the Internet) to their television. As with satellite and cable service providers, this STB delivers the service to the subscriber and also ensures that only paying subscribers are able to view the service. By connecting directly to the television, these services are more natural substitutes for traditional television services than PC-delivered services. While the PC is currently not a natural device for watching television, that might change in the future. Conversely, not many consumers are accustomed to connecting a device that is attached to their television into the Internet. The user must have a local data network set up that reaches the television. This factor currently may be an impediment to widespread deployment at least as onerous as the requirement to view content on the PC for the PC-based over-the-top services.

Some example services are described here.

Akimbo   Akimbo was one of the original hardware-based IPTV service providers. The Akimbo service requires an up-front cost for the hardware and a monthly fee for the service. Subscribers get access to a number of unique channels such as IFILM, MavTV, and Ripe TV. For an additional fee they can subscribe to premium channels, including music channels and the Naked News. In addition to the subscription service, Akimbo provides an on-demand service where premium movies can be downloaded to the device for a rental period.

TiVo   TiVo, which originated the concept of the digital video recorder, also acts as an over-the-top IPTV service provider. Broadband-enabled TiVo devices are capable of receiving video content from the Internet. TiVo has announced relationships with the Independent Film Channel (IFC), Rocketboom, and Netflix. IFC and Rocketboom contain specialized content usually not found on traditional broadcast networks. Because TiVo works in conjunction with a user's existing cable or satellite TV service, the nontraditional nature of its downloaded content is complementary.

XTV   XTV is a hardware-based over-the-top IPTV service that delivers adult content to an Internet-connected STB. As with other hardware-based services, fees are required for the service; pay-per-view movie options are available as well.

A Lack of Content?

Today, Akimbo and other hardware-based IPTV services appear to have limited content offerings. Most of the content currently available is from independent sources that appeal to a niche audience. More traditional video content on IPTV services remains scarce. The on-demand movie library of IPTV services such as Movielink and Vongo are smaller than cable VOD services or traditional video rental businesses.

It is understandable that content owners have not rushed to make their premium content available to new IPTV systems. They may be uncertain of the advantages of this new channel as compared to existing ones or even other models being developed for IPTV. It may be prudent for them to hold back on opening up their content libraries until the market stabilizes and the business case is clear. In addition to copy protection issues, neither the economic advantage nor potential threat to traditional distribution channels is clear. IPTV services can be direct replacements for cable and satellite services. To content owners, they are just new distribution channels with significantly smaller audiences.

Over-the-Top Services Facilitators   In addition to the companies providing various IPTV services, many others are facilitating the ability of these services to succeed. Hardware companies make it more economical to create STBs and other devices to receive IPTV content. Software companies provide the software platforms upon which IPTV services are developed. A number of standards bodies throughout the world are creating specifications for IPTV services and devices, making it easier for devices to interoperate and provide economies of scale. In this section we look at some of the facilitators that are making the emergence of IPTV services possible.

The Microsoft Media Center PC   Microsoft and its hardware partners are facilitating over-the-top services by providing a platform for Internet-delivered content. The Microsoft XP Media Center Edition and Media Center PC are designed to improve the ability to receive and view high-bandwidth digital audio-video content. The operating system and hardware have been optimized to improve the viewing experience. Microsoft hasn't released numbers on sales, but to date it appears that almost 2 million Media Center PCs have been sold and more and more hardware options are available to consumers. This is clearly a growing base of PCs ready to receive IPTV services.

Perhaps even more important than the hardware for the Media Center PC is the software platform for IPTV services that Microsoft provides. Developer tools make it easy for an IPTV service company to build upon this platform and make its service available to all media PCs. Companies wishing to enter the IPTV space will find an easy way to reach a large audience. Providing these tools drives developers toward the Microsoft platform, while Microsoft retains ultimate control of the software tools as well as the look and feel of the user interface. As the distribution model evolves, Microsoft may let the studios and broadband providers fight it out. Meanwhile, Microsoft will continue to develop what may become the de facto standard platform for viewing IPTV content.

The Video iPod and iTunes   After several years of denying that it was considering a video version of its popular iPod, Apple started offering the video iPod in late 2005. As mentioned, the iTunes service started offering video content for purchase, and Apple continues to announce content deals for iTunes. The success of the iPod has had a huge impact on the digital music business. A large installed base of video-capable iPods could do the same for IPTV services.

The Cost to Broadband Service Providers   Over-the-top services have the potential not only to increase demand for broadband services, but also to increase dramatically the average data consumption per user. As more users sign up for broadband to view Internet-delivered IPTV services, the more bandwidth they will consume on the service. It is estimated that almost 50 percent of high-speed data traffic is now video content, typically from peer-to-peer file sharing or streaming of video content from IPTV services. The rise in over-the-top IPTV services can increase the operational demands on broadband service operators without a corresponding increase in revenue per subscriber. A single digital movie download to the PC, for example, consumes about 1 GB of traffic, while an hour of television content would consume about 500 MB. It is not unreasonable to assume that a video download service subscriber would consume at least two movies per week and about an hour of television content per day, resulting in more than 20 GB of data downloaded per month. Movielink, for example, offers reasonable rates that would allow a subscriber to download multiple movies per month. The growing number of over-the-top service providers and facilitators will ensure a growing audience for video and other media services via broadband, and the subsequent increase in bandwidth usage in broadband networks. As a result, broadband service providers can expect data rates (and bandwidth utilization) to increase greatly from their current rates. This could lead to congestion on shared network architectures, as is the case with cable modems. IPTV services are bound to increase network usage throughout the system for all broadband providers.

The increasing bandwidth available from broadband providers is fueling an increase in video content being shared among users as well. File sharing applications such as BitTorrent allow broadband users to share large files easily. These files are increasingly digital versions of television shows and movies. Because a two-hour movie or television program may require multiple gigabytes, sharing these files throughout the Internet is bound to increase bandwidth consumption.

Broadband service providers are just starting to grapple with supporting this growing data consumption trend because of IPTV, without a corresponding increase in compensation, as they increase the scale of their networks to handle the additional network traffic. Service providers are considering an increase in fees to either consumers, via different tiers of service, or over-the-top service providers, via usage fees. Should the websites that generate, and profit from, the increase in bandwidth consumption pay more for access to broadband distribution networks? Do broadband service providers have a right to charge for increased bandwidth usage or will they be forced to be network neutral and charge all sources the same regardless of bandwidth consumption? Should the free market or the government regulate broadband service business models? Arguments for both sides are being debated in the court of public opinion, with well-paid lobbyists plying the halls of Washington trying to sway potential legislation.

New IPTV Distributors: Telco TV

Telephone network operators throughout the world are taking advantage of IPTV by entering the pay television market to compete directly with cable and satellite services. As the cable operators did decades before them, telephone companies will spend billions to enable their networks for IPTV. When this is completed, subscribers will be able to receive traditional broadcast television, premium pay channels, and VOD from their telephone companies.

Just as Voice over IP (VoIP) made it possible for broadband providers such as cable networks to offer traditional telephone services to subscribers, IPTV will make it possible for telephone operators to offer video services. Through IPTV, telephone operators will be able to match the "triple play" of cable offerings: video, broadband access, and telephone service. The next step in this arms race will naturally be the "quadruple play," with the addition of wireless telephony, or mobility, to the mix.

The stakes are enormous as cable, satellite, and now telephone companies vie for subscribers. Current ARPU (average revenues per user) for video services continue to climb and average more than $50 per month, while ARPU for (cable) broadband subscribers is about $40. Add telephony services to the mix, and a triple play consumer can bring in more than $100 per month in revenues. With more than 100 million households in the US, the potential market, in monthly subscriptions alone, is more than $100 billion per year. Adding advertising revenues increases the amount to almost $200 billion.

Deployments by Major US Telephone Companies   Consequently the traditional telephone operators are making large investments to enable IPTV services on their networks. AT&T/SBC has stated that it would spend $4 billion to upgrade its network of copper lines to support its Lightspeed initiative. Verizon's FiOS plan is even more ambitious. Some analysts believe Verizon may spend more than $20 billion to string fiber cable directly to homes. These two major telephone network operators are taking significantly different approaches to IPTV. AT&T/SBC's investment will extend high-bandwidth optical fiber to the neighborhood, and then use DSL over existing copper wires (also called twisted pair) to the home. The hybrid fiber-copper approach will be less costly to deploy than running fiber all the way to each subscriber's home, as Verizon is doing. When deployed, however, Verizon's fiber-to-the-home (FTTH) network provides a truly high-speed connection to subscribers, which can be used for IPTV and future IP-based services.

Verizon's FTTH approach will initially deliver television and IP-based services separately. Broadcast television channels will be delivered in the same way digital television is delivered today, via modulation of a radio frequency instead of over IP packets. This signal is sent down the optical fiber along with traditional broadband IP services. Therefore Verizon's initial television service is not technically IPTV, but a hybrid of digital television and IP-based services. Eventually the television services will become packet-based and transition to pure IPTV. The flexibility of the fiber network, however, means that Verizon can switch to all-IP–based television services in the future, yet roll out services immediately based on the proven technology used in cable.

The Franchising Debate

Cable operators in the US were required by state laws to negotiate with local municipalities for the right to deploy their service in the local market. State and local governments grant an operator rights to use public rights-of-way and utility poles and conduits, typically in exchange for a franchise fee on gross revenues. This process involved thousands of individual negotiations with each municipality requiring different adjustments to the service. One of the primary concerns for city governments was that the service operator makes the service available to all households, not just in well-to-do neighborhoods.

The major US telephone operators hope to roll out television services nationwide eventually. It might be difficult for them to negotiate thousands of individual agreements with every municipality in a timely manner. Consequently, the operators have been lobbying Washington for an exemption from local franchising rules and instead want a national franchising option. At the time of the writing of this book, the House of Representatives had passed a measure overhauling the 1996 Telecommunications Act. The measure allows telephone operators to obtain national franchises for video services. Under a national franchising agreement, both cable and telephone operators would pay a fixed percentage to the local municipality for use of public rights-of-way to provide their service. It is not clear if similar language will pass the Senate.

International IPTV Deployments   While the largest US telephone companies are laying out billions of dollars to implement IPTV to millions of customers, many international telephone operators have already rolled out services to their customers, including the following:

- PCCW in Hong Kong began offering television services over its DSL lines in 2003 and now reaches more than 500,000 IPTV customers with its NOW Broadband TV.

- Italy's FastWeb service provides IPTV to more than 300,000 customers throughout Italy. It timed the launch of its television services with the start of the football season, making a deal with the Italian National Football league for rights to games.

- In France three companies offer IPTV services over DSL: Neuf Telecom, Iliad's Free service, and France France Telecom's MaLigne TV. MaLigne TV has more than 200,000 subscribers.

- Deutsche Telekom plans to roll out broadband TV (IPTV) in Germany in 2006 starting in ten major German cities, including Berlin, Hamburg, Cologne, and Munich. The service will include broadcast TV, video on demand, digital video recording, and interactive television services.

- British Telecom (BT) announced plans to roll out IPTV services in 2006. The BT Vision service would combine digital terrestrial television services with IPTV for on-demand content.

International Telcos may have taken the lead in deployment of IPTV for various regulatory and technological reasons. On the technical side, achieving the bandwidth required to deliver IPTV over DSL lines requires relative short distances (called *loop lengths*) between the operator's central office and the subscriber's home. Denser housing populations, especially in parts of Asia, result in a larger subscriber base living close to the central offices. An IPTV service over DSL therefore can reach more subscribers than in the less dense markets often found in the US. As a result, US operators are either reducing loop lengths by extending fiber closer to the homes or going all the way to the homes with fiber and removing the distance limitations of DSL.

No Option but IPTV

Some analysts believe that telephone operators really have no choice but to deploy IPTV: as cable companies begin to steal landline telephone customers with VoIP offerings, telephone companies need to take advantage of their networks to offer video services and stem the tide of defections to cable. For some Telcos, entering the TV market is the only way to make up for the increasing losses of telephone subscribers to VoIP services from over-the-top voice providers such as Vonage and from the cable companies. By the end of 2005 Comcast had 1.3 million telephone customers with a goal of adding 1 million more in 2006. Time Warner Cable had almost 1 million voice customers, and Vonage had more than 1.5 million subscribers. These millions of customers were former customers of the Telcos. As VoIP services continue to take customers away, the major Telcos may have no choice but to offer television services to compete, or else continue a downward trend in subscriber base. An indication of the aggressive battle for subscribers can be found in a comment (Multichannel News at http://www.multichannel.com/article/CA6325061.html) from the CTO of Comcast Cable, David Fellows, who said telephone operators "have almost 95% of my telephone subscribers, and this is something I intend to correct over time."

The initial IPTV deployments by Telcos appear to be "me-too" services that offer packages similar to existing cable or satellite providers. While some may talk about the range of new services that IPTV could enable, such as interactive television, multiple viewing angles, and watching multiple channels on one screen, in reality the products to date from Telcos appear to be almost identical to current offerings from MVPD. The operators may be investing large amounts of capital to compete eventually for the relatively stable pool of TV households, ultimately driving margins down in the process.

IPTV Solutions Vendors   With billions of dollars to be spent on IPTV equipment by the major Telcos, it is no surprise that a number of eager hardware and software companies have created products to meet the demand. Incumbent suppliers and multiple startups are all vying for a piece of the pie.

Hardware vendors are offering network equipment such as fiber and DSL components to prepare networks for IPTV services. Large incumbent suppliers to the telecom industry such as Siemens, Lucent (which recently announced it would merge with Alcatel), Nortel Networks, and Cisco can be expected to supply much of this equipment. At the subscriber's home, new IPTV STBs will be supplied by the Telco. Traditional set-top suppliers such as Philips, Thomson, Motorola, and Scientific-Atlanta have announced a number of deals to provide millions of new set-tops. Newcomers such as Amino and 2Wire have developed innovative solutions as well and have seen some early deployments.

Middleware vendors supply the software platform upon which the IPTV service is built. A good middleware platform allows an operator to build and deploy new services quickly. To achieve this, a middleware should be hardware and operating system agnostic. This allows the operator to create the software for a new service and deploy it immediately across its hardware platforms instead of having to rewrite it multiple times to fit multiple operating systems. Other important factors for middleware include the ability to scale from a few thousand to millions of customers. As more and more customers use the service, there will be a subsequent increase in the number of transactions in the system. In addition, the software supporting the service must be able to handle the increased load. Microsoft has made a number of high-profile announcements with major operators supporting its IPTV platform, and trials using its middleware have begun in a number of locations internationally. A number of smaller middleware vendors have also currently deployed products with many smaller operators. One such vendor, Myrio (acquired by Siemens), has deployments with many small operators in the US as well as in Belgium and Thailand.

While the major telephone operators appear to be playing it safe by partnering with large, established vendors, many of the newer vendors are being deployed today with smaller operators internationally. As this market matures one can expect the consolidation of some and the disappearance of others, as operators make their choices.

New Sources of Content

The Internet has spawned many new forms of self-expression, from text-based blogs, to podcasts and video blogs. As a distribution medium, the Internet truly provides unprecedented access to millions of viewers for anyone who wishes to publish. In addition to creating new distributors or over-the-top content aggregators, IPTV may also lead to a new market for nontraditional video sources. User-generated content can now be published on the Internet for the whole world to see, giving unprecedented power to the masses.

There have been a number of early forays into creating new portals for user-generated and other video content via the Web. Google is rolling out the first phase of its Video Upload Program, which enables users to upload their personal videos to Google, where they will be indexed and integrated into search results. Google already offers the Picasa service for storing and sharing digital photos as well as the Blogger service for blogs. Video might be a natural extension to this line of services. Under the Video Upload Program, content owners will be able to control distribution rights themselves, setting a price for the video clips they upload. Eventually users will be able to search, preview, purchase, and play videos directly from Google's site. The company will take a percentage of all video purchases to cover some of its costs, and of course will provide advertising. Google is directly courting television stations and production facilities for this service as well.

Video blogs, the visual descendent of web blogs, continue to proliferate and offer a range of content. Some of the more popular sites have audiences that rival traditional media. For example, more than 100,000 viewers use their computers or TiVos to tune into a video blog called Rocketboom. YouTube (recently acquired by Google) and iFILM are destinations for short form video content, including independent short films, movie trailers, and infamous "viral" video clips that proliferate on the Web. A segment of the TV show "Crossfire" may have attracted more viewers to iFILM than the original television broadcast.

Brightcove is a startup hoping to take advantage of the demand for niche content on the web and people's desire to self-publish. The Brightcove home page states that owners of content will be empowered by its direct-to-consumer distribution channel. It claims that owners will profit more from publishing on its site than through "traditional" distribution channels. A company brief claims that in the future Internet video channels will be as prolific and diverse as websites are today. Brightcove also announced that its content will be available to TiVo subscribers.

Power Shifts in the Television Service Market

What is perhaps more important than the introduction of new service models is the fact that IPTV has the ability to change the power structure of the business of television radically. While IPTV is enabling new distribution models and new product markets, it is also shifting power bases within the traditional television services model. New distributors create competition, thereby shifting power to content owners and consumers. The convenience and portability of digital formats give users more power in how, when, and where they consume video services. And the interactive nature of IP makes content on demand the norm instead of the exception.

The Shift from Distributors to Content Providers

Because they did not sell their content directly to the consumer, content creators and owners depended on distributors to reach their customers. Conversely, distributors depend on content deals to provide an attractive service. This balance of power developed over years of negotiations and market development. IPTV has the potential to shift power to content owners in two different ways: by providing competition in the distributor market, and by offering content owners a way to reach consumers directly. Both give more options, and more power, to the content providers.

As described earlier, IPTV has introduced new entrants into the television services distribution market. These new entrants, either over-the-top service providers or facilities-based IPTV providers such as Telcos, provide alternatives to the content provider. The result of this competition gives content owners more choices for reaching consumers through distributors; as a result they acquire leverage in deals for content with these distributors.

The second way that IPTV shifts power to content owners is by offering them the ability to reach consumers directly. After decades of relying on other companies to make their content available to the consumer, Hollywood and television studios may be able to reach consumers through their own over-the-top services. These independent portals offer movies and television shows directly. By offering content directly, content owners may also be able to receive all potential revenues from advertising instead of sharing it with distributors. ABC's recently announced plan to make hit television shows available on the Internet leaves all national advertising intact, unlike the corresponding iTunes downloads. In addition, the viewer cannot fast-forward through the commercials as they can on a DVR.

It is not clear yet if a direct-to-the-consumer approach will be beneficial to content owners. Content aggregators offer some advantages that individual content owners cannot offer, such as one-stop shopping for a range of content, a simplified way to purchase multiple programs, and a single place for large advertisers to reach a broad audience. While the Internet offers the best chance for content owners to sell directly to consumers, it may not be the natural evolution of the industry. At one time, book publishers thought the Internet would allow them to bypass the retail booksellers by going direct to the customer; however, many consumers have simply shifted from brick-and-mortar booksellers to online booksellers, keeping the content aggregator in the loop.

Regardless of how it works out, the consumer typically stands to gain from any increase in competition and access to content. Analysts predict that incumbent distributors will be forced to lower prices in response to new entrants into local markets to retain subscribers. How much elasticity there is in the television services market has yet to be determined, but it is bound to change the way consumers pay for such services.

More Power to Consumers

IPTV also promises to shift power to consumers in ways other than lowering the cost of television services. The digital nature of IPTV services allows content to be much more portable than analog television was.

Shifting Time and Space DVRs from TiVo and other companies allow consumers to "time-shift" content. DVRs not only record many hours of television content but also provide convenient playback features not possible with VCR tape. In particular, users can pause live television while it is being recorded, or start watching a show from the beginning while it is still being broadcast. The instant access nature of digital recording provides these and other features that make it easier for consumers to view content when they find it convenient and no longer be beholden to the broadcast schedule. Users can shift prime time to any time that they wish.

Digital recording also makes it easier to skip or even remove advertising from recorded programs. Such ability certainly shifts power to the consumer, as they are no longer forced to watch commercials. While initially fearing the consequences to the advertising model, content owners are realizing they may be able to take advantage of digital technology and DVRs to enhance the advertising model. TiVo provides a number of new ways for advertisers to reach television viewers, perhaps in a more efficient, targeted way.

In addition to its time-shifting capabilities, the nature of digital television also makes it easier to "place-shift" content. Portable media devices such as the video iPod and other players make it easier for people to view video content far from their living room television sets. In a slightly different model, the Slingbox Personal Broadcaster from Sling Media lets users place-shift their satellite and cable television shows. The Slingbox STB works in the opposite direction of over-the-top IPTV services: it takes in television content from other sources and broadcasts it onto the Internet. It allows people who are traveling to watch the same television programs they would get if they were home. The user can be connected to the Internet, theoretically anywhere in the world, and receive the content being broadcast from their own home. Using a laptop or other Internet-connected device, the user controls the Slingbox in their home remotely and receives the video content transmitted by it.

The ability to place-shift television content may be a challenge to broadcasters who sometimes have contracts to schedule different events in different geographical regions. In particular, various sporting events have blackout locations where distributors cannot broadcast during the live event. Place-shifting allows consumers to circumvent these limitations in geography.

Everything on Demand   The nature of IP makes possible new IPTV services with interactivity not seen before with television services. Consumers are no longer forced to watch only what is broadcast but can take a more active role in what they see. In particular, users will more increasingly watch content on demand, choosing to watch content at a time that is convenient. As we described with DVRs, the digital recording of television content makes it easy to time-shift broadcast content.

But true on-demand content is enabled by IPTV. The iTunes and broadcaster web portal video download services make television shows available any time after their initial broadcast. The video download services of Movielink and CinemaNow make thousands of titles available almost instantaneously. If Netflix reaches the full potential of its name, by offering the ability to download movies from the Internet, its millions of subscribers could shift to IPTV services. Consumers truly will benefit from this shift in power as they move from being passive consumers to demanding consumers of video content.

New Advertising Models for IPTV

While the demise of the 30-second commercial spot in broadcast television has been predicted in the past, IPTV might just be able to put an end to, or at least marginalize, it. The interactivity and flexibility of IPTV content makes it possible to create more dynamic ways of including advertisements. The on-demand nature of IPTV results in content that is more customized for the user, and it is only natural that advertising also be customized to the viewer. And, finally, while not unique to IPTV, digital television makes it easier to fast-forward or skip over commercials entirely. Advertisers need to find new ways to compel users to view advertising. All of these will lead to new types of advertising models and cooperation with IPTV services to enable them.

The traditional linear avail in a broadcast program consists of a 30-second spot for a commercial. The content provider, typically a broadcast network, incorporates a fixed number of these within the program during commercial breaks. The network usually sells some of these avails to national advertisers and sells or trades the rest to the distributor. The distributor typically sells the avail to local advertisers. A complex system of selling these advertising slots has developed over the decades. Content creators rely on future sales of these slots to pay for the increasing cost of producing television shows. Conversely, distributors increasingly rely on advertising sales to pay for network operations. For example, in 2005 (per Comcast financial report for 2005) Comcast Cable generated $13.6 billion in revenue from video subscriptions, from which 10 percent, or $1.3 billion, came from advertising sales. In addition, advertising revenue growth was more than double that of video revenue growth.

The interactive and on-demand nature of IPTV means that instead of the shotgun approach to advertising—where all viewers receive the same advertisement in the program—commercials can be targeted to the viewer. The choice of which commercial to show can be based on geography, viewing habits, or personal information volunteered by the viewer. Internet shopping sites such as Amazon.com already tailor the web browsing experience to the user's past purchases and presumed personal preference. IPTV will bring some of the same personalized content to advertising in television content. IPTV distributors will be able to promise advertising avails that are more targeted and therefore more likely to reach the desired audience than traditional commercial avails.

The interactive nature of Internet-based services also extends to IPTV advertising in the form of telescoping advertisements. In a telescoping advertisement, a standard commercial offers the viewer an option to learn more about the product. If the user selects this option, he or she is taken to an extended version of the commercial. The user may also be given the option to request more information directly from the advertiser before being returned to the program. DVR products such as TiVo are particularly well positioned to provide telescoping advertisements because of their ability to pause live broadcasts.

Figure 1-6 illustrates some of the new advertising models. In targeted advertising, any of a number of commercials choices are inserted into the commercial spot. The commercial that is inserted is chosen based on the particular viewer's personal choices, and targeted for that individual. This should improve the chances that the commercial is relevant to the viewer and therefore has a higher probability of making a sale. In a tele-

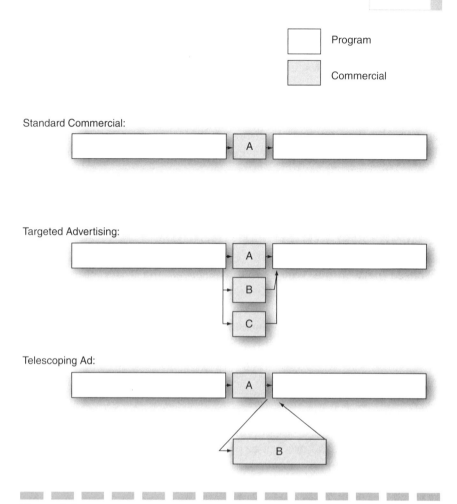

Figure 1-6
Some of the new types of advertising enabled by digital TV services: target advertisements that change depending on the viewer, and telescoping ads that allow the viewer to see a longer version if they are interested in the product.

scoping ad, the user actively requests additional information about the product. The length of the advertising window is increased as the user views the additional content. This form of advanced advertising is particularly useful in time-shift DVRs such as TiVo, where the user seamlessly returns to the program after the longer commercial without missing any of the program.

Operational Efficiency from IPTV

We mentioned that the constant improvement of computation efficiency and storage density made it economically possible to bring IPTV services and equipment to the consumer. While not as glamorous as new distributors and the ability to watch television anywhere, the lower costs and improved operational efficiencies that IPTV can provide to new and existing distribution networks will have a profound impact on the business of television.

Lower Costs of IP Equipment

IP-based networking equipment will lower the costs of operation throughout the distribution network. Because IPTV is based on the same protocols as the Internet, IPTV services can take advantage of equipment developed for the web backbone. As the explosive growth of the Internet and broadband continues, IPTV can follow the cost curve as IP network equipment continues to offer more bang for the buck.

At the content creation step, digital cameras and digital processing equipment are more convenient and cheaper than traditional film. IPTV content is easier to transport from origin back to production houses for editing. Content producers can also more rapidly turn raw material into the final product as computer workstations replace costly television splicing equipment.

In the distribution network, IP routers are indifferent to the nature of IP packets: these packets can be data or video. By using the same equipment for both types of services, an operator is able to create a simple, more efficient network that can be managed using the same tools. Operators no longer need to manage and maintain separate networks for data and video. Further down the pipe in the home, digital set-tops based on IPTV can be made cheaper than existing cable set-tops as radio-frequency tuners and converters are replaced with low-cost Ethernet and other IP network connectors.

Switched Digital Broadcast

In addition to lower cost equipment, IPTV also leads to efficiencies in bandwidth usage. Traditional broadcast video services transmit all available programs to all subscribers on the network all of the time. Given the variability in content across channels, it is highly likely that during some parts of the day many programs or channels are not being watched by any subscriber. With digital services, the number of possible programs carried by the network increases dramatically, and therefore, so does the probability that programs are being broadcast but no subscriber is actually watching.

In a switched digital broadcast model (Figure 1-7), programs are broadcast from the operator's transmission facility (called a *headend*)

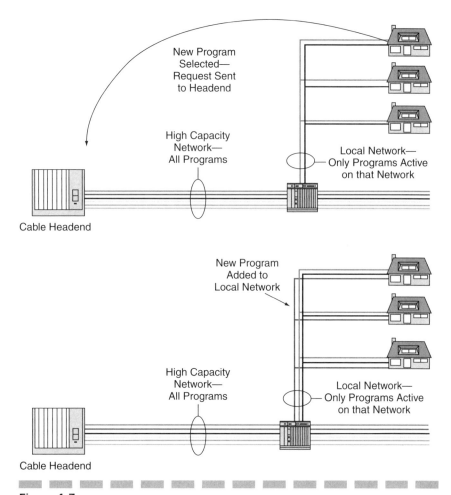

Figure 1-7

In a switched digital broadcast system, television channels are placed on the network only when specifically requested by a viewer, as opposed to being broadcast to every home.

onto the local network only when requested by a subscriber. When a subscriber selects a program for viewing via an interactive program guide, the application determines whether that program is currently being broadcast on the local network. If so, the STB simply tunes into that broadcast. If the program is currently not on the network, the STB makes a request to the server application to begin broadcasting that program on the network. When the subscriber switches to another program or is no longer watching the selected program, the server application is again notified. When the server application determines that no more subscribers are on the node viewing a particular program, it can remove it from the network and, thus, free up the bandwidth for other programs.

Switched broadcast, therefore, has the potential for reducing the amount of bandwidth required to support large numbers of television channels. With normal broadcast service, the amount of bandwidth required grows linearly with the number of programs being offered. All of the programs are broadcast to all of the homes. By switching channels, the amount of bandwidth required grows much more slowly as the number of channels increases. Only when different homes are watching different programs does the number of programs on the network increase. Statistically, most homes are watching only a small subset of available channels, usually the most popular ones. By not broadcasting the programs not being watched, the system operator can use the network bandwidth for other purposes.

The two-way nature of IP makes IPTV a natural platform for switched broadcast services. When a subscriber tunes to a channel a packet is sent up the network into the distribution system to request that the channel be placed on the network. This model is similar to how web content is served to a web browser at the request of the user. You select which content you want to see, and it is delivered to your PC. Content is not broadcast all the time to every PC waiting for someone to watch it.

IPTV for Business

IPTV isn't just for consumer entertainment; it has also been successfully applied to business applications. Over the years, many companies have incorporated video as a tool for communications as part of their day-to-day operations, but on a limited basis. Some companies that would have wanted to utilize video were unable to do so because of the cost associated with video operations. In the past, installing and maintaining a video distribution system within a company over a coaxial cable presented many challenges and difficulties. Debugging analog video problems over coaxial distribution systems required specialized skills for dealing with specialized video hardware. Also, the costs associated with running a mini-cable plant were often prohibitive, thus killing many new and innovative projects.

Thanks to the growing use of IP networking technology in almost every business, the costs for running IPTV systems are becoming more affordable, and many companies are either switching from analog video systems or rolling out new services based on digital IPTV. Today, with the advancements in IP technology and with most corporate and commercial buildings being wired (for example, with CAT5) for networking, installing an IP network is either essential or straightforward. Many of those older project concepts that were stalled due to prior limitations are now getting renewed attention. And because IPTV is based on the same technology used by existing data networks, it does not require the same level of dedicated hardware and dedicate support staff as analog TV did.

Examples of business applications in which IPTV can play a role include the following:

- **Digital signage.** With the increasing popularity of DVRs in consumer homes and the ability to skip past commercials, the value of advertising over broadcast television is decreasing. To counter this trend, advertisers are aggressively searching out new and innovative approaches to promote products to consumers. Digital signage is one such solution to this problem and has a significant amount of energy and momentum devoted to it. At an increasing rate, dynamic advertisements are popping up in places of commerce such as in stores, shopping malls, restaurants, and bars. IPTV enables mass deployment of commercial messaging to many locations instantaneously.

- **Distance learning.** Various professional fields have seen an increasing demand for distance learning, in particular the medical field, large corporations, and educational institutions. Distant learning includes the transmission of video (in classrooms, operating rooms, and so on) and interactive participation (including voice and text) with active participants. IPTV can reduce the cost of distance learning that was previously based on dedicated analog video hardware.

- **Corporate and business communications.** Video is an excellent mechanism for communication within a large corporation as well as with business partners. This might include product information, advertisement information, training, corporate communications (announcements, speeches, quarterly reports, and so on), net meetings, and relaying products/information to customers (for example, a financial company relaying stock prices to clients). IPTV over internal data networks allows large corporations to increase the effectiveness of internal communications.

- **Commercial airlines and hospitality suites.** IPTV is ideal for delivering broadcast and VOD content to these easily networked environments, again replacing video-specific systems with standard data networks.

- **Military and government.** Military and governments have a never-ending demand for secure video conferencing as well as other applications from secure mission coordination, image processing training, centrally stored data that can be securely accessed remotely, and traffic control.

These are some of the interesting applications for IPTV. We envision an increasing demand for IPTV networks as the technology matures and prices continue to lower.

The IPTV System Model

IPTV can be applied to many applications, ranging from facilities-based service operators that compete head-to-head with satellite and cable, to over-the-top IPTV services that allow consumers to watch audio and video content (streaming) over a broadband Internet connection, to business-to-business (B2B) applications that might include video enterprise, distance learning, and digital signage. In this chapter we will explore the system components required to implement the various IPTV systems. Note that the amount of IP video currently being delivered over broadband networks can easily be debated. Unfortunately, accurate information characterizing how common video over IP applications are on broadband networks is not available. While the general perception among service providers and the general public is that a majority of broadband traffic is for browsing the Web, e-mail, and sharing music, only anecdotal evidence indicates that video over IP traffic is now larger than music file sharing or other applications on the Internet and may actually make up almost half of all broadband traffic.

Broadband network operators generally do not examine the specific application mix of their customers. Most information regarding usage patterns is confined to characterizations of usage across general categories such as peer-to-peer (P2P) or HTTP-based web surfing. This information is not specific enough to describe the percentage of P2P packets, for example, that contain video versus music files. There are some indicators, however, that video over IP is already one of the primary sources of data traffic on residential broadband networks, perhaps accounting for 35 to 50 percent of all broadband traffic. If true, many of the technical hurdles clearly have been solved already to the degree that there is wide-scale consumer adoption of IPTV applications, albeit under a different service type than we will discuss in this chapter.

Broadcast Services, Unicast Services, and Switched Digital Video

Before we dive into a complete IPTV system architecture, it's important to review multicast and unicast services, their relevance, and how they relate to a switched digital video architecture.

Since the latter half of the 20th century, all television was broadcast television. Initially, consumers received television signals via antennas from off-air broadcast sources. Then cable television became popular and antennas were replaced with coax cable, but consumers continued to receive only broadcast services. Later, satellite video entered the scene, but still consumers received only broadcast services. Any commercial video operator must include broadcast programming as part of its product offering if it wants to stay competitive or stay in business. Furthermore, due to the fierce competition between cable, satellite, and now Telco video operators, video operators must include hundreds of channels of broadcast video to the consumers.

For terrestrial, satellite, and cable services, broadcast channels are transmitted to all customers via radio frequency (RF) waves. For IPTV, the method used for delivering broadcast channels to multiple customers simultaneously is more complicated. The building block or tool network operators use to enable broadcast services within their IPTV network is multicast. A multicast stream on an IP network allows multiple (if not all) homes within the network to connect and view it. This provides the same functionality as terrestrial, cable, and satellite broadcast services. Internet Protocol was not originally designed for broadcast communications. Providing multicast support requires additional protocols on top of IP and network equipment that recognizes and supports those additional protocols.

As competition grew among the video operators, they began to differentiate their services. Network operators that built bidirectional networks (and have available bandwidth) can deploy *unicast* services—content that is delivered to a single recipient instead of everyone on the network. Video on demand (VOD) is an example of a unicast service with which a consumer can watch a program intended only for them over the network. VOD utilizes the bidirectional capability of the network for signaling (select, purchase, and start) and control (pause, play, stop, rewind, and fast forward) of the movie or video stream. Depending on the network, the content can be distributed to the consumer's homes in various ways; for cable networks, it goes to all homes as does broadcast channel programming; for Telco networks it is present on the network till the last mile and then gets routed only to the home requiring it. The conditional access system within the cable networks ensures that only the home requesting the VOD movie has the ability to decrypt and view it. VOD is a natural application of a bidirectional IP network, with its ability to address a video stream for a single user along with the ability of a client to communicate concurrently with the VOD server while viewing the content.

An IPTV service provides both multicast and unicast television services via a switched digital video architecture. *Switched digital video* (SDV) refers to network architecture that switches and routes *selected* video data from the source (the service operator's headend) to the consumer's living room. As described in Chapter 1, the cable industry has done work in the field of SDV as well as telephone companies and has the potential to improve the efficiency of its cable network.

In an SDV network, video content is placed onto the network only when someone is watching it. Unicast services such as VOD might serve only one subscriber, while broadcast services could be serving thousands of subscribers. Let's walk through the process of selecting and watching a broadcast service on a SDV network. Suppose an IPTV subscriber is in her living room and wants to watch the NBC broadcast channel. Using her remote control she selects NBC, which causes the IP set-top box (STB) to send an Internet Group Management Protocol (IGMP) multicast join message (request) out of the house and into the IPTV access network. The access network will then direct the IP STB to join the multicast data stream if it is already flowing on the access network. If it is not already present at the access network, the request is communicated upstream to the central office. The IPTV network is continuously switching and routing data (including video, voice, and data services) from the source to the correct final destination. This is in contrast to original broadcast cable systems, where each broadcast channel is sent to everyone, whether someone is watching or not. The SDV system is quite elegant and efficiently utilizes the network's bandwidth as it routes IP packets only to where they are required. However, it greatly increases the complexity of the network.

Facilities-based IPTV System Architecture

To help you understand how a network operator would deploy a broadcast IPTV switched digital video network, we will explore a "typical" IPTV system architecture. An IPTV broadcast network can be divided into four sections (shown in Figure 2-1):

- **Content/Headend.** The source for much of the video content within the system. The central point within the network is the headend or super headend. This is where the broadcast programming and on-demand content is captured or ingested into the system.

- **Core Network.** Transports all of the system's content (that is, video, music, channel lineup, and data). The core network is the "backbone" for the IPTV broadcast system within the region of

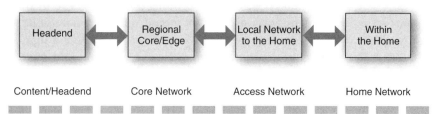

Figure 2-1
An IPTV broadcast network.

service. Also, local content and local advertisement insertion for each region could be inserted at the core network.

- **Access Network.** The "last mile" for the network operator. It provides the network connectivity of the IPTV services to consumer homes.

- **Home Network.** Where the IPTV service enters the home (via a router/gateway). It is also where the distribution of all of the data (voice, data, and video) takes place among all IP devices in the home.

Expanding the block diagram (see Figure 2-2) shows how content enters the system and how it flows all the way to consumer homes.

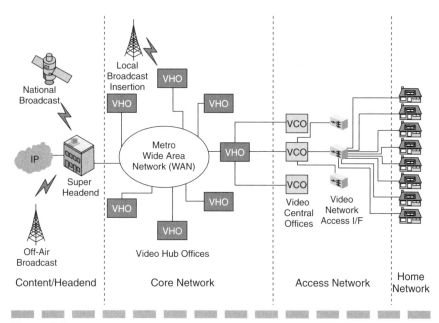

Figure 2-2
An IPTV system network.

Many smaller operators obtain content from a *content aggregator* that acquires the various programming in bulk and makes it available to many operators. Content may also come in pre-packaged from a digital satellite feed or content aggregator and all that is required is to "turn-it-around" and make it available on the network. The super headend (content/headend) is where the bulk of the network's content is captured and formatted for distribution within the network, including the broadcast and on-demand services. Multiple methods are used to obtain the content, such as receiving national feeds via satellite, local feeds via terrestrial (antenna), and content via metro-wide fiber-based networks.

After the content is captured within the headend, it is formatted for distribution within the system. This may include digitally encoding analog content for distribution or transcoding digital content for optimization purposes. The digital formats in use today include MPEG-2, MPEG-4 Advanced Video Codec (AVC), and VC-1. The various compressed bitstreams may also be groomed, removing elements not required for the network (for example, undesired channels or programs in the multiplexed transport, irrelevant system information, and so on), and multiplexed together into multiprogram transport stream. A statistical multiplexer, or rate shaper, may also be used to create the required bitrates for the distribution network.

For an IPTV system, the various multiplex program streams are then encapsulated in IP packets. The signals leave the super headend over an extremely high bandwidth wide area network (WAN) to the video hub offices (VHO). The WAN and VHOs constitute the *core network*. The WAN is the backbone of the core network and uses high-bandwidth IP transport formats such as gigabit Ethernet or ATM to connect the VHO site. The VHO sites are strategically located for regional coverage within the video service operators' combined area or customer base. The multicast streams enter the video hub via the WAN. The video hub may also have local receivers, which offer additional local content. Local content is processed much like national content, possibly getting digitally encoded, transcoded, or turned around. Therefore, these VHO sites may have headend equipment (for example, encoders, IP encapsulators, grooming equipment, and so on) used to process the local content. Each region will have its own unique channel lineup, which would include the numerous multicast broadcast channels and VOD channels. It should be noted that these channels may be encrypted for security purposes at either the super headend or the video hub. The video hub may also include the various back-end office equipment (that is, servers) necessary for billing, system management, data storage, and signal routing.

The IPTV data then travels from the VHO (core network) to (access network) video central offices (VCO) over a high bandwidth network. Each VCO will route data to video network access interfaces (for example, Digital Subscriber Line Access Multiplexers, or DSLAMs). In the Telco case, the DSLAMs route the desired video data from the network over a twisted-pair DSL line to the consumer's home.

Content/Headend

The heart of any IPTV system is the super headend (shown in Figure 2-3), which consists of various types of equipment designed to receive content, possibly reformat it as needed, and prepare it for distribution to a WAN. The components of an IPTV headend are very similar to those used for digital cable television headends. However, the equipment is typically based on standard PC server platforms used for most web applications instead of equipment specific to cable technology. Multiple vendors such as Dell, HP,

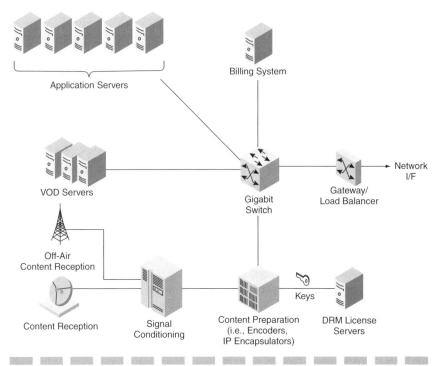

Figure 2-3
IPTV super headend equipment block diagram.

and IBM provide rack-mounted server equipment running any of a number of operating systems including Linux and Windows. This is one of the advantages of an IP standards-based approach.

The following functions are performed by the components in this block diagram:

- **Content reception.** Consists of components that receive both analog and digital video feeds either directly from the content provider or from a content aggregation facility such as provided by the National Digital Television Center (NDTC). This includes broadcast and on-demand services. Increasingly, the digital feeds are coming via high-speed fiber links instead of satellite.

- **Signal conditioning.** Consists of signal processing equipment designed to enhance the video signals coming in from the content reception equipment. This might include integrated receiver decoders (IRDs), noise reduction, and digital video processing products.

- **Content preparation.** The content encoders prepare the video streams in a format that is suitable for IP transport and reception by an IP STB. This will consist of either digitizing (and encoding) analog content or transcoding digital video content into the format used by the codec employed by the IPTV system—for example, either MPEG-2, Windows Media Video 9, Real Networks Video 10, or MPEG-4 AVC. Typical bitrates for standard definition television (SDTV) channels are 1.5 Mbps, and for high definition television (HDTV) 8 Mbps.

- **Digital rights management.** As part of the encoding process, the encryption component of the digital rights management (DRM) system encrypts the content and wraps it in a DRM container to prevent unauthorized usage of content. Figure 2-4 shows a block diagram of a typical content preparation system. It shows how content is received from satellite and off-air feeds and gets processed. The digital feeds either get transcoded (that is, into advanced compression) or rate converted for optimization purposes. Off-air feeds get digitally encoded into the desired digital format. All of the digital bitstreams (that originated from satellite and off-air feeds) then get IP encapsulated.

- **DRM license server.** Manages, authorizes, and reports content transactions as well as manages the encryption of content data. The server verifies content license requests and issues content licenses to trusted, authenticated DRM end user clients. It also provides auditing information to facilitate royalty payments.

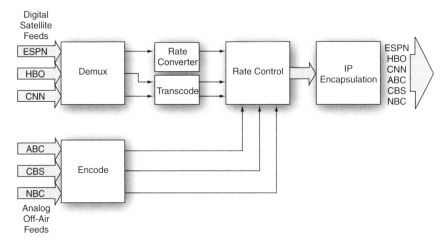

- **Demux:** Takes an MPTS and passes along an SPTS with the desired channel.
- **Encode:** Converts an analog video signal and digitally compresses it into a digital bitstream.
- **Transcode:** Converts a digital bitstream (e.g., MPEG-2) to an advanced compression format (e.g., AVC or VC-1).
- **Rate Converter:** Multi-pass digital (MPEG-2) compression to improve video quality.
- **Rate Control:** Final digital formatting which includes transport and clock resync.
- **IP Encapsulation:** Formats the digital streams within IP payloads suitable for delivery over an IP network.

Figure 2-4
Content preparation system.

- **VOD servers.** VOD or media servers are optimized to serve multiple streams simultaneously to clients. They are typically bandwidth-limited in the number of streams they can sustain and therefore must scale with expected usage and the number of subscribers to the service. Content may be stored on the server for multicast (a single stream sent simultaneously to multiple viewers) to an ensemble of viewers at a fixed time, or for unicast to individual users in a VOD system. Depending on the system architecture, VOD servers can reside either in the super headend or in the core network (VHO).

- **Application servers.** The application servers can vary greatly between IPTV deployments, depending on features, functionalities, scalability, middleware, system control, and so on. Application servers could include electronic program guide (EPG), Conditional Access System (CAS)/DRM servers–entitlement, navigation/ middleware server, IPTV portal or walled garden, e-mail, and remote diagnostics. Much like VOD servers, application servers can reside either in the super headend or in the core network (VHO).

- **Billing system.** The subscriber database contains subscriber-specific information with respect to the level of service the user is authorized to use and other information to be used for billing (such as addresses, credit card information, and so on.).

- **Gateway/load balancer.** Provides load balancing and session control and sends the data stream to the network interface.

Core Network

The core network (shown in Figure 2-5) consists of a fiber backbone (WAN) and various VHOs. The core network gets data from the super headend (content/headend) and delivers data to the access network. The primary purpose of the core network is to provide adequate bandwidth

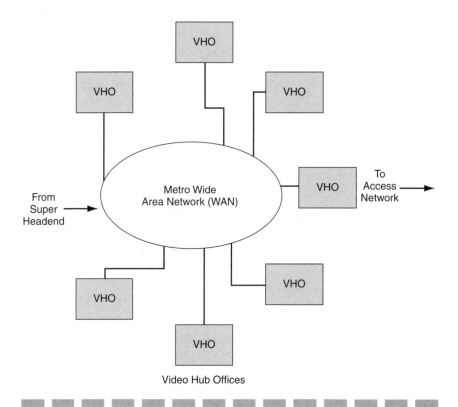

Figure 2-5
High-level architecture for the core network.

for all of the data and video network traffic between service areas and the national content (super headend) source. The core network also provides the capability for insertion of local content (including emergency alert system, or EAS) into each service area.

The core network must accommodate and provide adequate network bandwidth capacity as the system grows with more customers and more content. Figure 2-6 provides an analysis of the required IP traffic at a VHO. Note that these numbers can vary depending on each network operator's system, scale factors, and service parametrics. You can easily see how large the complete network traffic could be within the core network by multiplying the VHO total capacity (for example, 4 Gbps) by the required number of VHOs deployed within the system. For this reason, as well as future growth and scaling, we show the data services (Voice over IP [VoIP] and broadband data) residing on a separate fiber strand than the video data. Depending on the network implementation and bandwidth required, a network operator may choose to transport the video and data on the same or separate fiber networks.

The VHO (Figure 2-7) may look like a super headend, but it actually handles and processes content on a much smaller scale. From a content perspective, the VHO provides local information (such as EAS) and content (local broadcast) to the customer area it is serving as well as local ad insertion into national content.

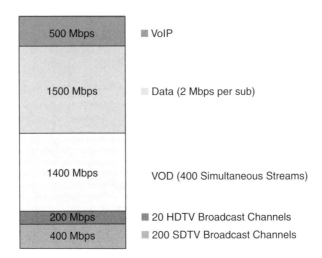

Total Transport Network Capacity 4000 Mbps

Figure 2-6
VHO IP capacity analysis.

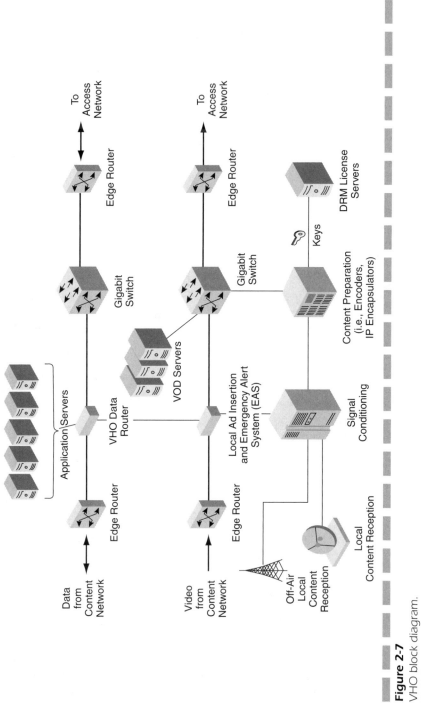

Figure 2-7
VHO block diagram.

Telco Access Network

The access network provides the network link from the core network (national content, local content and data) to consumer homes. It provides a network translation from the switched network (for example, fiber based) to whichever access technology the network operator uses to get data into customer homes as well as the last critical step in connecting homes to the overall network. The access network is often called the "last mile."

Some Telco network operators such as AT&T utilize DSL (Digital Subscriber Line) technologies to deliver their IPTV and broadband services to the homes over their access network. They can choose between various ADSL (asymmetric DSL) technologies (DSL, DSL2, DSL2+, and so on) or VDSL (very high bit-rate DSL) technology. Digital Subscriber Line Access Multiplexers (DSLAMs) transfer the signals from optical fiber to copper wire for DSL delivery. Because DSLAMs are often placed within local neighborhoods, these IPTV systems are sometimes called fiber-to-the-curb (FTTC) deployments.

Other Telco operators such as Verizon are deploying fiber-to-the-home (FTTH), in which optical fiber is used all the way to the consumer's home. FTTH provides high bandwidth all the way to the consumer and can deliver many services simultaneously; however, FTTH is typically a more expensive approach.

The access network for FTTC deployments (Figure 2-8) delivers the IPTV content from the core network via a WAN interface (for example, an optical interface) to Gigabit Ethernet switches. In FFTC deployments, these Ethernet switches connect to DSLAMs that provide consumers access to their data and content. DSLAMs can be located at the VCO or closer to the home within neighborhoods (apart from the VCO). The combination of the DSLAM and the Ethernet switch reduce the required bandwidth in the access network because these devices will route data that is intended for each port or subscriber. This way, the access network will not route the entire channel lineup to each consumer's home but only the channels that are actively being watched.

In an FTTH deployment, the access network is a transition from an active optical fiber network to a passive optical network (PON). The optical fiber carrying the various data and video services is repeatedly split within the PON using passive splitters until it reaches individual homes. A PON is less expensive to deploy and maintain than an active one. Because the last-mile access network contains most of the miles of fiber required to reach millions of homes, the less expensive PON architecture is used. There are many varieties of PON technology with var-

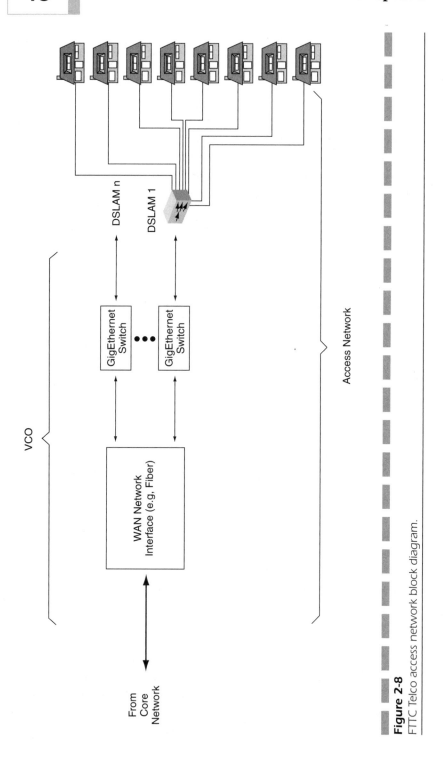

Figure 2-8

FTTC Telco access network block diagram.

ious bandwidths and networking technologies. These include asynchronous transfer mode PON (APON), Ethernet PON (EPON), and Gigabit PON (GPON).

Cable Access Network

The access network for a cable operator uses Quadrature Amplitude Modulation (QAM) modulated RF signals over coax cable. Just as DSL technology enables broadband data services over twisted-pair telephone wires, the DOCSIS (Data Over Cable Service Interface Specification) technology allows cable operators to deploy broadband services over their coax networks. With DOCSIS, part of their cable network becomes an IP network, which enables IP video streaming, video downloading, and so on. Therefore, a cable operator could deploy video services over an existing DOCSIS-based broadband network. Figure 2-9 shows a cable access network over the last mile to the consumer's home. DOCSIS specifies a Quadrature Phase Shift Keying (QPSK) modulated RF signal for the upstream return channel. A Cable Modem Termination System (CMTS) mediates between the IP-based core network and the RF coax plant, using QAM modulation for downstream communications and QPSK for upstream.

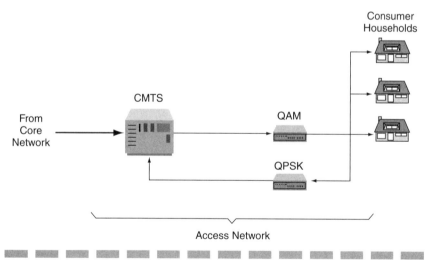

Figure 2-9
Cable access network block diagram.

Home Network

The typical home network (which will be covered in more detail in Chapter 5) consists of a broadband modem plus router (the combination of these two devices is a *residential gateway*); and client devices such as IPTV STBs and computers. The modem translates the modulation protocol of the access network (DSL for Telco, DOCSIS for cable) into one of the standard home networking technologies. Various physical-layer technologies are used for distributing broadband data within the home including wireless, CAT5 Ethernet, coax, phoneline, or powerline. Video distribution within the home presents additional challenges due to high bandwidth and quality of service requirements. In the end, the home network will be responsible for delivering IPTV data (for example, video content and data) to the television via an IP STB, and Internet data to computers within the home.

Content Security

Implicit in this model of an IPTV system is the use of an IP-based DRM system. Condtion access systems (CASs) have been deployed in traditional broadcast systems and often rely on the unidirectional characteristics of these networks to protect the content. Special security messages are transmitted in-band along with the content. If hackers or pirates are able to crack these messages and keys, the content would become compromised. Unlike CAS, DRM systems use two-way authentication methods, making them more secure than broadcast-only CA methods. An IP-based DRM system acts above the IP layer; therefore it is not integrated into transport-specific hardware such as current cable systems. With DRM, usage rights are held separate from the content. As a result, rights can be determined on a case-by-case or user-by-user basis at the time of decode request.

The IPTV network operator will review all content that flows throughout the system and determine which content requires content protection. Often, most of the content on the network will require some level of protection; otherwise, anyone could tap into the network and watch content without paying for it. Examples of content the network operator *would* want to protect includes high-value content, content that the content creators (that is, movie studios, cable channels, and so on) demand be protected; pay-per-view (PPV) or near-video-on-demand (NVOD), and VOD. Premium movie channels such as HBO that provide the latest released movies and popular programming clearly require protection. Examples of content the network operator *would not* want to protect (that is, encrypt) include channels that advertise the IPTV service or tell consumers how to sign up for the service (such as Barker channels), local channels (including public broadcasting), and advertisement channels (such as advertising the programming library for PPV, NVOD, and VOD). Content that is not protected is called *content in the clear*, meaning there is no encryption or protection scheme associated with it.

Digital Rights Management (DRM) DRM can effectively utilize the bidirectional IP network and secure IP protocols to provide the IPTV network operator a secure mechanism for delivering high-value content over a network in a protected manner. DRM can be implemented in many ways and multiple DRM vendors offer products for IPTV networks. Therefore, the IPTV system architect has various options available and can choose a solution that best fits his or her particular requirements.

Digital encryption is used to scramble the content and protect it from unauthorized viewing. The IPTV system architect will need to consider both the solution that encrypts content as it enters the system and the component that enables a subscriber to decrypt and view the content (as desired) in a seamless fashion.

Two types of content must be considered, each with its own special needs for encryption:

- **Non–real-time content.** Examples include VOD and PPV (NVOD), which are movies or special events that are prerecorded material. When this content enters the system, it is stored on a server for playback (such as a VOD server). Often, when the content is ingested into a server, the content protection system (DRM) encrypts and protects it as it is stored within the server's hard drives. This encryption can be accomplished with a DRM license server along with the VOD ingest server over a secure or local network. Therefore, DRM license servers should be co-located with the VOD servers to keep the communications secure. As indicated, VOD servers can reside in either the super headend (content network) or the VHO (core network). Depending on where the IPTV network operator places the VOD servers, they will need an ingestion strategy that may include the addition of a DRM server for content protection.

- **Real-time content.** Examples include linear programming such as broadcast channels (ESPN, HBO, and so on). These channels will be entering the system (primarily) at the super headend via the content reception equipment (satellite receiver, IRDs, and so on). After this material gets processed and encoded, it will be encrypted before it leaves the super headend. Therefore, the content protection system will need to interface with the content preparation equipment (digital encoders), resulting in an encrypted digital bitstream of the channel.

When consumers want to view content (via the decryption process in the home) that has been protected with DRM, the client devices will need to communicate with a DRM license server. Often VOD servers and DRM license servers are located within the core network (VHO) to minimize network traffic between the content network and the core network. However, this is dependent of the IPTV system architecture and can be located in either location. Figure 2-10 steps through a fictitious VOD purchase scenario to demonstrate a typical communication session between an IP STB, VOD server, and DRM license server.

1. Using the IP STB, the consumer navigates through the various user interface screens and ultimately purchases a VOD movie.

2. The IP STB sends a secure message to the DRM license server requesting a license (with decryption keys) to view the associated content or VOD movie.

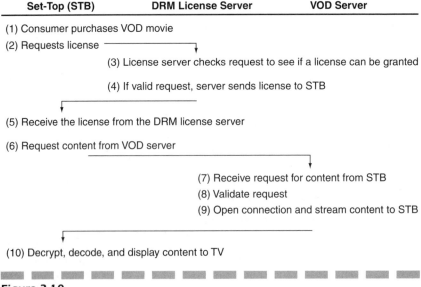

Figure 2-10
VOD purchase process of DRM-protected content.

3. The DRM license server receives the client request and checks its database to see if this subscriber is trusted, in good standing, and should be allowed to view VOD content.

4. If the DRM license server finds nothing wrong with the request, it will securely send an encrypted license to the IP STB.

5. The IP STB receives the license, decrypts it with its secure private keys, and stores it.

6. The IP STB is now able to view the VOD content and sends a request to the VOD server to start streaming the content.

7. The VOD server receives the request from the IP STB.

8. The VOD server processes the request, including a validation procedure to determine whether it has sufficient resources (for example, can the server stream another movie, does it have sufficient network bandwidth, and so on).

9. Once the VOD is able to support the request, it will open a network connection and stream the desired content to the IP STB.

10. The IP STB will start to receive the VOD stream, decrypt the packets, decode the bitstream, and render the content to the television.

Condition Access System (CAS)   The CAS system determines which subscribers (or, more precisely, which STBs in subscribers' homes) are permitted access to the content. CAS systems have been around a while and been deployed in large-scale systems from digital satellite to digital cable. For the most part, they effectively utilize a unidirectional network by transmitting in-band security packets (such as ECM [Entitlement Control Message], EMM [Entitlement Management Message], and so on) that provide a network operator a secure mechanism for delivering high-value content over their network.

As content enters the network (typically at the super headend), it gets processed with the CAS system's encryption system. Part of this process includes the creation of ECMs that client devices utilize to obtain valid keys for decryption of the content for playback. These ECMs are part of the content's transport (for example, MPEG-2 transport stream) and will have their own program identifier (PID). Broadcast content is real-time encoded with CAS processed simultaneously in the headend, resulting in a bitstream containing ECM packets as well as audio and video packets. As VOD content gets ingested into the VOD servers, it will be processed by the CAS system resulting in a bitstream (much like the broadcast content bitstream) containing ECM packets as well as audio and video packets.

Since a CAS system in a unidirectional network does not include a server for the client to communicate with, the system relies on embedded hardware (in a client device) to perform this function. Two common approaches for this are for the IP STB to include a smart card (SC) or an embedded security module. These two devices have an on-board micro-processor that communicates with the client device. The primary differ-ence between an SC and an embedded approach is that an SC is removable and can be easily replaced where an embedded module can-not. From a security perspective, an embedded approach is often more secure than an SC because it is difficult for a hacker to get to critical data and reverse-engineer the process. However, once a system gets hacked, the SC system can easily be updated by simply replacing the SC, where an embedded approach would require the entire STB to be replaced.

As with DRM, the IPTV system architect will need to accommodate a process that wants to encrypt content as it enters the system, and a process for subscribers to be able to decrypt and view the content. CAS protects the content by decrypting it in real-time after it is digitally encoded (before it leaves the super headend), and encrypting the non–real-time content as it gets ingested for storage at the VOD server or the PPV server.

When consumers want to view content that has been protected with CAS, the client devices need to communicate with either an SC or an embedded security module. Figure 2-11 steps through a fictitious PPV purchase scenario that demonstrates the required communication between an IP STB and an SC. A similar process would take place for a VOD purchase.

1. Using the IP STB, the consumer navigates through the various user interface screens and ultimately purchases a PPV movie.

2. The STB formats the purchase data and sends a purchase request to the SC, requesting addition of an entitlement to it for the upcoming PPV event.

3. The SC validates the request and stores the new entitlement in its nonvolatile memory. Note: At a later date the STB will communicate via its low-speed modem (via a telephone for satellite or via the coax for cable) to the billing system, registering the purchases the subscriber made so the network operator can bill the customer.

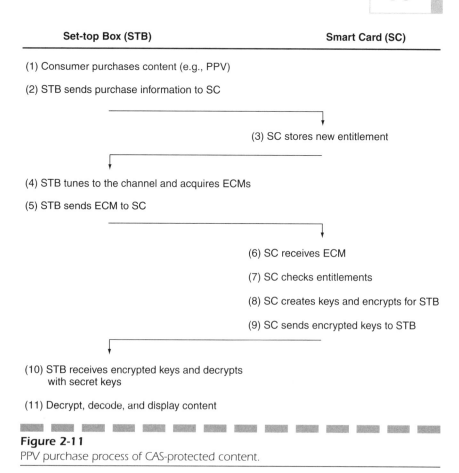

Figure 2-11
PPV purchase process of CAS-protected content.

4. When the PPV event starts, the STB will tune to the proper channel and start to acquire audio, video, and CA (that is, ECMs) packets.

5. When the STB receives an ECM, it will immediately send it to the SC to get keys for decrypting the content. Note: Any audio and video packets will be discarded because the STB does not yet have the keys required for decryption.

6. The SC will receive the ECM from the STB and start to process it.

7. The SC will check the ECM against its list of entitlements (programs it can watch). If the SC determines that the STB is entitled to watch the event, it will start to process the ECM.

8. The SC will take the associated decryption keys, re-encrypt them with a public/private key (shared by the STB), and package them in a message for the STB.

9. The SC will send the STB the message containing encrypted keys for viewing the PPV content.

10. The STB receives the message from the SC and processes it. The STB will then decrypt the encrypted keys with its portion of the public/private key, and store the decryption keys in a secure location within the STB hardware for decrypting content.

11. Once the STB has the correct decryption keys, it can start to process incoming audio and video packets, decrypt the content, decode it, and render it to the television.

Internet Television

As indicated earlier in this chapter, over-the-top Internet television differs greatly from facilities-based IPTV. Facilities-based IPTV is deployed over a private or managed network, where a level of quality of service (QoS) is provided. Internet television takes the opposite approach, leveraging the existing Internet infrastructure, using a "best effort" approach, and depending on a large customer base having broadband service. The cable and telephone companies are aggressively growing their IP networks, expanding broadband coverage, increasing broadband penetration (more than 40 million subscribers in the US), increasing available bandwidth to the home, and reducing the average cost for service. As this trend continues (especially increased bandwidth to the home), Internet television's capability increases as well.

Internet Television System Architecture

To understand how an over-the-top Internet television system could be deployed, we will explore a "concept" of an Internet television system or service. This system can be broken into three areas (shown in Figure 2-12):

- **Source.** Represents the sources of content the over-the-top Internet television system would provide with its service.

- **Distribution.** The distribution of our system includes the Internet and the broadband networks that bring the Internet into consumer homes today.

- **Consumers.** The residential home where the Internet television will be enjoyed.

Figure 2-12
High-level block diagram of an Internet television system.

We do not envision that Internet television systems will replace commercial systems (such as cable or satellite); instead, it will augment them with additional (niche) content. Niche content in which consumers are interested but is not typically included in commercial systems includes various Internet video sources such as local traffic cams, webcasts, podcasts, and so on. Because the intention of this "concept" system is to be a portal for the consumer's viewing, the system should incorporate a small set of popular broadcast channels (such as ESPN, CNN, and so on) that are always up, provide a guaranteed playback (supported format type and resolution), and provide higher quality video than normal web-based audio-video. The main purpose for these channels is to encourage consumers to use the system while they view frequently watched channels. Another key feature for this system includes a reliable portal EPG that will always connect and display the broadcast channels first, and then provide listings for previously watched web content. What is important is the fact that Internet television will most likely be an advertisement revenue–based business model that requires popular content and many "eyeballs."

Since the over-the-top Internet television service is targeted for the living room televisions and not hidden in the study (as computers often are), it will need to target consumer entertainment devices and not just computers. For example, graphics in the user interface will need to be designed for televisions and not just for computer monitors for four basic reasons: First, due to interlaced technology in television displays (versus progressive technology in computer monitors), graphical elements that appear fine on the computer may flicker on a television. Second, typical viewing distance of several feet versus one or two feet requires a user interface with visual elements (buttons) versus a textual one. Third, the client device needs to function like consumer electronics equipment, meaning the device works out of the box without the need for drivers to be downloaded and/or installed, or any other software maintenance functions. Fourth, the links in the EPG or portal should function, or at least show an indicator with a confidence level (for example, green = high, yellow = moderate, and red = risky). Consumers using this service in their living room will not tolerate or will quickly get irritated by EPG links that are not active or up to date.

Expanding the service block diagram (Figure 2-13), you can see how content flows through the system and how the Internet television portal controls the flow of data and the overall consumer experience.

The components in this system are as follows:

- **Internet broadband cable and Telco.** Over-the-top Internet television is based on the existing Internet infrastructure and relies on a large base of consumers who have broadband in their homes.

- **Internet television web portal.** The portal is the central point for this system. Consumers navigate to this default web page with their computer or IP STB. It provides them access to any and all content within the system (including Internet content).

- **Broadcast video.** Sources of real-time broadcast video with relatively low value or requiring no content protection.

- **Secure broadcast video.** Some high-value broadcast video requires content protection. If an Internet television system is able to include high-value content (for example, broadcast, VOD, and so on), the overall service becomes more valuable to the consumers, which could translate to more revenue for the operator of the system.

- **Unicast/VOD.** A number of channels or source content will be provided to the consumers via unicast. Most of the public Internet isn't multicast enabled yet, requiring content to be unicast to each subscriber. Not being able to take advantage of the bandwidth savings of multicast may limit the amount of broadcast content such a service can provide. VOD content, because it is of high value, will require content protection.

- **Websites.** Internet television isn't entirely about video. At the heart of Internet television are web functionality and the ability to leverage the millions of websites readily available to consumers. The concept we are reviewing has video integrated with websites to provide as rich and compelling a service as possible.

- **Blog sources.** Much like websites, including access to the ever popular blogs would be a nice touch from a service perspective.

- **Residential homes.** The residential homes are the endpoint in the service. Here is where the consumers will be using their IP client devices to access and enjoy the Internet television service.

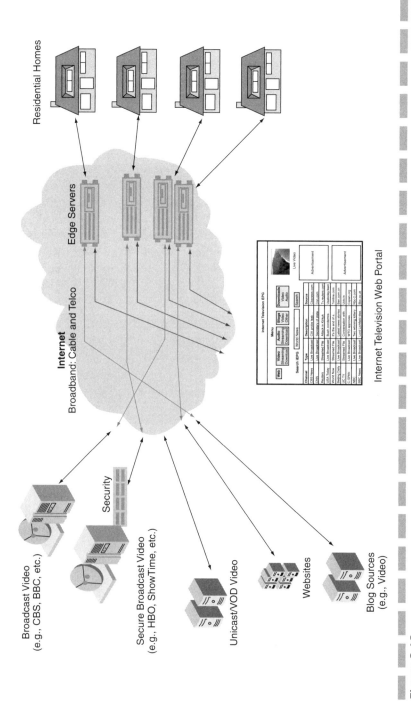

Figure 2-13

Internet television system architecture.

As stated above, the user interface (shown in Figure 2-14) is key to the consumer experience. It acts as a portal to all of the services being offered and controls the flow of data to the user. This figure also highlights some of the features for our "concept" over-the-top Internet television system:

- Streaming audio and video files from a server to the television. This includes web and broadcast content.

- Broadcast programming, including content available in cable and satellite systems.

- High-value VOD content. Comparable to cable, satellite, and DVD rentals.

- Internet radio.

- Downloading of high-value audio/video, and audio only (music) files. This downloading feature would compete head-to-head with the DVD rental market.

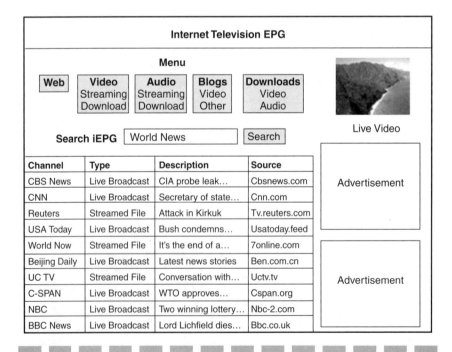

Figure 2-14
Internet television EPG portal.

- Integrate "Internet search" to the user interface to assist the user in finding content.
- Users can save customizable channel lineups.
- Video conferencing (such as via webcam).
- Web surfing at the television.
- Blogs.
- DVR.
- DHN support.
- Advertising.

Additional Applications for IPTV

IPTV isn't exclusively for home consumption. IPTV is a great candidate for businesses to utilize for projects that were considered too difficult or too expensive to implement with other technologies. IPTV simplifies the integration of video into applications, lowers CAPEX (capital expenditures that include purchase of new equipment) spending, and reduces maintenance and support costs. Numerous applications in the business world (both B2B and B2C) could utilize core IPTV technology, including video enterprise, digital signage, and distance learning, for example. This trend will continue to grow as more companies explore the advantages and capabilities IPTV provides and realize how IPTV can be applied. Thus, current IPTV business applications can be used in large corporations, department stores, grocery stores, convenience stores, gas stations, airlines, gambling facilities, and shopping malls.

Digital Signage

A typical digital signage system includes display devices, IPTV STBs, an IP network, and IPTV servers (see Figure 2-15) that have a network connection/interface (such as IP, satellite, and so on). The purpose of the system is to provide attention grabbing displays with content that is continuously changing, which research has shown to be a much more effective advertising approach versus static signs (such as billboards, posters, and so on). The types of advertising content displayed in a digi-

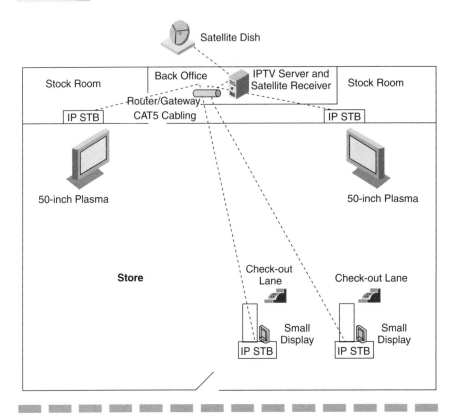

Figure 2-15
Basic IPTV digital signage system architecture.

tal sign include digital video (MPEG-2, AVC, or VC1), animated graphics (such as those built using Macromedia Flash), high-resolution glossy images (JPEG), and computer-generated images (PowerPoint, and so on) with rich text. Possibly the most important piece for digital signage is the display device; this is ultimately where the consumer sees the advertisement. These display devices can be large, high definition monitors (such as DLP, LCD, plasma, and projection), small to large televisions, small and portable LCD displays, or free-standing kiosks.

When building out an IPTV digital signage system (see Figure 2-16), the following system components are often required:

• **Display devices.** Some projects require large and expensive monitors throughout the store for maximum effect, while others require a mix of small displays (for example, at a cash register).

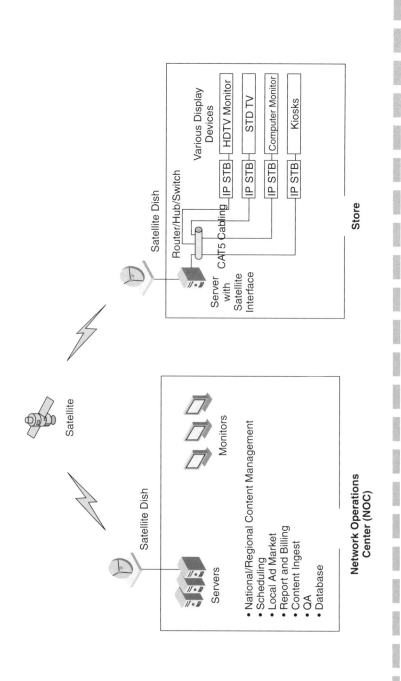

Figure 2-16
Complete end-to-end digital signage system.

Cost versus advertisement effect often plays a role in the final selection of display devices. Also, some digital signs include multiple screens side-by-side, creating an even larger display with interesting effects. Other interesting approaches include rotating a 16×9 HD plasma monitor 90 degrees. Creativity generates an infinite number of possible approaches, enhancing the attractiveness of digital displays.

- **IP STB.** Minimal user interface and is designed to present content (advertisements) to various display devices. The output signals on the IP STB vary: S-video, composite video, high definition component video, high definition multimedia interface (HDMI), and video graphics array (VGA). The network interface is primarily Ethernet or wireless (WiFi). Playlists dictate the content play-out and can be controlled locally (for example, via a hard drive), remotely from a server, or the STB can connect to a multicast or unicast stream and the server manages the video stream.

- **IP network.** Typically consists of IP devices connecting to CAT5 cabling (for Ethernet) or sometimes wireless devices for difficult to reach (with cables) places. However, wireless could present distribution problems with intermittent interference (for example, wireless phones, microwaves, and so on) and a good digital signage system must be robust with little to no required support.

- **Router/switch/hub.** Connect to the IP network providing routing capability for the entire IP network. This is critical for computers, IP STBs, and other hardware.

- **Server.** Instrumental in getting content into the system from remote locations, monitoring the health of the system (including a reporting mechanism), and controlling the IP STBs (for example, playlist, video scheduling, and so on). Often has either a satellite or broadband connection allowing for data/content ingest, and monitoring and control information to be sent back to the network operations center (NOC).

- **Network operations center (NOC).** A control center provided by a professional digital signage company to manage the systems in the field. The NOC provides the connection to the servers (in the stores) as well as the flow of content to them. The services the NOC supports are satellite uplink, scheduling, quality control, operations, reporting, and billing.

Enterprise Video

Enterprise video is a broad topic that includes many applications identified earlier. A good example of enterprise video that highlights the most common system elements required (see Figure 2-17) is a B2B communications IPTV system. In this example we show a financial company that invests clients' money (stocks, bonds, and so on). This company wants to distribute information that its analysts create to customers who walk into the regional offices.

The corporate headquarters is where their financial analysts reside. The analysts monitor the various financial markets and generate numerous reports, recommendations, and videos for their clients (investment strategies, retirement planning, college tuition savings plans, and so on). The content is created, reviewed, and approved at the headquarters. When the content is ready for distribution (daily), the headquarters office will transfer it to its regional offices over a broadband (or satellite) network.

Each regional office connects to the headquarters servers via the broadband network. The content could be pushed to the regional offices (headquarters sends it to each office) or pulled (regional office requests the files from the headquarters). Some of this content could also be tar-

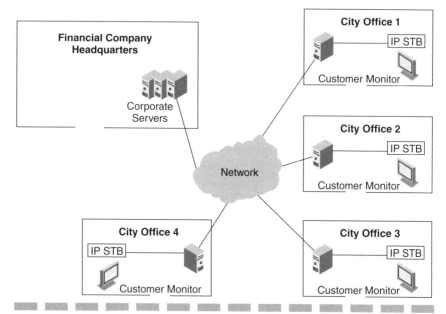

Figure 2-17
Enterprise video system diagram.

geted for certain regional offices (local stock tips) and not necessarily all of them. Once at the regional office, the content can be either transferred to the IP STB hard disk for local playback (along with a playlist) or streamed from the server over the IP network to the IP STB. Then clients can walk into the regional office and watch the daily clip while enjoying a cup of coffee.

Peer-To-Peer (P2P)

There can be no denying the fact that P2P has become so popular it has started to dominate the overall Internet traffic statistics. Consumers can easily obtain free, open source P2P software for viewing and uploading video content from PCs. Such software has been used to share computer games, music files, and increasingly video files.

P2P is a technology for sharing content among computers that are owned by individuals and not necessarily companies or corporations. These computers form P2P networks where once content enters the P2P network it can then be shared among other P2P clients within the network. This approach can greatly speed up the process or time required for a file transfer.

In a P2P network, content is not distributed from a single source to many homes directly. Instead, the source sends parts of the content to a handful of "seed" homes. These homes in turn feed parts of the content to other homes, and so on, until each home has every part of the entire file. A client application on the user's PC monitors which parts are needed and downloads the content in the background while simultaneously offering parts it has already downloaded to other client applications in other homes. A companion application allows anyone to create his or her own channel of video content and serve it onto the network. This application handles seeding parts of the content out into the network.

Some claim that P2P publishing means file size and cost are not issues anymore, so you can offer full-screen video with no bandwidth costs. In this distributed model, the content publisher needs to serve the content only to a few seed PCs, and the distributed software will spread it throughout the network. The cost model for distributing video content over the general Internet was disadvantageous because the unicast model did not scale well. The over-the-top service provider (Internet television providers) would have to increase server capacity and incur increased bandwidth costs as the number of subscribers increased. P2P or swarming technologies could effectively reduce these costs by seeding the content with a smaller number of subscribers who subsequently share the content with others. This effectively shifts the costs of over-the-top providers to the broadband service provider. The concept is illustrated in Figure 2-18.

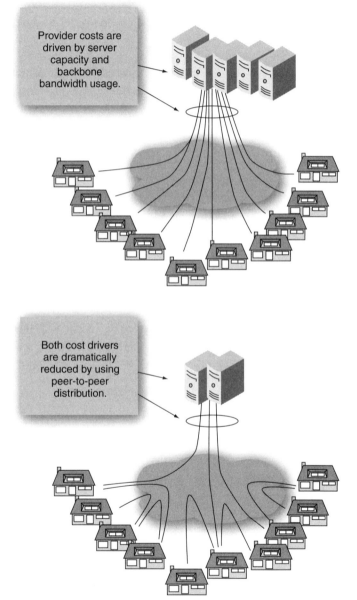

Figure 2-18

Instead of serving content individually to each subscriber, resulting in costs that scale with subscriber growth, the content can be seeded to fewer subscribers and then shared with others.

Provider costs are driven by server capacity and backbone bandwidth usage.

Both cost drivers are dramatically reduced by using peer-to-peer distribution.

Recognizing the questionable legality of such services if they were to be used to publish copyrighted or marked broadcast material, the open question is how the Motion Picture Association of America and National Association of Broadcasters will react if large numbers of people were to upload copyrighted and broadcast television content. Will they issue thousands of lawsuits like the Recording Industry Association of America does today to individuals who use this software? Will it be possible to pursue offshore websites creating channels for the service?

CHAPTER 3

The Technology of Internet Protocol Networks

As the title of this book implies, IPTV's foundation is the Internet Protocol (IP) upon which the Internet is based. IP forms a common international language that allows a range of devices, from refrigerators to supercomputers, to communicate anywhere in the world, over a range of physical media, including telephone wires, two-way radios, and optical fiber. A layered approach to IP allows this universality by making different components of a digital network independent, and therefore interchangeable. In its simplest form, IPTV services use IP to deliver digital audio and video bitstreams to consumer devices, ultimately to the television. However, IPTV is much more than a method of delivering digital bitstreams. It also forms the basis for command and control messages that allow consumers to select content and interact in a bidirectional manner with the service delivery system. While broadcast television is passive, IPTV has the ability to be interactive. This allows many new business models to be developed with a television service. We will examine some of these in later chapters.

We'll begin this chapter with an overview of the basics of the IP suite and how it delivers packets of data among devices. We will then dive deeper into some of the pertinent and more advanced protocols that IPTV utilizes in creating a television service. Finally, we will look at how the MPEG-2 and MPEG-4 bitstreams are transported using Internet protocols.

The Internet Protocol Suite

The IP suite is a set of communications protocols that forms the foundation for network communications. IP can be used to deliver data across a network from one digital device to another. While this peer-to-peer (P2P) model of communication is supported by IP, the more common use is in a client-server architecture. In a typical client-server transaction, the client computer requests data from a server computer. Web browsing is an example of the client-server model—for example, a company has a large commercial server hosting information about its products, and the client is a home computer requesting information from this server. These computers rely on standardized software stacks or protocol stacks to communicate between one another. The term *protocol stack* refers to a suite of networking protocols and the actual software stack that executes those protocols on a specific machine. And of course these protocol stacks are developed or compiled specifically for each computer make. In this way, an Apple computer running Mac OS X can communicate with an IBM server running Linux, or any other hundreds of combinations. The common IP language among these computers abstracts away the differences in operating systems, network connections, and hardware architectures (including central processing chips). As more and more consumer electronics devices, in particular televisions, include IP stacks, they will be able to participate in the vast information flow of information on the Internet, in particular IPTV services.

The Layer Model

The power and versatility of the Internet protocols is that they were developed in a modular, or layered, manner. Each layer is self-contained and communicates only with the layer above or below it. The communication between the layers in the stack is standardized while the details of the operations inside the layers are not. In this way, the software inside a layer can be written in any way the programmer prefers as long as it uses the standard communication protocols between layers. The power to this approach is that if the details of a single layer change, it does not affect the other layers.

Figure 3-1 shows a typical software layered approach, or *software stack*. The highest layer is typically an application in which the user may interact with the software. This is usually called the *user interface* (UI). At the lowest layer is the software that interacts with the computer's hardware. Examples of this might include a video driver that manipulates graphics hardware registers or an Ethernet driver that receives and transmits data. In between the upper and lower layers are additional layers designed to interact with one another. This is why software is often referred to as a *software stack*, as these layers are stacked one upon another to form a complete solution.

When two computers are communicating over a network, these systems have similar protocol stacks and are able to send data up or down their respective stacks using a common language. Figure 3-2 shows how two computers can communicate through Internet protocols because they both have the same common protocols and can pass data up or down their software stacks despite their differences in hardware and operating system. In this example, a home computer wants to request a certain web page from a server out on the Internet. That request will originate at the application layer (a web browser) and is

Figure 3-1
Typical
software
architecture
layered
approach.

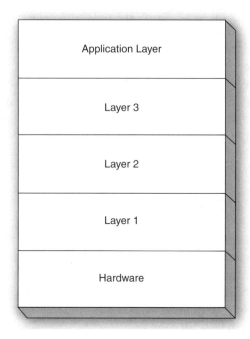

then sent down the home computer's IP software stack (software layers), which will prepare the data so the receiving server will understand the request. The data is sent from the home and makes its way through the Internet to the desired commercial server. The data will then enter the server and is sent through its IP stack, where the information (request) is extracted from the data packet. When the server decides to send the requested web page, it will initiate a response similar to the transmission the home computer made. It will send the desired web page data down its IP stack. This data will leave its computer and building, enter the Internet web, and ultimately make its way to the home computer. The home computer will receive this data, break it down, and send it up its software stack till it reaches the web browser (application) and render it to the monitor.

That may seem like a lot of work just to get to a web page, but that's how the core IP technology works. The Internet itself may contain dozens to hundreds of other devices that handle the data between the home and the server. Each of those devices will have its own IP stack, and the data will pass up and down each. Despite all of these transactions between software layers, you can typically gain access to a web page within a matter of seconds from making the request at the browser.

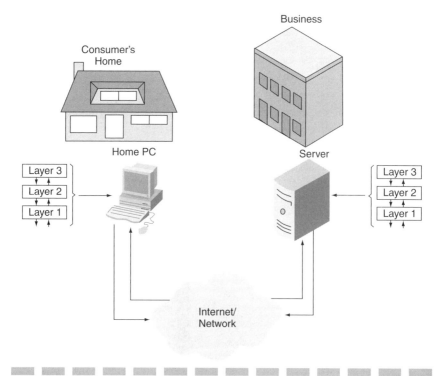

Figure 3-2
Passing data between two systems' protocol stacks.

The OSI Reference Model

The definition of the various layers used in Internet communications are based on the *Open System Interconnection* (OSI) standard or reference model. In fact, most, if not all, networks in operation today utilize the OSI reference model as their core architecture. OSI was developed by the International Organization for Standardization (ISO) back in the early 1980s. ISO is a global standards body formed to create technical standards and has representation from approximately 156 countries. The OSI model is based on seven layers that define how computers talk and transmit data. These seven layers are depicted in Figure 3-3.

- **Layer 1: Physical.** The physical layer defines a physical medium over which the communications will take place. For example, this would represent the cable or wireless interface being used. Protocols for the physical layer would include the timing of signals and the relative voltages on the wire.

Figure 3-3
OSI reference
model.

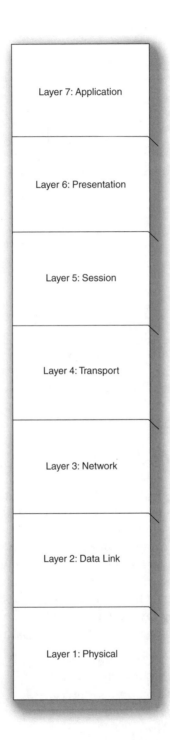

- **Layer 2: Data Link.** The data link layer defines data formatting to enable it to move through the network. Therefore, a network data packet could include parameters such as a checksum to verify integrity, source, and destination address, and the data itself. The data link layer has a *Maximum Transmission Unit* (MTU), or the largest amount of data within a single data packet or datagram allowed within the network. Also, this layer handles the physical and logical connections to the packet's destination by using a network interface.

- **Layer 3: Network.** The network layer is responsible for routing data throughout the entire system or from one network to another, enabling the data to be sent from the source to a destination. As such, the network layer is responsible for managing and directing data packets. For example, on the server side, this layer breaks up extremely large blocks of data that exceed the MTU of the data link layer into smaller transmittable blocks. The receiving computer's network layer would be responsible for reassembling the fragmented data.

- **Layer 4: Transport.** The transport layer manages the transmission method of the data within the network. For example, the desired transmission approach could mandate a reliable method of assuring delivery, such as requesting a retransmission of lost or corrupt data. Other roles or functions that may be performed at the transport layer include reordering of the data and error checking.

- **Layer 5: Session.** The session layer manages sessions between the two communicating computers within the network. For example, the session layer would deal with initiating a session and negotiating the parameters to be used when communicating. Other roles or functions that may be performed at the session layer include managing the ongoing session, requesting a change in parameters, and terminating a session.

- **Layer 6: Presentation.** The presentation layer deals with how the data elements will be transmitted. One way to think of this is the method of converting data from the originating computer's system unique model to a more conventional or standard method for any receiving computer system. This might include the ordering of bits and bytes within a number or converting floating point numbers.

- **Layer 7: Application.** The application layer is where data is managed and manipulated to perform network tasks or services. Examples of this could include web and e-mail access and file transfers. You can think of the application layer as the boundary between the user's experience and the underlying computer and network.

Figure 3-4 shows how Transmission Control Protocol (TCP), IP, and User Datagram Protocol (UDP) fit within the OSI model and how the application sits on top of the TCP/IP/UDP software stack and takes care of the session, presentation, and application layers.

We will focus on layers 3 and above with respect to IPTV. The lower layers define the physical medium upon which the Internet protocols communicate. Because of the layered approach to OSI, different physical solutions to layers 1 and 2 make no difference to layers 3 and above—that is, the lower layers can be interchanged without affecting the others. For example, wireless connections (WiFi or other) versus wired (Ethernet, DSL, or other) connections differ significantly in the implementation of layers 1 and 2, but the protocols in layers 3 and above are identical.

The Network Layer: IP   The network layer is based on IP and is designed to move data from one device to another on the network. More specifically, the layer adds the concept of a source and destination

	TCP/UDP/IP	OSI Model
Figure 3-4 How TCP/IP/UDP map to the OSI reference model.	Application	Layer 7: Application
		Layer 6: Presenation
		Layer 5: Session
	Transport (TCP, UDP, RTP)	Layer 4: Transport
		Layer 3: Network
	Network (IP, IGMP)	Layer 2: Data Link
	Link (Ethernet, WiFi)	Layer 1: Physical

address into the framework. Under IP, each device on a network has a unique digital address (its IP address). To send a digital message between any two computers on a network, the data is broken up into packets (Figure 3-5) in a manner similar to the MPEG-2 standard. At the beginning of each packet in the IP header are two IP addresses: the address of the source (or sender) computer and the address of the destination computer. This simple requirement enables the movement of data through the network, from the source, through intermediate routers, and finally to its destination. Each device on the network looks at the destination address in the IP header. If the address is for a different device, the receiving device passes the packet along to the next device until it eventually arrives at its destination. A good analogy for IP is sending a letter via a series of postcards: the letter is broken into small postcards, and each postcard has a source address and destination address attached to it. The postcards are then sent individually until they all reach their final destination.

IP was designed to transport data to remote devices over an unreliable network. If any one link in the web of connections on the network goes down, packets may find an alternative route to their destination. This is accomplished by duplicating packets; a device receiving a packet from a source destined for some other device may duplicate the packet and pass it along to two other devices on the network. Conversely, if a device is too busy at the moment, it might discard or drop packets that don't belong to it. As a consequence, packets may be duplicated in some places, dropped in others, and may or may not eventually reach their destination.

The Transport Layer: TCP, UDP   As its name implies, the transport layer is the mechanism responsible for getting the data to its destination. As such, the transport layer's tasks include reliability,

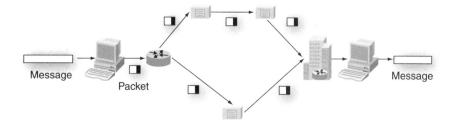

Figure 3-5
IP messages are broken into smaller packets and distributed across the network.

sequencing, and ensuring the right application receives the designated data. Again using the postcard analogy, under IP, the receiver may get duplicates of some postcards or never receive others. When re-creating the original letter, the receiver must put the postcards back in order, throw away duplicates, and request the missing ones. This is what the transport layer protocols do. While this type of delivery system may be acceptable for e-mail, it is not ideal for more time-critical usages such as television images.

The star of the transport layer would be Transmission Control Protocol (TCP). TCP is a reliable, connection-oriented protocol that guarantees reception and in-order delivery of data from a sender to a receiver. For example, under TCP, if a packet doesn't arrive in time and is assumed lost, a request will be sent to the sender to resend that packet. By handling this at the transport layer, all higher layers can safely assume that all parts of the message were delivered. TCP also distinguishes data for multiple applications (such as web server and e-mail server) running on the same host, routing packets to the appropriate application. TCP can provide other services such as monitoring the network traffic and possibly throttling data transmission to avoid or minimize network congestion.

User Datagram Protocol (UDP), on the other hand, is a connectionless protocol that provides a best effort in getting the data to its final destination. For many real-time applications (such as streaming A/V) that are time critical or time sensitive, UDP is often used instead of TCP. UDP minimizes overhead and is not affected by network data loss or delays. But unlike TCP, UDP is not a guaranteed transport mechanism, and if a packet gets lost anywhere along the line, the destination application will simply never get that data. Why would engineers design such as communication protocol? Broadcast IPTV services using IP multicast are actually a good example of how UDP might be preferred over TCP. A typical MPEG-2 compressed bitstream might deliver millions of bits per second, contained in thousands of IP packets. The sending device is broadcasting these thousands of packets potentially to hundreds of devices in the multicast group simultaneously. If a packet gets lost and is not received by one of the viewers, it would not make sense to halt the transmission while a request is made to resend that missing packet. In this scenario, it's easy to conceive that no progress could ever be made because of all of the thousands of possible retransmissions. Instead, the affected receiver does the best it can to recover from the missing data and continue with the transmission. Multicast really comes down to a "best effort" being made to broadcast data from a source to many destinations. Broadcast TV operates in a similar "best effort" fashion when exposed to a weak or lost signal. Analog video exhibits artifacts such as noise or ghosts, and digital satellite or cable displays digital artifacts such as macroblocking (pixellation).

The Application Layer   Typically applications that utilize TCP/IP/ UDP take care of the application layer, presentation layer, and session layer. The application layer is the software that interfaces directly to the TCP/IP/UDP stack. The application layer does not include these network protocol stacks, but simply utilizes them. This layer is the logic that involves making use of the network and underlying protocols to accomplish a user function such as e-mail or web browsing.

Figure 3-6 puts the various layers together by depicting a fictitious communication session between a client and a server over the Internet. In the figure, two "hops" occur between the client's machine and the server. Assume the client is a consumer using a PC, browsing a commercial server's catalog. She is shopping for a new pair of shoes and wants to see a web page that consists of all of the shoes that are currently on sale. The PC's web browser application initiates a request for a specific web page. This request traverses down the PC's network IP stack and out onto the Internet. The request makes its way to the first hop, which is a router. The router, like all Internet-connected devices, has its own IP stack. However, the packets in this case do not need to go past the network layer because this layer is where the network translation occurs. At this layer, the router device will know that this request is not destined for itself so it will send the request onto the next hop. The router will accomplish this by sending the request down its stack and back into the network. The second hop is similar to the first hop. The second router does not have to be an identical router, or even run the same operating system. However, each router has an IP stack following the same protocols.

Because literally millions of packets per second are traversing through these routers, there is a need for speed. These routers are designed to receive requests and send them on their way to the next hop as quickly as possible. Eventually, the request makes its way to the commercial shoe store's web server. The request will make its way up the server's IP protocol stack. The web server will parse the request, formulate a web page based on the details of the request, and send it down its IP stack and back out onto the network. This response does not need to follow the same path in which it came, but it can. Eventually the web page arrives at the requesting PC, travels up the IP stack, and gets rendered by the browser application on the shopper's monitor.

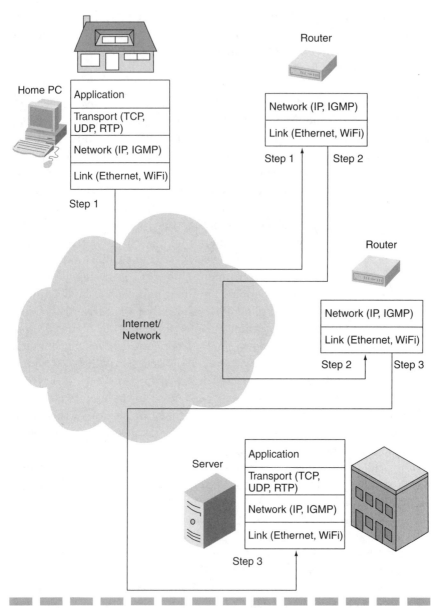

Figure 3-6
An example of a client-server session over the Internet.

Unicast versus Multicast

IP carries some additional protocols designed to perform additional networking functions. One such protocol is Internet Group Management Protocol (IGMP), which is used to manage multicast data. IP is primarily a *unicast* protocol; it was designed to convey messages from a single source device to a single destination device. However, IP also defines multicast addresses, destination addresses that represent more than one destination device. IGMP is used to define which devices are in which *multicast* group.

A unicast session is the conventional networking method two computers use to communicate with one another within a private one-on-one environment or session. The data exchanged between the two computers is intended for just these two machines and no others. Web browsing is a good example of an IP unicast session, with a client computer communicating to a web server possibly requesting web pages, and the web server sending the requested information or web pages back only to the originating web browsing machine. Unicast is the process of sending information to one destination only. If a machine or computer is required to send the same data to multiple destinations but within unicast sessions, the originating computer must replicate the data and send individual streams to each of the desired recipient computers.

From an IPTV perspective, video on demand (VOD) is a great example of a unicast application. Take, for example, a typical IPTV network that includes a (unicast) VOD server, the broadband network, and the client set-top box (STB) in a living room. The consumer would utilize the STB's user interface (UI) to exchange data with the VOD server. At this point, the consumer would initiate a unicast session with the VOD server. The client would ask for web pages depicting all available titles along with cost and receive them via the unicast session from the VOD server. At some point, the consumer finds a VOD title she wants to watch and then initiates the purchase process, which may include security interfaces, all via the client-server unicast session.

Once the VOD movie starts, the connection between the client and server is still a unicast session because this VOD clip is not intended for everyone, just the person who purchased it. Additionally it should be mentioned that VOD clips are typically protected with some type of Digital Rights Management (DRM) scheme to prevent anyone from stealing a clip or viewing it without paying for it, but we'll get into DRM later. Let's assume this consumer has paid for and is watching a VOD movie—

a Doris Day classic—and it is streaming over the network to her home within a unicast session. Since this movie is VOD, the consumer can utilize the back channel to communicate with the VOD server and issue commands. Don't forget that all of this is still unicast with just the consumer and the VOD server communicating. Let's say the phone rings and the consumer wants to pause the movie. She can simply use the remote control to send a command back to the server telling it to pause the movie. Because the network provides for unicast sessions, the server understands that this particular household wants the movie to be paused and does so by stopping the stream of data. Eventually, our Doris Day fan will hang up the phone and return to the movie. She could even rewind the movie a little to get back into the flow of the movie. The communication that enables the client to control the VOD server is accomplished with Internet protocols such as Real-Time Streaming Protocol (RTSP). We will discuss RTSP later in this chapter.

For each unicast VOD session, a separate stream of content exists on the network. This enables VOD, but a significant amount of bandwidth on the overall network is allocated for each consumer's VOD session. For example, if 1000 active movie sessions are underway, the network must accommodate 1000 separate streams. Each stream could be 5 Mbps (Megabits per second) for standard definition or upwards of 15 Mbps for high definition video. That could add up to a huge amount of bandwidth within the network.

Figure 3-7 shows a broadband network with three homes currently playing a VOD movie. Each of these homes has an active unicast session with a VOD server in the Telco headend. Three separate video bitstreams are flowing from the headend/VOD server to each house, along with a back channel for trick mode support (such as pause, play, fast-forward, and rewind).

Multicast, on the other hand, is the process of a single source sending data to multiple destinations (or broadcasting) at a single time. Broadcast television transmits its signal to many users simultaneously with no return communication from the user back to the broadcasting server. Each broadcast television channel would have a unique IP multicast group. Using IGMP, clients are able to receive the broadcast packets and enable the routing of the broadcast stream to their network device through the network. IGMP allows an individual host machine to "join" and "leave" multicast groups by responding to queries by a multicast capable router.

The multicast technique enables a video operator to add broadcast video to a network. It saves a tremendous amount of network bandwidth

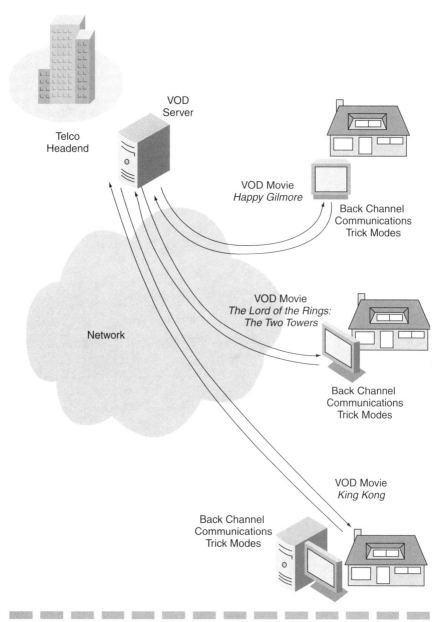

Figure 3-7
VOD using unicast in a broadband network.

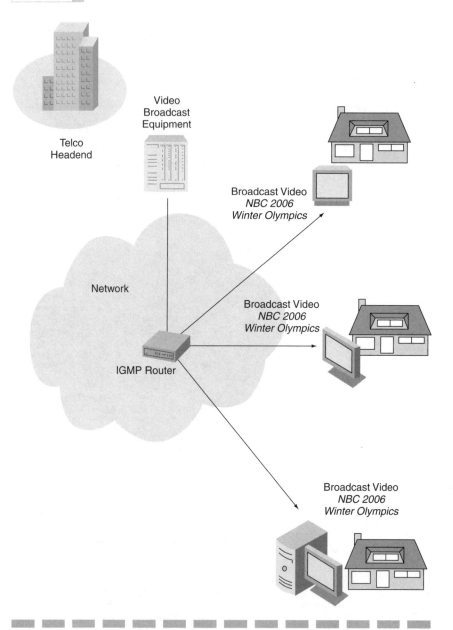

Telco
Headend

Video
Broadcast
Equipment

Broadcast Video
*NBC 2006
Winter Olympics*

Network

Broadcast Video
*NBC 2006
Winter Olympics*

IGMP Router

Broadcast Video
*NBC 2006
Winter Olympics*

Figure 3-8
Broadcast video using multicast in a broadband network.

over unicast, but there is no reliability mechanism so lost packets stay lost. Figure 3-8 shows a broadband network with three homes currently playing the same broadcast video stream (the 2006 Winter Olympics). Each of these homes has an active multicast session receiving the same video bitstream that originates from the Telco headend.

Where does this leave us with regard to multicast versus unicast? Think of these as tools the IPTV network operator should have in a tool chest. Each has its unique purpose in building out a video service. Unicast is the tool of choice for VOD services. Multicast is the tool of choice for broadcast services. Multicast has three advantages over unicast:

- **Saves network bandwidth.** By sending a common data stream out to many users at one time (versus several data streams to many users), multicast saves an enormous amount of network bandwidth.

- **Lowers network congestion.** Because multicast saves a lot of network bandwidth, it naturally saves a lot of network congestion, with fewer collisions and fewer lost or dropped packets at routers.

- **Saves on servers or source load.** With multicast, only one source is required to provide the stream instead of many sources.

For IGMP to be successful at obtaining the bandwidth savings of multicasting instead of unicasting data, every router element in between the source and destination devices must support IGMP. These routers track every request to join or leave the host group for a particular multicast address. Multicast can be applied in private networks where the network operator ensures that the routers within the network are all multicast enabled. Otherwise, the likelihood of users on the Internet being able to receive multicast services is low because most routers out in the Internet are not multicast enabled. Movements to enable multicast networks, such as Mbone (Multicasting backbone), a virtual multicast network with multicast-enabled routers, are in the works.

Multimedia over IP

Multimedia and networking is core to IPTV. Multimedia applications utilize various media types such as text, graphics, animations, audio, and video. Many network-based multimedia applications are available today, and many bright and imaginative minds are working on ideas for applications intended for high speed bidirectional networks. What new, innovative multimedia applications will come out of IPTV are yet to be seen. Some examples of multimedia applications include the following:

- **Video conferencing.** Video conferencing would make an interesting product differentiator for an IPTV service. It includes the real-time streaming of audio (voice) and video data over the broadband service and could be included within the IPTV STB.

- **Streaming audio.** Streaming audio is an existing multimedia application built into existing IPTV devices, which can be customized by the IPTV network operator with an attractive commercial audio package. Examples include Internet radio and audio webcast discussions.

- **Streaming audio and video.** Much like streaming audio, streaming audio and video is an existing multimedia application supported by IPTV devices. The IPTV network operator can bundle in attractive streaming AV services to help differentiate itself from competitors. Examples include education or in-class discussions, video webcasts, and on-demand archive programming.

- **Rich graphics and animations.** Graphics and animations provide a rich multimedia environment to aid in the adoption of advanced or new services (at the IPTV STB), such as interactive services.

- **Internet telephony.** Internet telephony is a growing multimedia application that requires streaming audio over a broadband network. This application enables IPTV network operators to offer a triple-play service (voice, data, and video) to their customers.

These applications are being applied to various products and services, ranging from distance learning, to business to business (B2B) services and business to consumer (B2C) services, to digital signage and collaboration.

Because networked multimedia applications are so important, it is critical for the IPTV network architect or content creator to understand the issues associated with multimedia networking as well as what tools are available to enable effective and compelling new applications. Following are three top issues for multimedia applications:

- **Network bandwidth.** Multimedia applications consume a large amount of network bandwidth. For example, a high quality MPEG-2 movie or broadcast stream could consume 4 to 5 Mbps. Advanced compression (MPEG-4/H.264/AVC/JVT or VC-1/WM9) would greatly improve these numbers and reduce the required bandwidth to approximately 1 to 2 Mbps. However, this is still a large amount of network bandwidth required for a single channel of content. Multiply this by a couple hundred channels and the service is consuming a huge amount of network bandwidth. Careful attention must be made when architecting the commercial IPTV service packages and network to ensure sufficient network bandwidth will be available to ensure scalability.

- **Real-time data flow.** Multimedia applications require real-time response. To stream a two-hour movie at the bit rates identified previously requires constant and consistent real-time processing. The receiver has multiple data buffers, including the input buffer and the decode buffer. It will be processing data in real time from these buffers, and the appropriate buffer levels must be maintained (as data gets consumed, new data must enter the buffer); otherwise, a buffer underflow condition could occur, resulting in broken audio/video. Breaks and interruptions in the content presentation are an unacceptable consumer experience. This puts a lot of pressure on reliable network delivery to process multimedia content in real time.

- **Bursts of network traffic.** Audio and video (multimedia data) content has a tendency to be delivered to the IPTV STB in bursts due to how the content gets digitally encoded or how the data gets routed through the IPTV network. This traffic pattern can play havoc with real-time processing. Some mechanism within the system must smooth out the data delivery to the receiver. Otherwise, if data comes in too fast, the input buffers will overflow, resulting in lost data for decoding. If data comes in too slow, this would result in data underflow, and the application will be starved of data. In either case, the resulting consumer experience will be unacceptable.

Video Streaming Protocols

The task of streaming and decoding digital audio and video over IP networks (suitable for viewing in the living room) provides a new set of challenges from traditional satellite and cable networks. For example, IP networks traditionally provide no real-time quality of service (QoS). Dropping packets, introducing delay or network jitter, has been typically acceptable as long as the data gets to its final destination. However, real-time digital video playback over IP networks cannot afford these disruptions. Additionally, a significant amount of network band-

width is required for video playback, which stresses the network even
further and can also introduce errors or dropped packets. To combat the
various problems associated with IP networks (for real-time streaming
of multimedia content), various Internet protocols have been developed
and proven out. These protocols address QoS, time (clock) management,
session management, VOD trick mode support, and so on. This section
provides a brief overview of some of these protocols.

The Protocol Stack for Streaming Media The software for a
streaming media device would incorporate all of the protocols shown in
Figure 3-9, which reside on top of the IP network layer and UDP transport layer. The relationships among the various protocols as discussed
in this section are also shown in this figure.

The following additional protocols on top of the TCP transport layer
may also be included to complete the software stack:

- **FTP.** In contrast to live broadcast or streaming of media content,
  non–real-time cached video services can be supported by the File
  Transport Protocol (FTP). Timing specific protocol layers such as
  RTP are not needed when using FTP.

- **TFTP/MTFTP.** Multicast Trivial File Transfer Protocol is a simple
  protocol used to transfer files and is implemented on top of UDP.
  This protocol is designed to have a small memory footprint and is
  easy to implement. Therefore, it lacks most of the features of regular
  FTP. This protocol is useful in booting machines that lack non-
  volatile memory or software downloads.

Figure 3-9
Various
streaming
media
protocols.

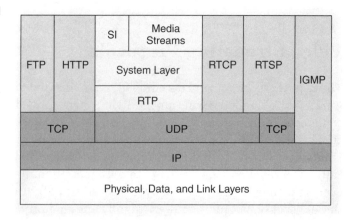

- **HTTP.** The Hypertext Transfer Protocol is the basis for web pages. A streaming video service would probably present web pages listing the services available and use a shopping cart to make purchases.

Intserv, Diffserv, and Quality of Service Due to networking, multimedia data can be affected in the following ways: dropped packets, jitter, delay, and simply errors or data being corrupted. The goal of QoS is to make sure the network can deliver data (end-to-end) with expected and predicted results. This includes latency, error rates, up-time, bandwidth, and network traffic loads. Without a QoS, multimedia applications could suffer greatly because they are extremely sensitive to interruptions, delays, and errors. Furthermore, QoS can be extremely important to a successful IPTV service within a congested network. Only service operators who also own and manage the IP network to the consumers' homes can guarantee QoS for the service. IPTV services that use the general Internet are not guaranteed of the QoS necessary for a good user experience.

Because of this importance, QoS has been a work in progress and continues to be an outstanding issue for IPTV or any networked multimedia application. The Internet Engineering Task Force (IETF) has developed two separate mechanisms designed to address QoS: intserv (Integrated Services) and diffserv (Differentiated Services). Intserv is an approach that places an emphasis at the routers within the network and involves reserving network resources along the data path within the system. All routers within the system implement intserv, and when applications require a real-time service, those applications need to utilize resource reservation (such as Resource Reservation Protocol). Protocols RSVP, RTP, RTCP, and RTSP (explained next) form a foundation for real-time services. Diffserv approaches the problem from a different perspective. Diffserv relies on the data being identified or marked with a "type of service" identifier and diffserv routers treat and prioritize the data according to the class of the data. Therefore, network resources (routers and switches) utilize internal buffers for various queuing schemes and react appropriately depending on how the data is identified.

Resource Reservation Protocol (RSVP) RSVP (RFC 2205) is designed to enable a receiver to reserve network resources through a network for an intserv service. The typical application for RSVP would be a real-time streaming service such as an audio/video clip. The receiver can request a specific quality of service for such a data stream. The receiver would use RSVP to negotiate with the appropriate network resources (such as routers) along with the desired parameters. Once reservations are set up, RSVP is responsible for maintaining router states and ultimately relinquishing the reservations. Following are the primary features of RSVP:

- RSVP flows are simplex, where RSVP reserve resources to send data in only one direction, from the sender to the receiver.

- RSVP supports both unicast and multicast network traffic and manages soft reservation states and adapts to changing membership and routes.

- RSVP is receiver oriented—the receiver initiates and maintains the data flow and the associated resource reservations with each node within the network that will carry the stream or data.

- RSVP provides opaque transport of traffic control and policy control parameters to adapt to new technologies.

Real-time Transport Protocol (RTP)   IP networks can be inherently unreliable and experience unpredictable jitter and delay. The multimedia data that travels on the IP networks must arrive on time and in the same order in which it was sent. RTP (RFC 3550) was designed to address the time-critical requirement of multimedia bitstreams and provides support of the transport of real-time data from the source to the receiver. In doing so, it provides a timestamp and sequence number to assist in dealing with these timing issues. Figure 3-10 shows an RTP packet encapsulated in UDP and IP. The RTP packet has a 12 byte header followed by the data payload containing the multimedia data such as a compressed bitstream. This diagram shows seven 188 byte transport packets that constitute the RTP payload. Within the RTP header is important information such as the timestamp associated with the data in the payload.

The timestamp is the most important piece of data for the real-time application. The source adds a timestamp when the data is first sampled and subsequent timestamps increase over time. The receiver can use the timestamp as a mechanism to determine when the data needs to be processed. Timestamps also provide a mechanism to aid in synchronization between services, such as audio and video. It should be noted that this synchronization is not intended for lip-sync and similar applications. Additional timestamps within the compressed bitstreams are intended for application layer synchronization (for example, PTS, or presentation timestamp for lip-sync).

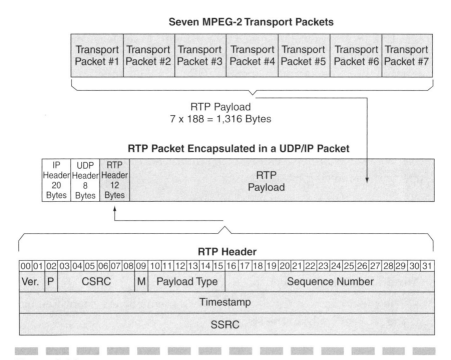

Figure 3-10
An RTP packet encapsulated in UDP/IP.

The sequence number can also be helpful in assisting the receiver in ordering packets. Remember that UDP is not a reliable transport mechanism and the order of the data is not guaranteed.

RTP is used for Session Initiation Protocol (SIP)–based IP telephony and H.323 solutions for video conferencing as well. RTP is both an IETF proposed standard (RFC 1889) and an International Telecommunication Union (ITU) standard (H.225.0).

Real-Time Control Protocol (RTCP)   RTCP (RFC 3550) is a control protocol designed to work with RTP and is defined within the RTP RFC. It is a mechanism used for QoS reporting and relies on a periodic transmission of control packets by all participants to send information regarding quality of the session or membership information. The primary function of RTCP is to provide feedback on the QoS of the RTP service. With this type of feedback information, the sending service can attempt to improve the QoS by taking certain corrective actions.

Real-Time Streaming Protocol (RTSP)   RTSP (RFC 2326) is an application-level protocol designed to work with lower-lever multimedia streaming protocols such as RTP. Its primary role is to provide control over streaming media much like a VCR, allowing functions such as pause or play. It is a great tool for VOD applications that have a unicast session between the client and the VOD server. The client can issue an RTSP PLAY command to start the movie, issue a PAUSE command to stop the movie temporarily, and so on. RTSP also provides the ability to choose delivery channels such as UDP, multicast UDP, and TCP. RTSP supports the following methods:

- **Options.** Enable the client and the server to communicate to the other party their supported options.

- **Describe.** The mechanism used by the server to communicate to the client the media object's (such as VOD movie) description.

- **Announce.** Serves two purposes:

  - The client can post the description of a media object (identified by the request URL) to the server.

  - The server can update the session description in real time.

- **Setup.** Enables the client to request the transport mechanism to be used for an identified media stream. Additionally, the client can change the transport parameters of an existing stream with this method.

- **Play.** Enables the client to tell the server to start sending the bitstream via the transport mechanism specified in a setup request. The client cannot issue a play request until the server has responded (previously) with a successful response from a setup request.

- **Pause.** Causes the media stream to be stopped temporarily. The server resources are typically not lost. However, the server may close a session and free resources if a timeout parameter (defined in the session header) is exceeded.

- **Teardown.** Stops the media stream delivery and frees all associated network resources associated with the session.

- **Get_Parameter.** This request retrieves the value of a parameter of a specified stream.

- **Set_Parameter.** This method enables the client to issue a request to set the value of a parameter of a specified stream.

- **Redirect.** Enables a server to inform a client that it must connect to another server. The redirect request contains the mandatory header location in which the client should issue requests for connection.

- **Record.** Initiates recording a range of media data according to the presentation description.

Session Description Protocol (SDP)   RFC 2327 defines the SDP, which is intended for describing multimedia sessions that include session announcement, session invitation, and other forms of session initiation. A common usage of SDP is for a client to announce a conference session by periodically multicasting an announcement packet to a well-known multicast address and port via the session announcement protocol.

Session Announcement Protocol (SAP)   RFC 2974 defines the SAP, a protocol used to communicate information regarding multicast sessions. An SAP announcer periodically sends a multicast announcement packet out to a well-known multicast address and port. These multicast announcements are of the same scope as the session it is announcing. This way, it is ensuring that those clients can join the multicast, and clients can listen to these announcements to determine whether they want to request the content.

Encapsulating Media Data into IP Packets

The satellite and cable industries were the early adopters of sending digital media into residential homes, and the tools available at the time were MPEG-2 digital bitstreams (MPEG-2 codec) along with MPEG-2 transport stream (TS). RTP, along with advanced compression, is the emerging technology for IPTV or IP networks. The natural progression of IPTV has been to leverage the more mature technology: MPEG-2 codec plus MPEG-2 TS encapsulated with IP, with a transition to advanced compression codec plus RTP encapsulated within IP. This section explores the two different approaches with a focus on required overhead for each.

Encapsulation of MPEG-2 Transport in IP   MPEG-2 transport streams consist of a series of 188 byte transport packets. The simplest way to transport these packets over IP is to insert seven of them into the payload of an IP packet. Ethernet's maximum MTU size is 1500 bytes; therefore, seven MPEG-2 transport packets will fit within the Ethernet frame and eight would exceed it. Figure 3-11 shows how MPEG-2 TS packets can be encapsulated within an UDP/IP packet.

IP Header 20 Bytes	UDP Header 8 Bytes	7 MPEG-2 TS Packets (1,316 Bytes)

Figure 3-11
MPEG-2 TS encapsulated in UDP/IP.

Sending MPEG-2 TS packets over UDP is the simplest method, but this requires sufficient QoS on the network to be effective. It is used extensively within the private networks of cable and telephone companies to deliver MPEG-2 transport streams throughout the system. For general delivery over the unmanaged Internet without QoS guarantees, streaming protocols such as RTP need to be used.

Encapsulation of RTP in IP Two approaches are used for transporting media data with RTP. The first approach would be identical to placing multiple MPEG-2 TS packets into an IP packet, with the exception of the MPEG-2 TS packets first being encapsulated in an RTP packet. Figure 3-10 showed how seven MPEG-2 TS packets were encapsulated within the RTP payload plus the RTP header and UDP/IP headers. The Digital Video Broadcasting over IP Infrastructure (DVB-IPI) group uses this approach.

The other approach is to transport Advanced Video Coding (AVC) data over RTP. RFC 3984 defines the RTP payload format for H.264 (AVC) video. The AVC specification defines a Video Coding Layer (VCL) and a Network Abstraction Layer (NAL). The VCL contains the signal processing functionality of the codec. The output of the VCL is slices that contain an integer number of macroblocks of video data. The NAL encoder encapsulates the slice output of the VCL encoder into NAL units. NAL units are suitable for transmission over networks via RTP and are the smallest possible entity that can be decoded without knowledge of other NAL units. An NAL unit consists of a 1 byte header and payload, and these NAL units are carefully mapped into RTP payloads.

Channel Change Delay

A key requirement in a commercial IPTV service is fast channel change, sometimes referred to as *channel zapping*. Channel zapping occurs when someone starts cycling rapidly through the channels with the remote control and an IP STB. Most consumers expect to see video within a second. If the device changes channel too slowly, consumers can get annoyed and may opt to discontinue the service.

Because IPTV relies on a complex digital switched network and a complex IP software stack, many bottlenecks can occur within the IP end-to-end system, which could adversely affect the time it takes to change channels. Figure 3-12 shows a simplified network diagram of a typical IPTV system. It shows all of the main components in which audio/video data needs to flow through to make its way to the consumer's home. Additionally, when a channel change is selected, the client needs to signal over the bidirectional network back to the network/system to request the necessary routing for the A/V data.

Figure 3-13 represents a typical timeline for an IPTV channel change within a multicast commercial offering. For this example, ignore the time required within the client software to render a UI screen (such as a grid guide) from which someone can change channels. Also, assume the channel lineup is cached within the client machine. The client is booted up and streaming a channel of video to the television.

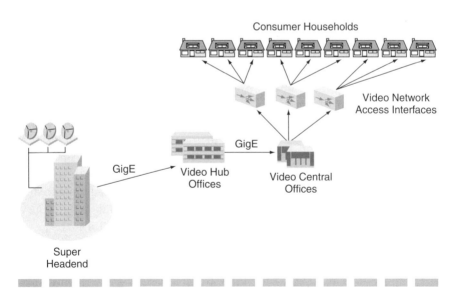

Figure 3-12
Network diagram of an IPTV system.

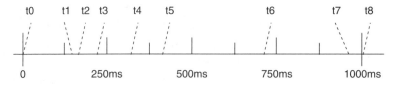

t0 = Channel change selected

t1 = Set-top issues IGMP (multicast) leave → duration ~150ms

t2 = Set-top issues IGMP (multicast) join → duration ~15ms

t3 = Data path routed (e.g., GW, DSLAM, distribution network) → duration ~50ms

t4 = Process system information (e.g., PAT/PMT parsing) → duration → ~100ms

t5 = Decryption keys (if required) → duration ~100ms

t6 = Dejitter buffer fills and reaches threshold → duration ~300ms

t7 = Time to start decoding (e.g., first sequence header) → duration ~250ms

t8 = Decoding of data and display first frame → duration ~35ms

Figure 3-13
IPTV channel change timeline.

Following is a description of the process shown in Figure 3-13:

- **t0.** t0 is the moment in time that the consumer selects the appropriate button on the remote control in which a channel change is initiated.

- **t1.** The client has to tell the network and server to stop sending the current A/V stream. If this step never takes place and the client asks for another A/V stream, the network will stream a second stream to the home. In fact, without IGMP leave requests, the system would continuously ask for more and more streams. The equipment in the home, starting with the router and gateway, will get swamped with too much data and eventually start to drop packets, which will affect video quality. Therefore, t1 is all about the client telling the network to stop streaming data, and this step typically takes approximately 150 milliseconds (ms). Note that some routers are enabled to handle instantaneous leave commands, which could dramatically reduce the time for t1. However, not all networks employ routers with this feature. For this example, we are factoring in the time required for a router that does not support instantaneous leave commands.

- **t2.** Once the client has stopped the multicast stream (with an IGMP leave request), the client will join a different multicast session. This is accomplished with an IGMP join request. The time required for this can be relatively small. Note that, in general, the fewer hops the IGMP requests need to travel the quicker the turnaround time will be for the network to stop the flow or route new data. This is also true for t1.

- **t3.** This is the time required for the system to flow the content to the home; 50 ms is a reasonable time required for this task. The system usually is able to route multicast video streams efficiently through the network to the consumer's home, so the typical time required for this is (usually) relatively small. With a Telco system, if the Video Network Access equipment or DSLAM (Digital Subscriber Line Access Multiplexer) already has the multicast data available, it can simply route that data with the new request. Otherwise, the DSLAM will need to request this data traffic from an upstream router.

- **t4.** The client is now receiving data at the Ethernet jack. The client must start to parse the incoming data for relevant system data (such as channel information, digital format descriptions, and so on). This data will be used later for the demux/decode steps.

- **t5.** If the system has implemented Conditional Access (CA) or DRM, the client will need to get the proper decryption keys from either an in-band or an out-of-band mechanism. Once the decryption system is configured with valid keys, when data comes to the client it will get decrypted and stored in a buffer for demux/decoding. This step is required only if the incoming content is protected and has different keys than the previous channel.

- **t6.** A step that will consume a relatively large amount of time is the filling of a dejitter buffer with A/V data. Because the data is flowing over an IP network, the data comes to the client in bursts. To combat this, the client usually implements a large dejitter buffer. The size of this buffer is driven by the overall system requirements that are derived from the system architecture. For this example, we have selected a 300 ms dejitter buffer.

- **t7.** Many factors are involved in the time required to start decoding, and an important one is the time before an MPEG Intra frame (I-frame) arrives. I-frames are the only frames that contain enough information for the decoder to build a complete picture suitable for rendering. Depending on the digital encoder's settings, the I-frame spacing can vary. Sequence headers contain the necessary information describing parameters within a sequence of pictures. The decoder must search for a sequence header and the first I-frame before it can decode and render any meaningful pictures to the television. For this example, we assume that these sequence headers arrive every 500 ms. Depending on when the client starts to buffer incoming data, the time it has to wait for a new I-frame can be anywhere from 0 to 500 ms. On average the client will have to wait 250 ms for the sequence header of an I-frame to arrive. You can probably see that this time will vary from channel change to channel change, and that this time will be a relatively large amount of time. Also, these I-frames can easily contain five times the amount of bits than the other frames in the video sequence. So the network architect wants to minimize the number of large I-frames within the system to maximize network bandwidth. But the spacing of these I-frames directly relates to the time required for channel change.

- **t8.** The time for the client to decode an I-frame is extremely small. The bulk of t8's time is spent aligning the picture with the vertical blanking and the proper field (odd versus even field).

Using this system, it's going to take approximately 1 second for every channel change. Of course, the time will vary slightly from channel change to channel change. But an average of 1 second would be a reasonable expectation placed on an IP STB. Also, a 1 second channel change is a pretty good response and would provide a relatively good consumer experience. However, many areas can easily push this time upward toward 2 seconds. Network architects need to pay careful attention to all of these parameters because they could lead to a pleasant or unpleasant consumer experience with respect to channel change.

The Technology of Digital Television

To understand the technology behind IPTV, you must first understand the technology behind the second half of the acronym: *digital television*. As with photography and music, television is becoming digital media for consumers. The many advantages of digital formats, in creation, storage, and transmission, are replacing the decades-old analog television format. After decades of little technological change, television began its transition towards digital in the 1990s and is the basis for national satellite television services, digital cable television, and HDTV broadcasts.

This chapter begins with the technology behind digital images, the basis of digital television. Understanding the venerable analog television format can help you better understand its transformation to digital. The essential compression technologies required to make digital television practical are also covered. Readers not interested in all of the technical details may want to skip to the chapter summary.

▮▮ Digital Images

Television is a series of individual images, each displayed for about 1/30 of a second. Likewise, digital television is a series of digital images displayed in sequence. This section examines the properties of digital images and applies not only to digital television but to digital cameras as well.

A digital image consists of a large number of individual colored points of light called *pixels*. If you look closely at any digital display from a computer, or at a printed digital picture, you can see that it is made up of millions of little colored squares. The concept of pixels is familiar to anyone with a digital camera: the number of pixels defines the resolution of the resulting images.

Images are two-dimensional and therefore require an array of pixels organized along rows and columns, or by a series of horizontal lines, each with the same number of pixels per line. The number and density of pixels is related to the resolution of the image. Because an image has two dimensions, the resolution could be different in each dimension. For example, an image could consist of 100,000 pixels, arranged as 250 horizontal lines of 400 pixels each. The total resolution of an image is the product of the number of pixels per line and the number of lines. Digital cameras typically produce digital images with millions of pixels. A standard digital television screen consists of 720 pixels per line and 480 lines, resulting in 345,600 pixels. High definition digital television (HDTV) screens have higher resolutions consisting of several million pixels. However, most digital cameras still have many times more pixels, resulting in higher resolution images than a single television frame.

Another important factor is the ratio of the number of horizontal pixels to the number of vertical pixels. This *aspect ratio* defines the rectangular shape of the resulting image. One of the features of HDTV is the change in aspect ratio from the standard definition television 4:3 ratio to the high definition 16:9 ratio. The larger aspect ratio results in wider images with a wider viewing angle. The wider aspect ratio of HDTV images is meant to resemble the movie theatre experience more closely.

Some examples of digital images and their resolutions are contained in Table 4-1.

Table 4-1   *Digital Images and Details*

Digital Image	Horizontal Resolution	Vertical Resolution	Number of Pixels	Aspect Ratio
One standard definition television frame	720	480	345,600	4:3
One HDTV frame	1920	1080	2 million	16:9
3-megapixel digital camera	2000	1500	3 million	4:3
8-megapixel digital camera	3264	2448	8 million	4:3

Color

Because of the way the human eye works, the color of an object can be completely described by a triplet of three numbers. For example, the color of an object could be described by three numbers representing the relative amount of red, green, and blue (RGB) light it gives off, or it could be described by three numbers representing its brightness, the hue of its color, and the relative saturation of that hue (pale blue to vivid blue, for example). In a color digital image, each pixel has three numbers associated with it, and multiple ways are used to represent these numbers. These different representations are called *color spaces*. Describing a pixel by the relative amount of red, green, and blue colors uses the RGB color space. A pixel that is made up of a 100 percent red component, 0 percent blue, and 0 percent green is a pure red pixel, while one that is composed of a 100 percent red component, 100 percent green component, and 0 percent blue would be a pure yellow pixel. Any pixel with equal amounts of red, green, and blue would appear white or gray depending on the brightness of the pixel. For example, combining 100 percent of red, green, and blue produces a pure white pixel, while 50 percent of each color results in a gray pixel.

The color space used in the analog and digital television signal is called the YUV space, where the number Y represents the relative brightness or luminance of the pixel. The luminance value separates the brightness components from the color component. In the RGB space, the brightness of a pixel depended on the relative amounts of the three color components. In the YUV space, the brightness is completely described by the Y value, and the values of U and V then represent the color information, regardless of its brightness. Interestingly Y, U, and V can be computed from the R, G, and B values via this set of equations:

$$Y = 0.587 \times G + 0.114 \times B + 0.299 \times R$$
$$U = 0.493 \times (B - Y)$$
$$V = 0.877 \times (R - Y)$$

From these equations, you can see that the two chrominance values U and V are found by subtracting the luminance Y from the amount of blue and red, respectively.

With a computer or digital camera, the fact that each pixel is described by three values means that three binary numbers are assigned to each pixel. Those numbers could be stored as 8 bit numbers each or even a higher number of bits. The more bits assigned per pixel, the finer the differences between values and the more colors that can be accurately represented in the image. Professional images typically assign 8 bits per color element, resulting in 24 bits per pixel or more than 16 million possible colors. The number of bits per pixel is sometimes called the *color depth* or *pixel depth* of the digital image. The color information can be stored in RGB space with 8 bits per color, or in the digital television format YUV space with 8 bits per luminance and chrominance value.

The various parameters of a digital image are summarized in the following table:

Parameter	Definition
Image resolution	The total number of pixels making up the image. It is the product of the number of vertical lines (vertical resolution) by the number of pixels per line (horizontal resolution).
Pixel depth	The number of bits used per pixel. There are three numbers per color pixel, so the total pixel depth is the sum of three individual color component depths.
Aspect ratio	The ratio of width to height of either the image or the number of individual pixels. Standard definition television has a 4:3 ratio while HDTV formats use 16:9.

Given all of these factors, you can compute how many bytes it takes to represent a full digital image. This number is the size of the uncompressed or raw image. The amount of memory required for uncompressed digital video is large, because a digital image is produced 30 times a second. Therefore, compression is used to reduce significantly the number of bytes required to represent a sequence of digital frames in digital television streams.

Table 4-2 expands on Table 4-1 to show color depth and image size (in bytes):

Table 4-2 Expanded Table Showing Color Depth and Image Sizes

Digital Image	Horizontal Resolution	Vertical Resolution	Number of Pixels	Aspect Ratio	Color Depth	Bytes per Image
One standard definition television frame	720	480	346,000	4:3	12 bits	518,000
One HDTV frame	1920	1080	2 million	16:9	24 bits	6.2 million
3-megapixel camera	2000	1500	3 million	4:3	24 bits	9 million
8-megapixel camera	3264	2448	8 million	4:3	24 bits	24 million
One minute of HDTV	1920×30 ×60	1080×30 ×60	3.7 billion	16:9	24 bits	11.2 billion (11 GB)

The Advantages of Digital over Analog

Today's world is a digital world. Phonographic record albums and cassette tapes have been replaced by CDs and MP3, film-based cameras have been eclipsed by digital cameras, and more than 40 million homes in the US receive digital television services. Earlier, we listed some of the advantages of digital television. Following are some of the advantages of digital media in general over analog media:

- **More immune to noise in transmission.** Analog media uses the magnitude of the signal to convey information. When this signal is transmitted over the air or over a wire, noise and other forms of signal degradation can occur, affecting the information. With digital signals, only 1s and 0s are transmitted in the signal. Small deformations to the signal do not affect the ability to read those bits on the receiving end. It takes a lot more signal degradation to affect a digital signal than an analog one (see Figure 4-1). For television, this means no ghosting, snow, or fading with poor reception (although digital television signals do introduce their own "artifacts" from poor signals).

- **No degradation in copies.** Making copies of analog signals usually results in a copy that is of poorer quality than the original. Some signal is always lost in the copying process. Because digital signals are just a series of 1s and 0s and less affected by signal degradation, is it possible to make copies that are exact duplicates of the original. This makes it easier to mass-produce copies, something that is both a boon and bane to content creators as a single unprotected or unencrypted copy can be shared among millions of people.

- **Longer storage lifetime.** Related to the relative immunity to noise, digital media may last longer in archives than analog media because the normal degradation that occurs with time will affect a digital signal less than an analog one.

- **Can be digitally compressed.** Digital media signals can be compressed before being stored or transmitted. Compression techniques remove redundant data contained in the signal and therefore take less room than their analog counterparts. Today about ten digital television signals can be transmitted in the same bandwidth as one analog signal.

- **Additional data services can be added.** It is easier to add data to digital media than analog media. For example, labeling an analog

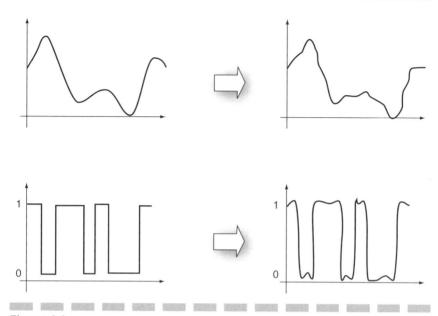

Figure 4-1

Analog signals degrade when even a small amount of noise is added to them; however, the information in a digital signal (just 1s and 0s) is preserved in the presence of small amounts of noise and is not degraded.

video tape as to what it contains involves mechanically writing on the tape or splicing in some video information. With a digital file, you can easily attach and modify additional bits of information known as *metadata*.

- **Easier editing.** With a digital signal it is easier to add, subtract, or modify content. Creating a "mix tape" of your favorite songs is certainly easier with your computer than it was with a phonograph and tape player.

Analog Television

Before we dive into the digital television standards, it is helpful to understand the analog television standard. Many aspects of the analog standard carry over into the digital standard. While the limitations of the analog technology do not apply to the digital signal, the techniques used to create the analog standard have digital counterparts. For example, the concepts of line resolution, color separation, and vertical blanking interval are characteristics of the analog signal and in the digitization process become parts of the digital signal as well.

The National Television System Committee (NTSC) standard was formed in 1941. It defined an acceptable visual quality level given the limitations of technology at the time. It was an excellent compromise between image quality, technical capabilities, and cost to enable a huge consumer market. Its success can be measured by the fact that it has remained a standard for so long and launched such a huge commercial market. Except for the introduction of color, closed captioning, and stereo sound, the television standard has remained virtually unchanged for decades. But like all technical standards, NTSC enables interoperability among manufacturers and a huge number of compatible devices but inhibits innovation. New capabilities and features most likely are outside of the standard and therefore cannot be introduced unless the standard is extended or a new one created.

Some might say that the success of the standard leads to the stagnation of television technology. We'll leave that discussion to others and look at the standard itself. We will focus on the NTSC standard for this book, but readers should note two other major systems are used for analog television throughout the world. The PAL (Phase Alternating Line) and SECAM (*Sequentiel Couleur Avec Memoire*) systems have frame rates of 25 frames per second (FPS) along with 625 scan lines for each frame compared to the NTSC 30 fps and 525 scan lines per frame. SECAM is used in France and parts of Eastern Europe, while most of Western Europe uses the PAL system. Asia and Africa primarily use PAL, while Japan and Korea use NTSC (who not coincidentally also produce most of the television sets for the US).

The NTSC analog signal is a continuous high frequency waveform modulated into one of a series of 6 MHz–wide channels. The waveform is actually a composite signal formed by a number of separate waveforms: these include a signal that indicates the pixel brightness at each location on the television screen, a separate higher frequency signal that indicates the pixel color, stereo audio, and a series of signals used for calibration and timing synchronization. More recently another signal was added that includes closed caption data for the hearing impaired. The digitization process will have to take these components apart and digitize them individually.

If you have ever looked closely at your television screen, you may have noticed that the picture is actually made up of a series of discrete horizontal lines. In a traditional cathode ray tube (CRT) television, each line is formed by moving an electron beam horizontally across the face of the television. The intensity of the beam determines how bright the phosphorous on the surface of the screen is excited. The NTSC standard is 525 horizontal lines, but not all of them are visible on the television screen. The horizontal line varies continuously in brightness and color as it crosses the screen. The complete set of horizontal lines is called a frame. A new frame is produced approximately 30 times a second, or every 33 ms (milliseconds). Therefore, each of the 525 horizontal lines crosses the television screen in about 63 ms (microseconds).

A new frame is produced by starting in the upper left corner of the television screen and scanning to the right (let's call that line number 1). What may be unexpected is that the beam does not continue down to the next line vertically (line 2), but skips a line and continues two lines down to line 3. This line skipping is repeated to produce half of the lines in the frame, in this case all of the odd lines. The beam finishes at the lower right of the screen and then moves back up to the upper left to draw line 2. It then continues with all of the odd lines to form the complete frame. Even though it draws only half of the frame at a line, this occurs so quickly that the viewer's eye does not notice and instead combines the two halves into a single frame.

Figure 4-2 shows the path the electron beam traces across the television screen as it creates a frame. A horizontal scan creates a single line across the screen. The beam must then be shut off as it sweeps back to the left side of the screen and moves down two lines. After creating a whole field (either the even or the odd lines in the frame), the beam must then traverse back up to the upper left corner of the screen to start the next field. The time period during this movement of the beam diagonally across the screen is called the vertical blanking interval, or VBI. The color coding of the three different elements of the formation of a frame, horizontal scans, vertical scan, and the VBI will carry over into the figures below on the NTSC analog signal.

Each half of the interlaced NTSC frame is called a field (the odd field and the even field). And a field is drawn approximately 60 times a second, or about 16 ms. The frame created by drawing each field separately is called an interlaced frame. If each line were to be drawn in order, the frame would be called a progressive frame. Progressive frames are used on computers and some HDTV formats.

Historically, the NTSC frame is interlaced because the technology at the time the standard was developed could not draw each line of the frame in order fast enough to avoid visible flicker. If the drawing process is too slow, the viewer's eye will actually see the frame being drawn and

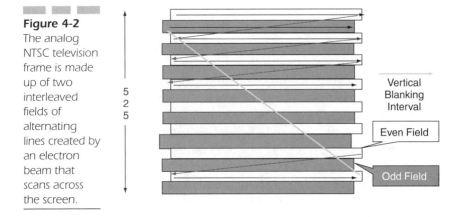

Figure 4-2
The analog NTSC television frame is made up of two interleaved fields of alternating lines created by an electron beam that scans across the screen.

therefore destroy the illusion of continuous frames. When personal computers arrived, the technology had advanced significantly and computer monitors used progressive scanning to create a single frame. It is also easier for a computer to represent a single progressive frames than two interlaced fields in its memory.

The NTSC Scan Line

As described in the preceding section, the electron beam in the CRT scans across the television picture tube to create a series of frames. As the beam crosses the picture tube horizontally, its creates a single horizontal line of pixels. Using an oscilloscope, we can graph the change in electronic potential (magnitude) with time to visualize the NTSC signal. A full-strength NTSC signal will vary in amplitude between –300 millivolts (mV) and 700 mV depending on the brightness of the image.

The magnitude of the signal roughly corresponds to the strength of the electron beam as it traverses the television screen. The strength of the beam is then directly proportional to the brightness of the screen as the beam hits the phosphorous in the glass. Figure 4-3 is a representation of an NTSC signal during the period when the beam scans a single horizontal line across the television screen. Given that a frame has 525 lines and each frame is drawn in 33.33 ms, the amount of time in the graph in the figure corresponds to 63.5 μs.

The signal's magnitude for a single scan line begins with a short negative pulse. This is called a sync pulse and indicates to the television that it's time to start a new line. The electron beam is sent across the screen from the end of the previous line during this sync pulse time period. The

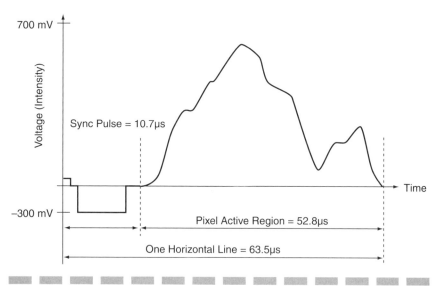

Figure 4-3
The NTSC signal corresponding to a single horizontal scan line across a television frame.

electron beam must be shut off during this period so that the beam does not cause a visible streak as it moves diagonally to the start of the next line. The sync pulse is just one of the set of code pulses in the NTSC signal that are used to signal timing information to the television.

The signal corresponding to the final horizontal line is unique. It must signal to the television that the field is complete and therefore the electron beam needs to move diagonally back to the upper left corner of the screen. The signal for this scan line is shown in Figure 4-4. It consists of a series of unique sync pulses that last for nine scan lines, followed by eleven blank lines. Again because the signal is zero or negative during the nine sync lines the beam does not draw anything on the screen during this interval. Instead of showing twenty black lines at the top of the screen, your television usually hides them under the plastic frame holding the glass screen. Because the lines are hidden, information can be added to the waveform during the VBI to send additional information such as closed caption data.

The NTSC Frame

Some of the 525 horizontal scan lines of a complete NTSC frame, like the final lines of a field, are synchronization signals, while the majority

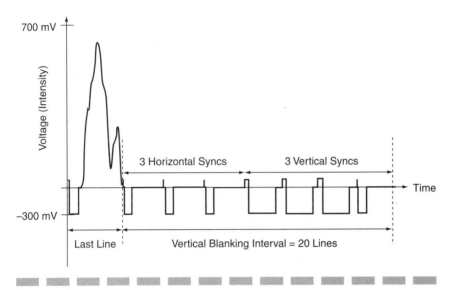

Figure 4-4
The final scan line in the NTSC signal showing the sync pulses contained in the vertical blanking interval.

represent pixel information. A complete NTSC frame is shown in Figure 4-5. It is indicated by 20 lines of sync pulses during the VBI, signaling the start of a new frame, followed by the first field of pixel information, another 20-line VBI, and then the second field, for a total of 525 lines. The two fields together form a single frame. Because the two VBIs do not contain picture information, only 480 of the 525 lines are "active" in that they contain pixel information (brightness and color) to form the picture. The remaining lines contain sync pulses and encoded data that do not contribute to the visible parts of the frame.

The Vertical Blanking Interval As stated earlier, the VBI was created to signal the start of a new field, and also to give the electron beam time to return to the top left of the screen. Electron beam technology has improved considerably and therefore not as much time is required to return the beam to the top. Instead of letting that time go to waste, several data services have been added to the signal during the vertical blanking intervals. It is possible to insert two bytes per line, after error correction, within each VBI. Since there are two VBIs per frame (lines 1–20 and 263–283) and 30 frames per second, the raw bitrate is 60 bps. Because the VBI scan lines are not visible to the user,

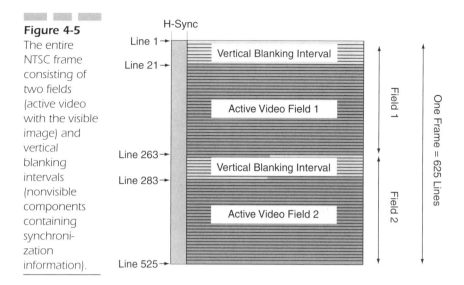

Figure 4-5
The entire NTSC frame consisting of two fields (active video with the visible image) and vertical blanking intervals (nonvisible components containing synchronization information).

adding these signals will not change the television picture. Some of the uses of the VBI lines are listed here:

- Lines 1–9 and 263–272. Still used for the frame sync signal and to give the beam time to return
- Lines 20, 283. Station identification information
- Line 21. Closed caption data
- Line 284. Extended data services

Even though the bitrates of information in the VBI are low, some commercial enterprises have developed around using the data services to broadcast data to millions of analog television customers. The digital television and IPTV standards include provisions for many high bandwidth data services to accompany the audio/visual elements of a television service.

Color in the NTSC Signal

Color was introduced to the analog television standard in the 1960s. With a substantial installed base of black-and-white television, color signals had to be added to the composite signal in a manner that would not affect existing black-and-white TV's. The engineers at the time came up with an ingenious solution whereby two high frequency color signals were added on top of the luminance signal. These high frequency signals were ignored by the older black-and-white televisions.

The YUV color space was chosen for the color television standard because the black-and-white signal already contains the luminance (Y) value of the pixels in the image. Therefore only the U and V signals needed to be added to define the unique color of each pixel. The U and V signals look similar to the luminance signal for a single line: they vary in magnitude as the signal sweeps across a single line. The U and V signals are not simply added to the luminance signal, since then they would interfere with the brightness of the image. Instead, each of the U and V signals is multiplied by a separate high frequency carrier wave before adding to the luminance signal. The frequency of these two carrier waves is 3.58 MHz and they are 90 degrees out of phase from each other. These higher frequency modulated waves average out to zero over the period of a single spot on the television, therefore not affecting the brightness of the spot. Color televisions look for the 3.58 MHz carrier wave and by the phase of the carrier wave determine the values of U and V for that pixel. Just before the active region of a line, during the sync pulse, the color carrier is set to zero phase so the TV can calibrate the phase to get an accurate color reading. This is shown in Figure 4-6.

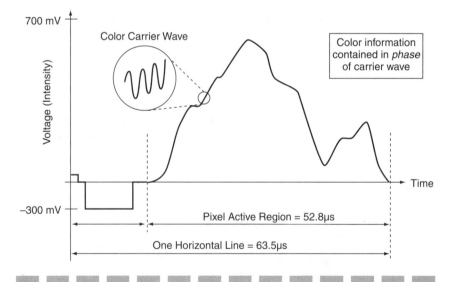

Figure 4-6
Color information is an NTSC signal in encoded by the phase of a carrier wave added to the brightness signal.

The Analog Audio Signal

Like the color information, the audio signal in the NTSC standard is modulated by a carrier wave and added to the luminance and color signals. The carrier wave is at 4.5 MHz relative to the luminance signal. While the modulation is higher than the color signals, the effective bandwidth is much smaller. Audio signals are limited to about 15 kHz of bandwidth, which is less than CD-quality audio that contains two channels with 22.05 kHz of bandwidth.

The original standard had only one channel, or mono audio. In the 1980s, two additional audio channels were added. The first additional audio channel is used to produce stereo sound. To produce stereo from the original mono channel, the second channel sends the difference between the left and right channel, or L–R. The original mono channel contains the sum of the left and right channels, or L+R. By adding and subtracting these two channels, the television receiver is able to recover the independent left and right channels. This clever method allows stereo sound to be transmitted with only one additional channel while maintaining backward compatibility with the original mono receivers. The second additional audio channel is used for carrying the secondary audio program (SAP), typically a (mono) second language version of the audio track for the program.

Putting It All Together: The Composite NTSC Signal

You now know that the analog NTSC signal consists of many separate signals added together: image brightness, color information, audio signals, and data services. Figure 4-7 shows the respective signals, and how they are multiplied by carrier waves and then combined to form the composite signal. At the receiving end, the television must take apart the composite signal to regain the luminance, color, and audio signals.

The Digitization of Analog Television

After more than 50 years of analog television, digital technology has reached the stage where it is economically feasible to work with digital

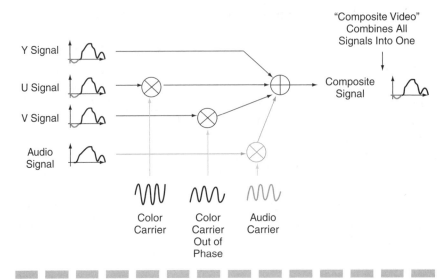

Figure 4-7
The NTSC composite signal consisting of the combination of luminance, chrominance, and audio signals into a single 6 MHz–wide waveform.

television signals instead of analog. However, because a vast amount of existing production equipment, recorded content, and consumers' televisions are still based on the NTSC analog standard, the process of converting between analog and digital television signals is important. It is also useful to review this process to understand some of the nuances of IPTV.

The process of converting analog television signals into digital ones is called *digitization*. Digitization of the NTSC video signal produces a series of digital bits, on the order of hundreds of millions of bits per second. This "bitstream" is the digital equivalent of the NTSC waveform.

The vast amount of data within the digital television bitstream is difficult even for the most advanced computers to manipulate. It is also not feasible to store that much information economically on most digital recording media. Thus, we will spend some time studying the important process of digital video compression, where the raw bitstream is reduced by a factor of 100 into a lower bitrate compressed bitstream.

Sampling and Quantization

More and more content today is captured in digital format and never has to undergo the digitization process. However, you may find it helpful to review the digitization process to help you understand digital television signals. Since the vast majority of television and movie content is still in analog form, most digital television transmissions use analog content that is digitized and delivered as a digital signal.

Two important parameters determine how an analog signal is turned into a digital signal: the sampling rate and the quantization level. For analog media such as music and video, the resulting quality of the signal when it is turned back into an analog signal for consumption depends on the choice of these parameters.

The sampling rate is the number of discrete samples of the analog signal taken per second. Figure 4-8 shows a single line of the NTSC analog signal sampled every T milliseconds. T is called the sample period. The sampling frequency is equal to $1/T$ and is measured in units of Hertz. The value of the analog signal is measured only at the sampling points. Any change in the signal between the sampling points is lost.

The choice of how often to sample the signal depends on the bandwidth of the analog signal. A mathematical formula called the Nyquist theorem states that a signal with bandwidth Fb must be sampled at a frequency Fs greater than or equal to $2 \times$ Fb to capture every frequency within the signal. Sampling at less than this Nyquist frequency can result in a loss of some of the information in the original signal. It can also introduce new information, called artifacts, which were not in the original signal. We saw earlier in the chapter that the NTSC signal is bandwidth limited to 6 MHz before transmission. The Nyquist sampling

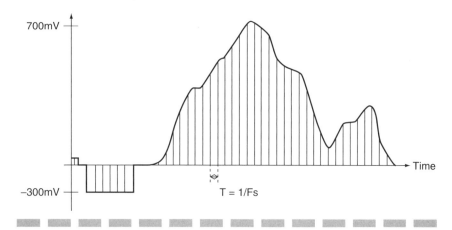

Figure 4-8
The sampling process records the value of a continuous signal at discrete points in time.

frequency would then be 12 MHz. For technical reasons, the sampling rate for digitizing NTSC analog signals is actually Fs = 13.5 MHz.

The second part of the digitization process is the quantization of the signal samples. Quantization determines how many bits of information are allocated to each sample of the analog signal. An analog signal theoretically is a continuous value and therefore could take on any possible value in its range. The quantization process limits the range of possible values. In the binary system of computers, the range of values is always some multiple of 2. The continuous signal is matched to the nearest integer value in the range from 0 to $2^q - 1$, where q is number of bits per sample. Figure 4-9 shows the quantization of the sampled NTSC signal.

As you can see in the figure, the digitization process samples the continuous analog signal only at a discrete set of points in time and quantizes the magnitude into only a finite set of possible values. The quantization process throws away some fidelity from the original analog signal as it limits the possible range to only 2^q values. Some nuances of the original continuous signal might indeed be lost in the process. For most people, the advantages of digital formats outweigh the possible loss of finer details from the digitization process.

CCIR 601 Digitization Standard

In digitizing the NTSC signal, a wide range of different sampling rates and quantizations can be used. Also, the NTSC signal is a composite signal con-

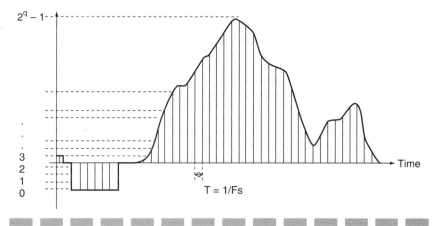

Figure 4-9

Quantization reduces the possible values of the continuous signal to a finite set of values from 0 to $2^q - 1$, where q is the bit depth of the digital signal.

sisting of separate luminance, color, audio, and synchronization signals. Each signal can be sampled and quantized independently, increasing the number of possible parameters used in the process. To standardize the digitization process, *Comite Consultatif International en Radiodiffusion* (CCIR) Recommendation 601 defines a set of encoding parameters. The standard contains a series of different combinations of sampling rates and quantization called formats, with different formats used for different purposes.

Three different sampling formats are of interest to this discussion. The first format is designed for professional or studio use. It offers the highest fidelity of the analog signal. The other two formats are for consumer or home use. They offer less fidelity but are still better than analog VCR recordings in terms of picture quality.

For all three formats, the sampling rates for each component of the composite signal are some multiple of a common base sampling frequency of Fs = 3.375 MHz. The Nyquist sampling rate of 13.5 MHz is four times this base frequency. Some parts of the composite signal will be sampled at less than 13.5 MHz. The Nyquist theorem indicates that this results in a loss of fidelity from the original signal. However, it results in fewer bits and the tradeoff for the loss of image quality is acceptable for consumer use. Each sampling format can also be quantized with either 8 or 10-bit samples. The 10-bit samples have more fidelity but again result in more bits. We look at the three formats of interest in the following sections.

CCIR 601 4:4:4 Format   In this format the luminance (Y) and two chrominance signals (U and V) are each sampled at 4 × Fs = 13.5 MHz. There are therefore 40.5 million samples each second. If each sample is quantized to 10 bits, the resulting bitrate is 405 Mbps. This format preserves much of the detail of the original analog signal and is used in professional video equipment.

CCIR 601 4:2:2 Format   In this format the luminance signal is sampled at 4 × Fs = 13.5 MHz, while the two chrominance signals are sampled at 2 × Fs = 6.75 MHz. This is half the sample rate of the 4:4:4 format. There are two luminance samples for every chrominance pair sample. The resulting sample data rate is 27 M samples/sec, and the resulting bitrates are 216 or 270 Mbps at 8 and 10 bits per sample respectively. This format is used in the professional digital video tape recorder formats called D1 and D5.

CCIR 601 4:2:0 Format   This format is derived from the 4:2:2 format. After sampling the chrominance values for every two luminance samples, the chrominance values from consecutive lines are averaged. The resulting sampling rate is 20.25 M samples/sec and the resulting bitrate for 8 bit samples is 164 Mbps. The consumer-grade 4:2:0 format is used for DVDs and HDTV broadcasts.

601 Color Sampling

The three formats differ by how often the color is sampled. The human visual system is less sensitive to changes in color than it is in luminance. Therefore it is possible to have less color information than luminance information without a large degradation in image quality. When the chrominance (color) signals are sampled at a lower rate than luminance, what is the spatial relationship between the samples? Figure 4-10 shows how the color samples are taken with respect to the luminance samples for the three formats. In the 4:4:4 format, each pixel has its own luminance and chrominance sample. In 4:2:2 sampling, a single color sample is shared by two horizontally adjacent luminance samples. This means that these two pixels are the same color but possibly different brightness. Finally, in the 4:2:0 format, four adjacent pixels share a single set of color values.

Each format uses a different number of bits per pixel on average and therefore the pixel bit depth is different for each format. This color subsampling is actually the first step toward reducing the size of the uncompressed digital television bitstream. The digitized television signal will produce a huge amount of digital data that needs to be reduced to a practical size. While each reduction in the number of bits will lead to some

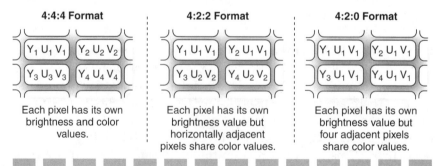

Figure 4-10

Three of the color sampling formats under the 601 standard. As color sampling decreases, adjacent colors share the same color values but have independent luminance values.

loss of fidelity, techniques were developed to minimize the perceived loss in quality. This simple process of sharing color information between pixels already cuts the number of bits per pixel, and therefore the total number of bytes required to represent the image, in half.

Sampling Format	Average Bits per Pixel
4:4:4	24 bits
4:2:2	16 bits
4:2:0	12 bits

Horizontal and Vertical Sampling

In all of the CCIR 601 formats, the luminance signal is sampled at 13.5 MHz. Each line of the television frame is contained in 63.5 µs of the signal, with the first 10.7 µs being the sync pulse and the rest the active interval or actual brightness values for the image. At the sampling rate of 13.5 MHz, the active region will be sampled 720 times (Figure 4-11).

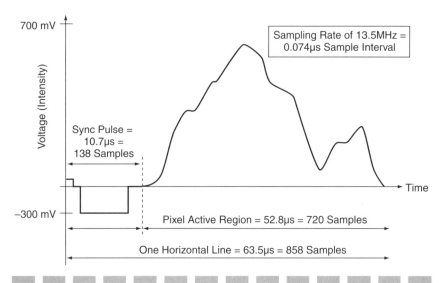

Figure 4-11
A single line of analog television is sampled to produce 720 active pixels per line.

That is, for each horizontal line of the frame the digital version will contain 720 pixels. This is the horizontal resolution of the digital image. Because of the increased picture size and quality of HDTV, the number of pixels in a horizontal line is significantly greater for HDTV formats. The two HDTV formats have 1280 and 1920 pixels per horizontal line, for example.

In the vertical dimension of the 525 lines in the NTSC signal, the active region consists of only 480 lines. The remaining 45 lines consist of two vertical blanking interface, which are 21–1/2 lines each and not visible on the screen. In all the standard definitions, NTSC signal digitization produces $720 \times 480 = 345,600$ pixels as shown graphically in Figure 4-12. Each pixel has a unique luminance sample and depending on the format used has either a unique or shared chrominance sample. For the 4:2:0 format with an average of 12 bits of information per pixel, the NTSC frame is digitized to 518,400 bytes.

Quantization

The three CCIR 601 formats can take samples of the analog signal with either 8 bit or 10 bit quantization. The analog NTSC signal ranges from –300 to 700 mV, with pixel values in the active region ranging from about 50 to 700 mV. Negative values are used for synchronization and not pixel information.

Figure 4-12
Sampling a
single analog
television
frame
produces 720
pixels on 480
lines in the
active region.

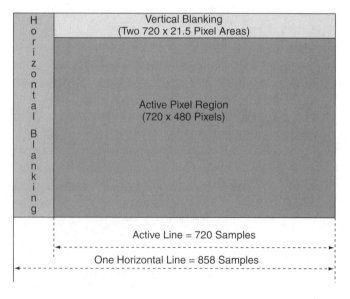

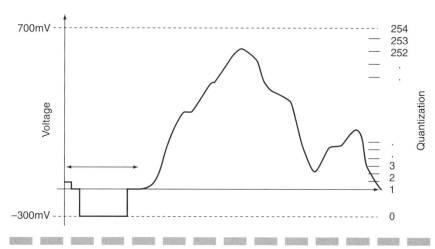

Figure 4-13
The analog television signal is quantized to 8 bits, resulting in 256 possible values for the signal.

For 8 bit samples the 50 to 700 mV active range is quantized to values from 1 to 254. In this quantization, black pixels are ideally mapped to the value 1 while bright white are given the value 254. Negative values, which indicate synchronization information, are mapped to 0 or 255 depending on the sync signal (horizontal or vertical). The mapping from signal voltage to an 8 bit (256 unique values) quantization level is shown in Figure 4-13.

Audio Digitization

The audio channels from an analog television signal are also digitized. The quantization and sampling rate for audio is distinctly different than for video. For one, the audio signal is one-dimensional (sound amplitude as a function of time) while the video signal is two-dimensional (horizontal and vertical brightness signal as a function of time). Also, the audio component is made up of three different channels, the mono L+R, stereo difference L–R, and SAP channels. In this section, we look at how the audio from an analog television signal is digitized. As with the video, the digital audio signal is later compressed to reduce the number of bits per second used.

Audio Sampling Rate   The detectable frequency range for human hearing is roughly from 20 Hz to 20 kHz, with the upper end decreasing with age (and the number of rock concerts attended). The Nyquist theorem says that any sampling frequency above 40 should be sufficient for capturing every audible frequency in an audio signal. Some common sampling rates for digital audio equipment are shown in this table:

Format	Sampling Rate
Digital answering machine	8 kHz
Music CD	44.1 kHz
DVD movie soundtrack	48 kHz
DVD audio format	96 kHz

The 8 kHz sampling rate of a digital answering machine means that frequencies above 4 kHz are not accurately captured in the digital signal. This lower rate matches the sampling rate throughout the telephone system. Anyone who has ever listened to music over the telephone, typically while on hold, knows how the low sampling rate results in poor audio quality for music but is sufficient for capturing the human voice. Future digital telephones, particularly those using Voice over Internet Protocol (VoIP), have the ability to sample the signal at a much higher rate, approaching music CD quality. However, as long as the signal has to traverse the plain old telephone system (POTS) somewhere in the connection between the two end devices, the signal will revert back to 8 kHz sampling quality. Conversely, the 96 kHz sampling rate of the high quality DVD audio discs can capture frequencies up to 48 kHz, which may be beyond the range of human hearing. Audio purists believe however that while not consciously audible, the true music experience requires these very high frequency components.

In the CCIR 601 digitization standard, each audio channel in the composite television signal is sampled at 48 kHz. As shown in Figure 4-14 the 48 kHz clock can be derived directly from the 27 MHz clock by downsampling by 8, by 9, and by 125 successively. According to the Nyquist theorem, this sampling rate is higher than is necessary but it results in exactly 1600 audio samples per video frame. This allows a common clock to be used for both video and audio sampling.

Audio Quantization Human hearing has a phenomenal response range (the range of sound frequencies and amplitudes that are audible). Sounds can be detected across six orders of magnitude in sound wave pressure. Sound waves with pressure as small as 0.00001 Newtons/cm^2

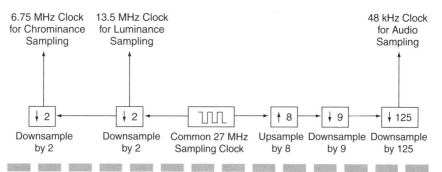

Figure 4-14
The audio channels in the NTSC analog signal are sampled at a rate derived from the common 27 MHz sampling clock for video. This results in the same number of audio samples per video frame helping to keep the audio and video in sync during playback.

to those with more than 10 Newtons/cm² can be heard. Trying to quantize this range would require at least 20 bits of precision per sample. The perceived volume of an audio signal, however, is not linearly related to the amount of pressure in the sound wave. Instead, the perceived loudness tracks the log of the pressure. Therefore, sampling the magnitude of the pressure wave of the sound requires some nonlinear manipulation before quantization. This makes it possible to use fewer than 20 bits per sample to achieve accurate representations of the analog signal. The 601 standard uses 16 bits to sample the audio channels. Quantization rates from some digital audio technologies are shown in the following table.

Technology	Bits per Sample
Telephone	8
Music CD	16
Digitized analog television	16
DVD-audio	24

Multichannel Audio   The analog television standard included two-channel stereo audio and a single mono SAP. New digital media formats such as DVDs and HDTV include multichannel audio that drives up to five different speakers. These additional channels include left and right surround and a center speaker in additional to the left and right stereo

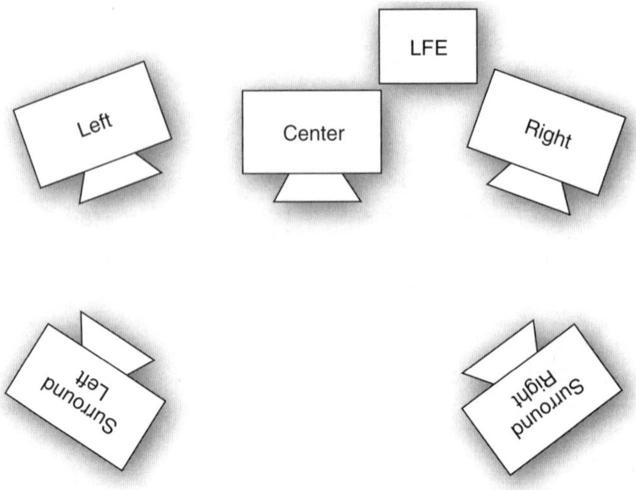

Figure 4-15
Speaker
placement for
5.1 channel
audio
including a
low frequency
enhancement
subwoofer.

speakers. One of the additional channels is typically a low frequency
enhancement (LFE) channel, whose speaker is also known as a subwoofer. The LFE typically has a response range of only 3 to 120 Hz, the
very low end of the 20 to 20 kHz human hearing range. Because frequencies this low are not perceived as directional by the human ear, the
LFE can be placed anywhere in the room and not pointed in any particular direction. Figure 4-15 shows a typical 5.1 multichannel surround
sound placement. The designation *5.1* indicates five full response speakers and one LFE.

Combing the sampling rate, bits per channel quantization, and the
number of channels, we get the effective bitrate for the digitized audio
streams as shown in this table:

Audio Technology	Sampling Rate	Quantization	Number of Channels	Data Rate
Telephone answering machine	8 kHz	8 bit	1	64 kbps
Music CD	44.1 kHz	16	2	1.4 Mbps
Digitized analog television	48 kHz	16	3	2.3 Mbps
DVD-audio	96 kHz	24	6	13.8 Mbps

Digital Video Compression

The digital media revolution would not have occurred without the development of digital compression technologies. Simply digitizing analog television signals results in data rates that are too large to work with. Processors found in personal computers and consumer electronics are not fast enough to manipulate the data and storage devices such as hard drives would fill up too quickly or be too expensive to be practical. Compression technologies reduce the effective bitrates of digital media to a level that consumer-grade processing power can handle, and storage requirements that are not prohibitively expensive.

The process of delivering compressed digital video is shown in Figure 4-16. In this generalized figure, analog content from either a live video camera or film creates a series of analog video frames. These are digitized into a sequence of uncompressed frames in a high-bandwidth bitstream. The compression stage reduces the bandwidth of the uncompressed bitstream so it is easier to store and transmit. At the receiving end, the compressed bitstream is decoded back into an uncompressed digital bitstream. The uncompressed video can be delivered

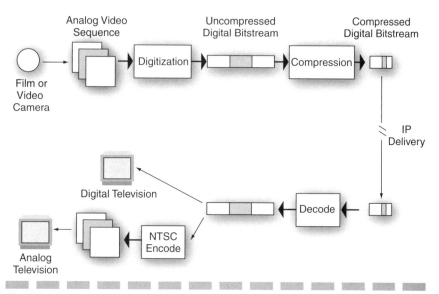

Figure 4-16

The generalized process of compressing digital video bitstreams for delivery over IP networks where they are decoded (decompressed) back into either digital or analog video.

directly to a digital television for display, or converted into analog NTSC video for delivery to an analog television. We will focus on the compression stage of this process in this section.

The Need for Compression

As we saw in the digitization of analog television, the digitization of an analog standard definition NTSC signal via the 8 bit CCIR 601 standard produces a continuous stream of digital bits on the order of 216 mps. An hour of digitized standard definition television would therefore produce 97.2 GB. HDTV has even higher bitrates and therefore higher storage requirements. One HDTV format produces more than 5300 GB per hour of uncompressed digital signal. These kinds of data rates are prohibitive in terms of storage requirements, transmission bandwidth requirements, and processor demands.

Storage Requirements   While the price of digital storage has decreased significantly, it would still be prohibitively expensive to store a reasonable amount of uncompressed television data. A two-hour standard definition television program would require almost 200 GB. A DVD-ROM disc holds only 4.7 GB or just a few minutes of uncompressed video. The fact that more than three hours of compressed video can be stored on a single DVD-ROM disc attests to the power of the compression process. Digital video recorders such as TiVo use hard disk drives for recording television content. As of this writing, hard drive capacity costs about 50 cents per gigabyte. Storing uncompressed digital television signals would cost almost $50, and only a few hours could be stored on a typical 128 GB drive. Even though capacity costs continue to decrease dramatically, storing uncompressed signals will remain prohibitively expensive for some time to come.

Bandwidth Requirements   Transmitting 216 Mbps of uncompressed data over any significant distance is extremely difficult with today's technology. Even some of the highest bandwidth digital channels, such as the connection between a hard drive and the CPU in a computer, would be maxed out at these data rates. Transmitting over longer distance is impossible with commercial networking technologies. Cable and DSL broadband data services are in the order of only a few Mbps while conventional Ethernet within a local area network (LAN) is capable of only 10 or in some cases 100 Mbps. An IPTV service that attempts to distribute digital television signals over broadband and Ethernet is going to require drastically reduced bitrates to work.

Processing Power Watching digital television requires reading the digital pixels and re-creating the images. Sometimes additional processing is also required, such as changing the size of the image to fit a particular window, or playing the video quicker to fast-forward through an uninteresting part. Simply retrieving each pixel to perform some processing operation requires significant computational power. For example, an HDTV frame consisting of 1920×1080 pixels takes more than 2 million computer operations to read from memory and transfer to the video output buffer. If the number of operations required to be performed on each pixel grows, it may require many billions of operations per second from the processor.

Video Compression Formats

Having established the need for reducing the bitrate of digital television through compression, several different commercial formats can be used to achieve this compression. Currently MPEG-2 is the dominant format used in commercial digital television services; however, several other formats are also widely deployed:

- **Motion JPEG.** Compresses each frame of the television frame independently. It results in compression ratios of about 3:1 for CCIR 601 digital frames.
- **DV25.** Used in many consumer camcorders and offers slightly better compression, with each frame still independently compressed. The resulting bitrate is 25 Mbps.
- **MPEG-1.** MPEG formats take advantage of spatial and temporal redundancies between frames to achieve higher compression ratios. MPEG-1 also uses lower pixel resolutions, discarding about 3/4 of the pixels before compressing the remaining pixels.
- **MPEG-2.** The dominant compression format for digital television takes advantage of interframe redundancy to achieve compression ratios of more than 50:1 but maintains the visual quality of the original, unlike MPEG-1.
- **Wavelet/fractal.** Use wavelet basis instead of DCT (Discrete Cosine Transform; more on this later).

- **MPEG-4 AVC, Windows Media/VC-1, RealVideo 10, and other advanced codecs.** These new formats include even more sophisticated tools than MPEG-2 to achieve higher compression ratios without losing image quality. They are just beginning to come into wide commercial deployment.

The various compression formats vary in how much they reduce the bandwidth of raw digital video. Figure 4-17 shows how some of the formats compare to the uncompressed video rate. The horizontal axis of this graph is on a logarithmic scale, so while MPEG-2 appears to be about one-half the length of uncompressed video in the graph, MPEG-2 actually produces a digital bitstream that is almost 100 times smaller than uncompressed video. Below the horizontal axis we show the maximum bitrates of some consumer devices such as CD drives, and broadband services such as DSL and cable modems. As can be seen on the horizontal axis, only the MPEG formats achieve bitrates low enough to be transmitted over DSL or across a DVD disc interface.

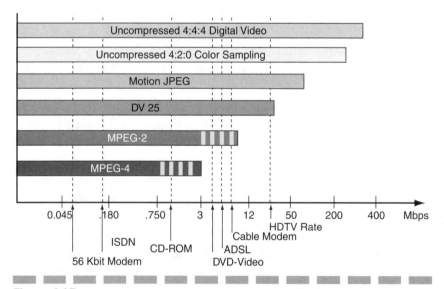

Figure 4-17

A comparison of the resulting bitrates for a number of compression formats versus the uncompressed digital bitstream for a standard definition digital television signal.

The Key to Compression: Removing Redundancy

Compression algorithms are able to reduce the size of a video bitstream significantly because video typically contains duplicate or redundant information both within and between frames. Image and video compression algorithms can take advantage of several types of redundancy to reduce the size of the resulting bitstream. We examine some of these here.

Spatial Redundancy   Neighboring pixels in an image often have similar values: the color or brightness of an object typically does not vary significantly over small areas. Instead of encoding each pixel individually, a compression algorithm could save bits by encoding only the difference between neighboring pixels. That difference is typically a smaller value than the full range of possible pixel values and therefore can be encoded in fewer bits.

Natural images often contain repeating patterns. These patterns could be encoded once and then repeated as needed, resulting in fewer bits.

Temporal Redundancy   Under the NTSC standard, 30 television fps is the norm. During the 33 milliseconds between frames, most of the image changes little or moves slightly from one place to another. Compression algorithms often encode only the small changes or the direction that a part of the image moved between frames. These changes typically require fewer bits than representing the image all over again. The MPEG standards obtain a significant amount of their encoding efficiency by encoding just the directions each little part of the image moved between frames instead of repeating all the pixels.

Coding Redundancy   Some patterns and motions are more common than others in natural images. The most frequent patterns can be encoded more efficiently than less frequent ones. This form of variable length, or Huffman coding, assigns fewer bits to more common codes. For example, when encoding the motion of things between two frames in sequence, the most common motions are small movements to the left or right. Large movements, especially in the vertical direction, are much less frequent. Encoding the small motions with a few bits and the large ones with more bits results in a more efficient system than encoding all of them with the same number of bits.

Psycho-visual Redundancy   The most efficient compression algorithms take advantage of human biology as well. Not all visual patterns are equally visible to the human eye. For example, fine details under low light or low contrast may not be visible. Efficient algorithms remove psycho-visual redundant patterns that are not visible to the human eye.

Lossless and Lossy Compression   Compression algorithms can be grouped into lossless and lossy algorithms. With a lossless compression algorithm, it is possible completely to re-create the original, uncompressed images from the compressed bitstream. These algorithms make the most faithful reproduction of the information. Lossy algorithms on the other hand destroy some information such that it is impossible to recover fully the original images. Lossy algorithms, while sometimes reducing image quality, produce the most efficient compression algorithms. MPEG-2 and most other video compression algorithms are lossy compression systems. The algorithms try to limit the lost information to parts of the image least noticeable by the human observer.

The MPEG-2 Video Compression Standard

The MPEG-2 compression standard is currently the most widely used compression format for digital television services. It is used by satellite, cable, and broadcast operators as well as the DVD format. The HDTV broadcast standard is also based on the MPEG-2 standard. MPEG stands for the Moving Picture Experts Group. Its home page can be found at http://www.chiariglione.org/mpeg/.

In this section we examine some of the key elements of the MPEG-2 compression algorithm and how it is able to achieve two orders of magnitude of compression for standard definition television bitstreams. Because of this compression the digital television bitstream is reduced from more than 200 Mbps to between 2 and 8 Mbps. Whole books are devoted to video compression in general and the MPEG-2 standard in particular. For our purposes, we will review the basic steps in the algorithm. Most video compression systems, including the newer advanced codecs, use similar methods to MPEG-2.

Subsampling   The MPEG-2 standard can be used for video streams of different image sizes. This includes not only the 720×480 pixel standard definition television size but a number of smaller and larger image sizes as well. In the CCIR 601 standard, NTSC analog standard definition television signals are digitized into a series of images that are 720×480 pixels. Because MPEG-2 can be used on a smaller image size, one way to achieve compression is to reduce the size first, or subsample the digital images for each frame. Typically, standard definition video images under MPEG-2 are subsampled to a number of size formats, in particular these:

- 720×480 (full size)
- 640×480
- 544×480
- 352×480
- 352×240 (the MPEG-1 default size)

Subsampling the television images immediately reduces the number of bits in the resulting bitstream, but at some cost to the image quality. Since the television screen always has a fixed aspect ratio, formats such as 544×480 require the pixels to be non-square—that is, the image is stretched horizontally to match the aspect ratio of the television.

Recall that another type of subsampling is involved in the digitization process itself: color subsampling. Here the color information for each pixel is shared among neighboring pixels, as we saw in the various CCIR 601 color formats. For example, the 4:2:0 format cuts in half the average number of bits per pixel.

Discrete Cosine Transform   After reducing the size of the image, the algorithm breaks it up into a mosaic of small 64 pixel squares, each 8 pixels to a side. A transform operation is performed on each of these squares independently. The transform is used in the MPEG compression algorithms, both MPEG-1 and MPEG-2, as well as the JPEG image compression algorithm—the Discrete Cosine Transform, or DCT. The DCT converts the values for the 64 pixels in the 8×8 square into 64 other numbers representing the spatial frequency components of the square.

DCT Quantization   Spatial frequency components of the DCT can be thought of as the tiny checkerboard patterns that make up the image. The human visual system perceives these checkerboard patterns differently depending on their contrast and frequency. Low contrast, high frequency components are difficult or impossible to see, especially at a distance. These patterns represent a form of psycho-visual redundancy and can be removed from the image with little or no loss in perceived image quality.

The quantization stage reduces or removes many components from the DCT; in particular, it removes those components that are not visible and reduces the number of bits on those that are. This stage is where most of the *"loss"* of the *lossy* compression takes place. These patterns cannot be recovered from the resulting bitstream.

Figure 4-18 shows a single image that has been quantized to various levels. The higher the quantization, the higher the compression ratio and the more bits are removed from the bitstream. However, this can lead to a loss in image quality, as shown in the figure.

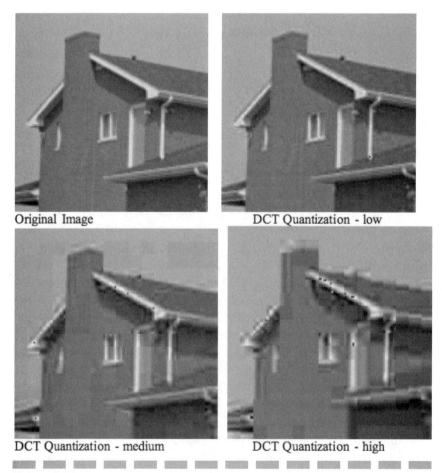

Original Image   DCT Quantization - low

DCT Quantization - medium   DCT Quantization - high

Figure 4-18
Increasing the quantization, and increasing the compression ratio, in the MPEG algorithm leads to lower image quality and the introduction of a number of MPEG artifacts.

DCT Quantization Artifacts The quantization of the DCT components can lead to visible artifacts in the resulting image, particularly if the algorithm is attempting to increase the compression efficiency and reduce the bitstream to as few bits as possible. Digital television experts have developed a number of terms to describe some of the common artifacts due to the DCT quantization:

- **Blockiness.** If quantization is too aggressive, the 8×8 block is reduced to a single uniform color. The boundaries between these blocks will become apparent and distracting.
- **Ringing.** Sharp contrast edges will have phantom edges parallel to the real one, similar to ghosting in analog television.
- **Mosquitoes.** In video sequences, edge ringing will change from frame to frame. This can result in strange motion around edges as if small insects were buzzing about.

The next time you look closely at an MPEG compressed video stream you might recognize some of these. Hollywood usually takes great care in producing MPEG-2 bitstreams for DVDs that minimize the artifacts of the compression process.

Motion Estimation and Frame Types The most significant compression of bits in the MPEG algorithm comes from removing the temporal redundancy between successive frames in the image. During the 33 ms between image frames, a large part of the image might remain the same. Consider a sequence of frames where the background image is stationary and an object moves across the field of view, as in Figure 4-19. Most of the pixels don't change from frame to frame due to the stationary background and short time interval between frames. In this example, a single object moves in front of a stationary background. Most of the pixels between the frames are identical. In fact, the middle frame of this three-frame sequence can be completely described by copying most pixels from the first frame and a few from the third frame. Describing the second frame as the composition of elements of the first and third frames would require many fewer bits than completely describing every pixel in the second frame. This is the basis for the frame-based interpolation used in MPEG-2.

MPEG-2 breaks up the sequence of images into three types of frames. The first are Intra, or I-frames. I-frames are completely described using the techniques already mentioned: DCT transform and quantization. The resulting series of bits can be used to re-create the frame in its entirety.

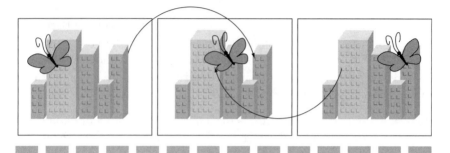

Figure 4-19
Each frame in a television signal comes just 33 ms apart and in that period many pixels may remain the same or change very little. In this example the middle frame can be completely described by copying parts of the previous and subsequent frames.

I-frames serve as anchor points in the bitstream. The other two types of frames are Predictive, or P-frames, and Bidirectional, or B-frames. Where possible, these frames are defined by taking parts of other frames and copying them over. For each block within the frame, a corresponding match is looked for in other frames. If a close match is found, it is copied over to create the block; if no match is found, the block is compressed just like an I-frame. P-frames search for matching components in previous I- or P-frames, while B-frames take parts of I- or P-frames that occurred earlier in the sequence or will occur in the future. The middle frame in Figure 4-19 is an example of a B-frame: it can be created by taking parts of the previous frame and the next frame. The three types of frames are illustrated in Figure 4-20, where a sequence of four frames is shown. The I-frame begins the sequence and is constructed from its compressed bits. The P-frame at the end of the sequence is constructed from parts of the I-frame at the beginning of the sequence. The two B-frames are constructed from parts of the I- and P-frames.

The advantage of creating frames from other blocks in other frames is that it is not necessary to send all of the information to describe each pixel in the block. Instead, a block can be described by motion "vectors" that point to which parts of other frames to copy from to create the block. Because B- and P-frames are created from copying parts of other frames, they require many fewer bits to describe than I-frames. Because B-frames can copy parts of images from both forward and backward in time, they are more likely to find matching regions and require even fewer bits than P-frames, which can only look backward in time.

Recall that the uncompressed digital frame required more than 7 million bits to define every pixel. In a standard definition digital television

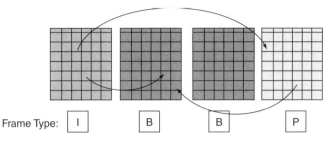

Figure 4-20
MPEG defines three types of frames. I- or Intra frames are self-contained while B- and P-frames are composed of parts of other frames.

Frame Type: I   B   B   P

signal, it may take about 400 kbits to define an I-frame, 100 kbits to define a P-frame, and as little as 50 kbits to define a B-frame. You can see that if we use more B- and P-frames in the sequence we can save even more bits. However, I-frames are needed to start the decoding process and establish at least the first frame in a sequence. Because B- and P-frames need at least one frame to copy parts from, there must be occasional I-frames to start the process.

Macroblock Matching   The little patches of image that are copied from other frames to make up the B-and P-frames are called *macroblocks*. Each macroblock is a 16×16 pixel square (comprising four 8×8 pixel blocks from the DCT stage). To create a B-frame in the encoding process, the encoder must find macroblocks in other frames that closely match the pixels in the original macroblock. The closer the match between all pixels in the macroblock the better the image will appear. While there may not be exact matches because pixels change slightly between frames, relatively close matches are usually found. The best MPEG encoders find the closest matches and therefore preserve the image quality by minimizing the difference between the original pixels and the copied macroblock.

Most MPEG encoder algorithms find the best match by searching within an area around the original macroblock and trying every possible match within that area. For example, to find a match for a macroblock near the center of a B-frame, the algorithm will search for a match within a rectangle around the center of adjacent I- or P-frames. The technique is shown in Figure 4-21.

The larger the search area, the more likely it is to find a good match for the macroblock. Current state of the art is a search range of 416×254 pixels, which is almost the entire image. However, this takes a lot of com-

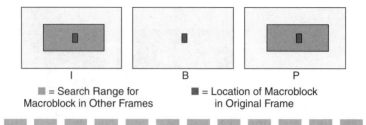

I   B   P

■ = Search Range for   ■ = Location of Macroblock
Macroblock in Other Frames   in Original Frame

Figure 4-21
Searching for a matching macroblock in a previous I-frame and subsequent P-frame
by searching in an area about the location of the macroblock in the original frame.
Such searches can take millions of computational operations.

putational horsepower. To perform MPEG encoding in real-time typically requires a dedicated Application Specific Integrated Circuit (ASIC). It is possible, but more difficult to do on general purpose CPUs as found in personal computers.

The advanced codecs described later in this chapter introduce new searching tools such as fractional pixel searches that require even more computational power. However, they result in higher quality images using fewer bits.

Group of Pictures (GOP) and Grouping Hierarchy   While there are bit-saving advantages to using as many B- and P-frames as possible in the compression of the digital bitstream, it is necessary to insert I-frames now and then. I-frames are not created from other frames but are created from compressed pixel information. They are not dependent on other frames to create them like B- and P-frames. Supposed a sequence consisted of only one I-frame at the start and then an infinite series of B- and P-frames. The B- and P-frames can be described by the other B- and P-frames plus that first I-frame. But all of the subsequent frames are now dependent on that first frame. If you wanted to know just one frame somewhere in the middle of the sequence you would have to know all of the previous frames back to the first I-frame to describe it.

Requiring the decoding device to remember all of the previous frames would be totally impractical for consumer usage. Imagine tuning to a particular channel in the middle of the day and then requiring every frame since the start of the broadcast to start watching the channel. Therefore I-frames are inserted periodically in the MPEG sequence so that you can start decoding from that I-frame and do not need all of the frames that came before it to create it. In a way, the I-frames are starting points in the bitstream to begin the decoding process. When tuning to a new digital channel, the decoder must wait for an I-frame to arrive before decoding can begin. Since I-frames take the most bits, there must be a compromise between the frequency of I-frames and how long you have to wait for one to begin decoding. Too many I-frames and the bitstream is too large, too few and you have to wait a long time for one to arrive. Typical usage is to insert an I-frame every 15 frames. At 30 fps this is an I-frame every 500 ms.

Out of Order Encoding   Because the B- and P-frames are made up of macroblocks copied from previous or even future frames, to create B- and P-frames you must already have the other frames on which they depend. So while video frames come into the MPEG encoder in a particular order, they are compressed, transmitted, and then decoded in a different order. For a single group of pictures, an I-frame must be sent to the decoder first followed by the P-frames and then finally the B-frames. So even though a B-frame might come right after the first I-frame in the sequence, it cannot be created until future P-frames have been delivered and decoded first. This change in ordering of frames is illustrated in Figure 4-22.

In summary, the MPEG-2 video compression process takes a digital television signal with a bitrate of 216 Mbps and a constant number of bits per frame and creates another, smaller digital signal of around 2 to 8 Mbps with variable number of bits per frame. The algorithm takes a

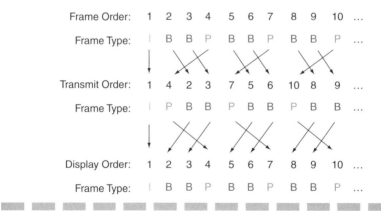

Figure 4-22
In MPEG-2 the order in which frames are transmitted is different than the order in which they are actually displayed. B-frames need past and future I- and P-frames to arrive at the decoder first even though the B-frame is displayed before them.

series of frames and breaks them up into groups of pictures, where within the group there is one or more I-frame and multiple P- and B-frames. Each frame type uses a different number of bits depending on the frame type and how many matching macroblocks were found. Also, the uncompressed digital bitstream contained each frame in order while the compressed MPEG-2 bitstream has the frames out of order. These steps are illustrated in Figure 4-23.

Out of order encoding combined with the need to start with an I-frame has important consequences for the implementation of a digital television service. The compressed digital bitstream is sent bit by bit over many miles of distribution network before reaching the decoder device. There will be a delay as the decoder waits for the bits associated with an entire frame. Once all of the bits for a frame are received, they are decoded (decompressed) back into a single frame. Because frames are sent out of order, some frames such as B-frames have to wait until later frames are received and decoded before they can be created. In addition, the decoder must wait for an I-frame to arrive to begin the decoding process, and therefore typically discards B- and P-frames until an I-frame arrives.

Each of the steps takes time and introduces a delay between when the compressed bitstream is sent, received, and finally displayed. Waiting for an I-frame may take up to 500 ms. Bit buffers are used to collect incoming bits and must receive entire frames before transferring to the decode. In addition, the buffer must account for jitter in the transmission channel and therefore wait slightly longer. Finally the decode and out of order processing can take another half second. The result is that unlike analog television where frames can be presented as soon as the signal is acquired, digital television streams may take longer to become visible to

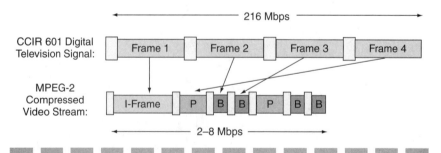

Figure 4-23
The MPEG-2 video compression algorithm takes a digitized television bitstream with fixed-size uniform frames and creates a smaller bitstream with variable size frames that are in a different order than the original frames.

the user after acquiring the desired channel. The delay can be considerable for systems such as IPTV over DSL where a new MPEG-2 stream must be initiated to the particular user when a channel change is requested. We examine these delays in more detail in Appendix A.

Run Length and Entropy Encoding   After encoding the pixels for I-frames and finding the macroblock matches for B- and P-frames, MPEG uses a technique called *entropy encoding*, or *variable length coding (VLC)*, to reduce the number of bits even more. For most content, it turns out that the macroblock motion vectors are usually small values representing small motions of objects during the 33 ms between frames. It is rare that a large motion vector is found to be the best match in the macroblock search. In VLC, fewer bits are used to encode the most common motion vectors and more bits are used for the less frequent vectors.

An important byproduct of using VLC and motion vectors, as well as with DCT compression, is that small errors or mistakes in the code can lead to large errors in the resulting images. The original uncompressed digital image was not so fragile; if a single bit was incorrect it would affect only a single pixel. The compressed MPEG-2 stream however is fragile; a single bit error can affect many pixels across multiple frames. For example, an error in an I-frame can corrupt many pixels in that frame and those errors are copied into other B- and P-frames, which propagate the error.

The fact that the MPEG bitstream is fragile is important when dealing with transmission methods that might introduce errors when transmitting the digital signals through a broadcast system. Some additional effort is required to minimize the number of bits that get corrupted in the process, particularly when using Internet protocols, where accuracy of bit packets is not guaranteed.

MPEG-2 Profiles and Levels   The MPEG-2 compression standard can be used for a range of applications, from small digital images on a cell phone screen to large screen HDTV. The standard includes a range of tools, some more complex than others, such as the use of B-frames that need to be transmitted and decoded out of order. It wouldn't be practical for an MPEG-2 decoder to have to accommodate the full range of applications with their different parameters and complex tools. For example, the ability to render HDTV on a cell phone would not make economic sense. The creators of the MPEG-2 standard had this consideration in mind when they defined subsets of the decoding parameters, called *levels*, and subsets of the encoding tools, called *profiles*.

An MPEG-2 profile defines which encoding tools can be used. The simple profile, for example, does not allow the more complicated B-frames while the high profile includes all of the tools in the MPEG-2 toolkit. Different profiles correspond to different levels of algorithmic complexity, and therefore differing requirements of computation load on the decoder. For applications requiring small, low-cost decoder components such as on a mobile phone, simpler profiles help keep the computational requirements low.

The MPEG-2 levels place constraints on various parameters such as the maximum number of horizontal and vertical pixels in a frame and the maximum bitrate of the MPEG-2 stream. The larger the possible image size, the more memory and processing power is required in the decoder. If the application is best served by constraining the size parameters of the digital images, limiting the application to a specific level reduces the decoder requirements. Some examples of the MPEG-2 profiles and levels are listed in the following table:

MPEG-2 Profile Name	Frame Types Allowed	Color Format
Simple profile	P, I	4:2:0
Main profile	P, I, B	4:2:0
High profile	P, I, B	4:2:2

MPEG-2 Level Name	Maximum Pixels per Line	Maximum Number of Lines	Maximum Bitrate (Mbit/s)
Low level	352	288	4
Main level	720	576	15
High level	1920	1152	80

The simple and main profiles are typically used for consumer applications while the high profile is used for professional applications such as in the content production process. The low level is suitable for small screens such as cell phones while the high level is required for high definition video. The consumer DVD movie format is based on the MPEG-2 Main Profile at Main Level (MP@ML) and the broadcast HDTV standard is based on the MPEG-2 Main Profile at High Level (MP@HL). The advanced codecs such as MPEG-4 have even more profiles and levels customized to different applications. Various IPTV applications also need to choose which level and profile they will be based on such that every decoder knows what to expect and be prepared to decode.

Variable and Constant Bitrate Encoding   A lot of flexibility was intentionally built into the MPEG-2 video compression standard. Many different parameters can be "tweaked" in the compression algorithm. By changing these parameters, the amount of compression can be balanced with the resulting image quality. For example, the algorithm could be instructed to use more I-frames and less quantization in the encoding process, resulting in higher image quality but a higher resulting bitrate as well.

Various parameters can be changed during the encoding process to increase or decrease the number of bits used over time. Some parts of a movie or television show might require more bits than other parts to maintain a high quality picture. Therefore, the number of bits per second of video changes with time. Conversely, it might be beneficial to maintain a constant encoded bitrate over time so that the storage and transmission capacity required are known. These two different approaches to encoding, constant bitrate and variable bitrate, are described next.

Constant Bitrate Encoding   With constant bitrate (CBR) encoding, various parameters in the encoding algorithm are changed over time to create a resulting MPEG-2 bitstream that uses a constant number of bits per second. This format has a number of beneficial characteristics:

- The bandwidth in terms of bits per second required to transmit t he compressed bitstream is constant. This is important for transmission channels, such as satellite transponders, that have limited bandwidth, or where it is necessary to fit an integral number of bitstreams into a fixed bandwidth channel. For example, if a satellite transponder is capable of transmitting 30 Mbits of total data, then compressing programs to a fixed rate of 3 Mbits means exactly 10 programs can be transmitted on each transponder.
- The resulting size of a compressed piece of content is a strict function of its length. It is therefore possible to know how many hours of content can be stored within a given amount of memory storage.

CBR encoding has some disadvantages, however. By using the same number of bits regardless of the material, the resulting quality will be variable. If the material is complicated and does not compress efficiently, the resulting quality decreases. If the material is relatively simple and compresses efficiently, more bits are used than necessary.

Variable Bitrate Encoding   In variable bitrate (VBR) encoding, the instantaneous bitrate of the resulting MPEG-2 bitstream is variable over time. Depending on the content, different frames can have more or fewer bits used to encode them. If material at a particular time is complicated, more bits can be used to keep quality high, while if the material is simple and compresses efficiently, fewer bits can be used. Typically VBR encoders work under two constraints: to keep the maximum bitrate below a given maximum, and to keep the average bitrate over time close to a target goal. If the average bitrate over time is achieved, VBR encoding still produces a predictable amount of storage as a function of the length of the content. Figure 4-24 qualitatively illustrates variable bitrate encoding.

Statistical Multiplexing Multiple Channels   Perhaps the most efficient encoding of multiple video streams with MPEG-2 mixes elements of both CBR and VBR encoding. If only a single compressed digital television channel is to be carried over a limited capacity (<8 Mbps) digital pipe, then CBR encoding is often used to maximize the capacity of the pipe. However, if the pipe can fit multiple channels (>10 Mbps capacity), each channel can be encoded with VBR encoding under the constraint that the sum of the bitrate from all of the channels at any one time is a constant rate. With this system, each channel takes advantage

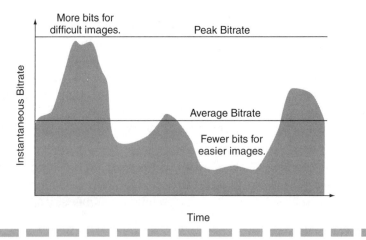

Figure 4-24
Variable bitrate encoding uses more bits to encode frames when the images are difficult to compress and fewer bits when the frames are easier to compress, attempting to remain below a peak rate and maintaining an average rate over time.

of VBR encoding to improve the image quality, yet the sum of the channels always fits within the capacity of the pipe. The MPEG-2 encoding functions for each channel trade capacity between them depending on the relative complexity of the content they are encoding. Figure 4-25 illustrates the model. A channel with relatively simple content will be able to give up some bits to another channel with more complicated content. When there are a sufficient number of channels to be encoded, statistically not all of the channels would contain difficult content at the same time, and at least a few channels will have easy content and a few will have difficult content. This statistical multiplexing (stat-mux) of multiple channels can be used in broadcast systems such as cable and satellite where multiple channels are merged into a single digital pipe. Narrowcast systems such as DSL can contain only one or two television channels and therefore cannot take advantage of stat-mux to improve compression efficiency.

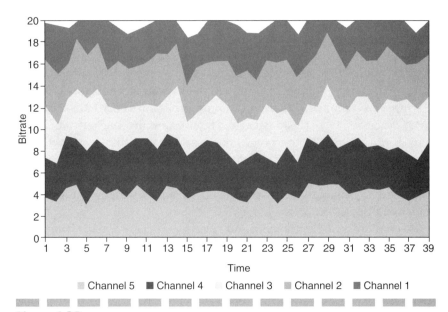

Figure 4-25
Statistical multiplexing allows each channel to take advantage of VBR encoding while the sum of the channels remains within a constant bitrate limit. Here, five VBR encoded channels are contained in a 20 Mbps capacity pipe, each with varying instantaneous encoding rate with a constant combined maximum.

The System Layer

The MPEG-2 standard is actually much more than just its audio and video compression algorithms. It also includes information on how to package and transmit the compressed digital content, in particular in a manner conducive to presenting multichannel television services. The MPEG-2 standard contains three parts: the audio compression standard, the video compression standard, and the system layer standard. The MPEG-2 system layer standard is a generic system for combining digital services and has been applied to applications beyond digital television because of its versatility. The system layer describes how the various audio and video streams are integrated into programs or channels, how multiple channels are multiplexed into a single service, and how a decoder (a television, PC, cell phone, or other device) can quickly identify and extract the particular program it is looking for from that service.

Compressed audio and video bitstreams are long continuous streams that can contain literally billions of bits. A single program such as a television channel might contain a single video and a few related audio streams (a main stereo audio channel, secondary audio channel, and possibly others for example). In order for these different streams to be transmitted over a digital channel they must be merged into a single stream of bits. It is not practical to transmit all of the video bits, and then the separate audio bits, and wait for them all to be received before the consumer can start watching TV. Instead, the various streams must be broken into small chunks, or packets, and multiplexed. The MPEG-2 system layer describes how these separate bitstreams are packetized, interleaved into programs, the programs interleaved with other programs, and how they are mixed with additional information that is used to separate out the desired audio and video components from the mix. This hierarchy from elementary streams to transport stream multiplex is shown in Figure 4-26.

The compressed digital audio and video streams are called elementary streams. These are broken into small packets, called *packetized elementary streams (PES)*. The various streams from a single program are interleaved into program streams. Finally all of the programs are interleaved, along with descriptive data, into a transport stream. The descriptive data includes information about the digital channels contained within the transport stream such as which audio and video streams are grouped into the various programs, as well as descriptive information to be presented to the user as the closed captioning.

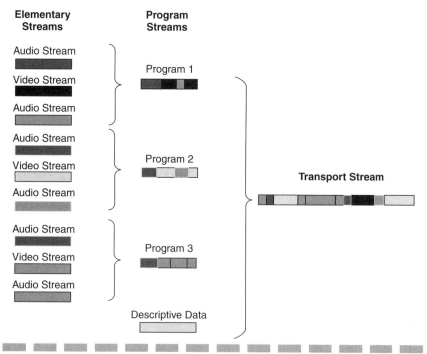

Figure 4-26
The MPEG system layer hierarchy where elementary streams are packetized and combined into program streams that are further packetized and combined into transport streams along with additional descriptive information.

Packetized Elementary Streams Packetization is used in the MPEG system layer standard to combine various elementary streams into a single interleaved bitstream. In packetization, the long, continuous elementary bitstreams are broken up into many small groups of bits (called *packets*). A small set of bits called a *header* is then added in front of each packet. When the various packets from many different elementary streams are combined into a single stream, the header indicates where one packet ends and another begins. The packet header also contains a unique identifier indicating to which elementary stream the attached packet belongs. Figure 4-27 illustrates how an elementary stream is packetized into packets with headers. The resulting stream of packets is the PES.

In the MPEG-2 standard, the PES header is 6 bytes long. It contains a unique 24 bit string of bits that indicates the start of a new PES packet. This unique code can appear only at the start of a PES header.

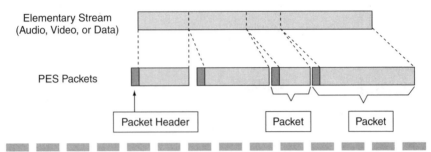

Figure 4-27
A PES is created by breaking up an elementary stream, which is either compressed audio, video, or data, into small packets and appending identifying headers in front of each packet.

Following this is the stream identifier indicating from which elementary stream this packet originated. The header also contains information on the length of the packet that follows the header. This information could be used to skip ahead in the bitstream to the next packet. The format of the packet header is shown in Figure 4-28.

Program Streams A *program* is a collection of audio and video signals that form a cohesive whole. For example, a DVD movie contains a program that may have a main video track and several audio tracks for

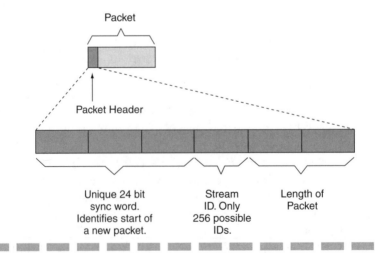

Figure 4-28
The PES packet header, which indicates the start of a new PES packet and contains information on the source and length of the data that follows.

different languages and commentary. An MPEG-2 program stream contains at least one video and one audio elementary stream, but it can contain up to 16 video streams, 32 audio streams, and 16 data streams. The various data streams in a program stream typically contain descriptive information about the program—for example, indicating where the various chapters in a DVD movie start and end. MPEG-2 program streams are primarily used for storage of a single program such as on DVD-ROM or a movie downloaded to a PC.

A program stream is created by interleaving the various video, audio, and data PES packets. The resulting stream of PES packets is then itself packetized; it is broken up into chunks called *packs*. These packs are usually 2048 bytes, or 2 KB, long. This length corresponds to one block of data on rotating media such as hard drives or DVDs. This is no coincidence, as the program stream format in MPEG-2 was created with such usage models in mind. The 2 KB pack size makes it convenient for storing and retrieving programs off of rotating media and was chosen with a service such as DVD movies in mind. Program stream pack creation from elementary streams is shown in Figure 4-29.

As with PES packets, a program stream pack also has a header added in front to provide information about the pack. Like the PES header, a unique string of bits in the pack header indicates the start of a new pack in the bitstream. The pack header also includes a new element called the *System Clock Reference (SCR)*. For the various audio and video packets to be played correctly by the decoding device, the decoder needs to know the time each pack is to be presented. The SCR is used by the decoder to synchronize its own clock with the original signal used in the encoding system. In this way the decoder knows when it is supposed to present the data in the pack to the user.

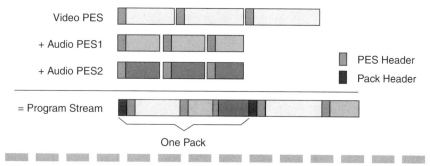

Figure 4-29
An MPEG-2 program stream is created from multiple packetized elementary streams and is then itself broken up into packs.

This clock synchronization is important in presenting digital movie or television programs; the decoder must present new frames every 33 ms and cannot skip a frame because data is coming in faster than it is being decoded, or pause on a frame if data is coming in slower than it is being decoded. If the data is being streamed from a hard drive in a PC, for example, the SCR can be used to either slow down or speed up the reading of data off of the disk such that the constant rate of 30 fps is maintained by the decoder. If the data is arriving from a broadcast system such as a satellite, the SCR is used by the decoder to make sure it is in sync with the transmission system and will not run ahead or behind the source. The elements of the pack header are shown in Figure 4-30.

Decoding Buffer Model   Multiplexing the various PES packets into a program stream at the source and de-multiplexing them on the receiving end is not a trivial process. When we watch television, the audio and video come at the same time: when we see an actor speak a line we expect her voice to be heard at the exact same time as her lips move. But the multiplexing process sends video and audio packets one at a time. If the audio arrives first, it must be held in a buffer until the video packet has arrived so they can be presented at the same time. Built within the MPEG-2 standard is a model of the various decoding buffers such that the order of packets in the program stream can be created to guarantee that the proper audio and video data will be delivered in time.

Figure 4-31 shows the program stream decoding process. The multiplexed bitstream enters the decoder and the audio and video packets are sent to their respective buffers. Once the buffers have the required data, they get decoded and presented simultaneously. The two graphs show how full the two buffers are as a function of time. Each one fills a little

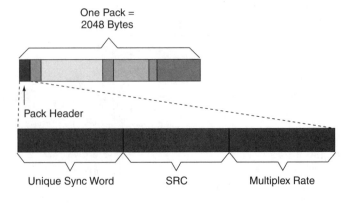

Figure 4-30
The program stream pack header contains the SCR used to synchronize the clock in the decoding process with the encoded data.

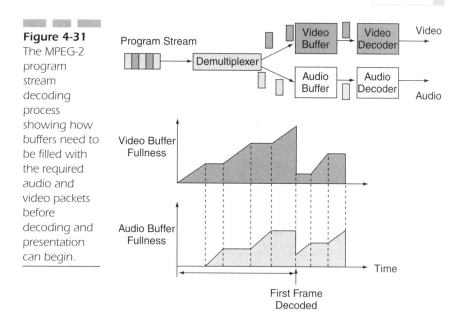

Figure 4-31
The MPEG-2 program stream decoding process showing how buffers need to be filled with the required audio and video packets before decoding and presentation can begin.

more as a packet arrives. Once enough data is present to create the first frame, both buffers are drained and the content is presented. The secret in the multiplexing process is to guarantee that the buffers always have sufficient data to present both audio and video simultaneously without requiring prohibitively large buffers.

A decode buffer is always required in the digital television decoding process. Since it takes time for this buffer to fill, a delay occurs between when the bitstream starts to arrive and when the first frame of video and bit of audio can be presented. If the digital television doesn't start receiving the bits until the channel is "tuned in," changing the channel can cause some delay while the new channel is tuned in, and the bitstream is buffered. In fact, this may be one of the disadvantages of digital television over analog. Some IPTV vendors are specifically working on solutions to decrease the delay in channel changing on digital channels.

Transport Streams   The final layer of the MPEG-2 system layer hierarchy is the transport stream. MPEG-2 transport streams are used in digital cable, digital satellite, and HDTV broadcast systems. An MPEG-2 transport stream contains one or more program streams along with additional information describing the various program streams it contains. A transport stream may contain one program, in which case it is called a single program transport stream (SPTS) or possibly dozens of separate programs in a multiprogram transport stream (MPTS). Typically an MPTS contains several different programs, plus descriptive information, and the whole MPTS is delivered as a single bitstream over cable or satellite broadcast systems.

As with program streams, transport streams are formed by breaking up either elementary streams or program streams (or both) into packets. In this case, the packets are a fixed 188 bytes including a 4 byte transport stream header. Figure 4-32 illustrates how a series of transport stream packets are created from three program streams and one data stream. Because the transport stream packets are only 188 bytes long, it may take many packets to transport just one program stream pack (recall that packs may be 2048 bytes long).

The transport stream header contains a unique code, or sync word, followed by a 2 byte program identifier (PID). Like the stream identifier in the program stream header, the PID identifies from which program the data that follows the transport stream header came. The PID could refer to one of the programs in the transport stream or one of the data streams. Certain PID values are reserved for specific data streams, as you will see in the following section. The remaining bits in the header are flags that indicate various properties about the packet. Since the length of the packet is fixed, there is no need to include the length of the data following the header as in the program stream header. The elements of the transport stream header are illustrated in Figure 4-33.

The MPEG-2 system layer specification is extremely versatile. It is used not only for MPEG-2 program streams but other data and audio/video formats as well. For example, in cable systems it carries IP

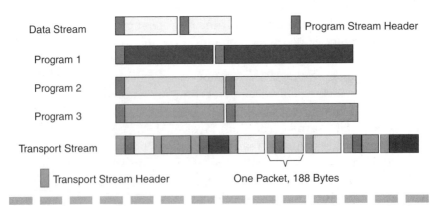

Figure 4-32
An MPEG-2 transport stream consists of many 188 byte packets that can contain parts of several program streams and data streams multiplexed together.

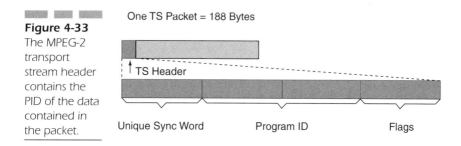

Figure 4-33
The MPEG-2
transport
stream header
contains the
PID of the data
contained in
the packet.

One TS Packet = 188 Bytes

TS Header

Unique Sync Word   Program ID   Flags

packets using a system called Data Over Cable Service Interface Specification (DOCSIS). In the rather complex Digital Storage Media Command and Control (DSM-CC) specification, the MPEG-2 system layer is used to control digital video servers and deliver a broadcast file system. Even the MPEG-4 AVC advanced audio and video compression formats still use the MPEG-2 system layer to encapsulate and deliver their packets.

PID, PAT, PMT, and Other Tables   Since a transport stream can contain dozens of programs, each containing multiple elementary streams of video, audio, and data, MPEG-2 defines a system for being able to identify the various programs within the transport stream and which elementary streams each program contains. A series of tables called *system tables* are inserted into the transport stream as elementary data streams to describe the contents of the transport stream. The transport packets containing these system tables are identified by unique PIDs. A decoder can immediately identify and extract the system tables, which enables the decoder to identify and extract the various programs in which it is interested.

The primary system table is the program allocation table (PAT). It is always contained in packets with PID value zero. The PAT is a table identifying the programs contained within the transport stream. For each program, the PAT lists a PID value for another table called the program map table (PMT). One PMT exists for each program in the multiplex. The PMT is a table that lists the PID numbers for every elementary stream within the program associated with that PMT. The connection between PAT and PMT is shown in Figure 4-34.

Another important set of tables that contains useful information about the programs contained in the transport stream is defined by the Program and System Information Protocol (PSIP) specification. PSIP provides information about current and upcoming programs on the various digital television channels, for example, "Program 32 will show an episode of 'Seinfeld' at 8:00 this evening." This information can be used

Program Assocation Table (PAT)

Program	PID of PMT
HBO	0 x 0023
KTVU-16	0 x 0024
Golf Network	0 x 0025
...	...
...	...

Program Map Table (PMT) for HBO

PID	Stream
0 x 1234	Video
0 x 2345	Main Audio
0 x 3456	Secondary Audio
...	...

Figure 4-34

The PAT identifies the programs in the transport stream multiplex and the PID to the associated PMT, which lists all of the service streams within a program and their associated transport PID.

to create an electronic program guide (EPG) that a user would navigate to select current programs to watch or future programs to record. PSIP is used within the terrestrial HDTV broadcast system to enable HDTV-ready televisions to present programming information to the user.

Video Formats Based on MPEG-2

The MPEG-2 set of standards defines how to compress and package digital television services. However, it does not completely define a service, or in some cases, it is more general than is necessary. A number of digital video services and products are based on the MPEG-2 standards. These products typically operate within some subset of the full MPEG-2 standard. Industry standards bodies typically place some restrictions on the large number of tools within MPEG-2 and add device-specific extensions to define the product and service. These restrictions provide interoperability among devices and lower complexity by limiting the scope of possible features. DVD videos, digital cable television, digital broadcast satellite, and HDTV are all based on the MPEG-2 standards but have associated industry standards that define a subset of the full MPEG-2 standard, while sometimes also introducing additional components specific to the industry. In this section we will look at some of these industry standards and how they relate to the core MPEG-2.

DVD Video Format   The Digital Versatile Disc (DVD) format uses the MPEG-2 program stream format to define how a digital movie is stored on a 4.7 GB optical medium. The DVD specification was created within the DVD Forum, an organization composed of companies with a mutual interest in creating a market for the format. DVDs use a subset of the possible MPEG-2 MP@ML (standard definition) encoding parameters. In particular it places restrictions on the image resolutions, bitrates, the number and placement of I-frames, and the particular audio formats that can be used. These constraints make it easier for a DVD player to know what to expect when playing a DVD and not have to plan for all possible audio and video codec options.

In addition to restrictions, the DVD format also extends the MPEG-2 standards by introducing data formats for navigating the contents of the DVD. These include menu screens, navigation buttons, video "loopset," and simple interactive operations. Even simple games can be created using the data formats defined in the DVD specifications.

Digital Broadcast Television   The digital broadcast system in North America and Korea is defined by the Advanced Television Systems Committee (ATSC), while most of Europe, Asia, and Australia use a system defined by the Digital Video Broadcasting (DVB) Project. The ATSC broadcast system, defined in the ATSC A/53 standard, uses MPEG-2 compression for video, but restricts image size to a subset of the MP@ML (standard definition) and MP@HL (high definition) image formats. In fact ATSC limits digital broadcasts to just 18 different possible image resolutions listed in Table 4-3.

The European DVB project also uses the MP@ML (standard definition) and MP@HL (high definition) MPEG-2 image formats as constrained by the DVB-T specification. Both DVB and ATSC use MPEG-2 transport streams to broadcast multiple programs. The two systems differ primarily in the radio frequency signal modulation schemes. ATSC uses Vestigial Side-Band (VSB) modulation while DVB uses Orthogonal Frequency-Division Multiplexing (OFDM). There has been much technical debate on which modulation scheme is better. Regardless of the modulation scheme used, both are carrying MPEG-2 transport streams to consumers' homes.

Both ATSC and the DVB Project also make extensions to the MPEG-2 standards to complete the broadcast television system. The ATSC A/65 standard adds system information in the form of PSIP tables. This metadata standard includes program description information for present and future programs on the television service. DVB defines the system information (DVB-SI) as well as a common scrambling algorithm (DVB-CSA), and interactive application platform (DVB-MHP) for digital television services. All of these standards are based on but extend the MPEG-2 system layer standard.

Table 4-3 Image Formats in the ATSC Digital Television Broadcast Standard

Resolution	Format Name	Number of Vertical Lines	Number of Horizontal Pixels	Aspect Ratio	Scan Mode	Frame Rate
HDTV	1080p	1080	1920	16:9	Progressive	24
		1080	1920	16:9	Progressive	30
	1080i	1080	1920	16:9	Interlaced	30
	720p	720	1280	16:9	Progressive	24
		720	1280	16:9	Progressive	30
		720	1280	16:9	Progressive	60
EDTV	480p	480	704	16:9	Progressive	24
		480	704	16:9	Progressive	30
		480	704	16:9	Progressive	60
		480	704	4:3	Progressive	24
		480	704	4:3	Progressive	30
		480	704	4:3	Progressive	60
		480	640	4:3	Progressive	24
		480	640	4:3	Progressive	30
		480	640	4:3	Progressive	60
SDTV	480i	480	704	16:9	Interlaced	30
		480	704	4:3	Interlaced	30
		480	640	4:3	Interlaced	30

Digital Cable Television   Cable operators began offering digital television services in the 1990s to their customers. The digital television transmitted over the coax cable is in the MPEG-2 transport stream format. Encoding formats for digital cable systems are based on the ATSC broadcast standard and therefore use both the MP@ML (standard definition) and MP@HL (high definition) images in a MPEG-2 transport stream. Cable uses a modulation scheme on the cable plant called Quadrature amplitude modulation (QAM). The 256-QAM modulation scheme is capable of carrying 38.8 Mbps of MPEG-2 transport stream data, which can carry more than 10 standard definition or multiple HDTV programs on just one channel.

Other Video Compression Standards

MPEG-2 isn't the only compression format used for digital video. Earlier formats such as MPEG-1 were used in a range of consumer electronics devices and some early video on the web. A number of newer formats, also called "advanced codecs," provide better compression than MPEG-2. Some of these, such as MPEG-4 AVC, are important to IPTV because they make it possible to deliver HDTV quality video over DSL protocols. This has allowed telephone operators to deliver video services over copper telephone wires. In this section we look at some of the more popular video compression formats.

MPEG-1   The first audio/video codec standard from MPEG was the MPEG-1 standard. While the standard includes many of the same video compression techniques of MPEG-2, it had limitations that constrained the resulting image quality. In particular, image resolution was limited to less than full CCIR-601 size, the standard dealt only with progressive frames and not the interlaced frames of analog television, and compressed stream bitrates were also limited.

Despite these limitations, MPEG-1 is still widely used for some computer video content. It is also the basis for the VideoCD, or VCD, format, which uses audio CD-ROM discs to store MPEG-1 content. The resulting video quality is comparable or less than analog VCRs but the technology was less expensive than the later DVD-ROM format. Also the CD-ROM format holds only about 70 minutes of video, requiring the use of multiple discs for a full-length movie. The format was particularly popular in Asia.

While MPEG-1 video did not reach large commercial deployment in the West, the MPEG-1 Layer 3 audio encoding format, also known as

MP3, became a commercial success for both PC-based audio recording and portable media players such as the Apple iPod.

MPEG-4 and Other Advanced Codecs Advanced codecs improve on the compression efficiency of the earlier compression algorithms such as MPEG-2. These codecs take advantage of improvements in compression theory as well as the increased computational power available to consumer electronics and personal computers. The advanced codecs will be capable of doubling the compression efficiency, or cutting in half the required bitrate, for the same quality as MPEG-2. These codecs have also extended the range of uses beyond MPEG-2's focus on movie and television content. For example, MPEG-4 has many new profiles for mobility and levels geared for low bandwidth and small screen applications such as video on cell phones. It also includes additions for high quality video at high bitrates for use in the production and distribution of high definition content.

MPEG-4 Initially MPEG-4 began as much more than just an efficient compression standard. It included additional features such as interactivity, allowing the viewer to interact with the audio/visual stream, perhaps changing elements of the stream beyond the traditional playback of content in a linear fashion. Some early concepts for MPEG-4 included synthetic or virtual components added to the scene, with those components compressed separately from the background component. A video of a sporting event for example might include virtual stadium venues that could be changed by the user or the broadcaster depending on the audience. However, it wasn't clear what the economic advantage of these extra features were, especially given the additional cost due to the complexity of the algorithm. At the same time, the new compression tools improved the efficiency, making it possible to produce higher quality video at lower bitrates, or to enable small, efficient video on new platforms such as cell phones, which have strict bandwidth requirements. The two approaches were at odds with each other; adding to the complexity and novel elements of the emerging standard versus improving efficiency and reducing the scope for smaller devices.

In the same time period as the development of MPEG-4, the International Telecommunication Union (ITU) was developing the next generation of audio/video compression within the ITU Telecommunication Standardization Sector (ITU-T). The ITU line of compression standards included the previous standards for video conferencing: H.262 and H.263. The ITU standards historically were geared for lower bandwidth applications such as video conferencing. The content was often less constrained by image fidelity as well, typically being used for business purposes and not Hollywood movies. The work within the ITU was focused on improved efficiency and smaller screen formats.

As they did with the MPEG-2 standard, the ITU and MPEG communities came together and formed the Joint Video Team (JVT) to merge their efforts into a single standard. The result is a compromise between exclusively improving compression efficiency and the inclusion of multiple new tools and interactivity. The standard agreed to in 2003 goes by many names. Within the MPEG forum it is MPEG-4 Part 10 and within ITU-T it is know as H.264. It is also known as AVC for Advanced Video Coding. Luckily the various names refer to a single standard currently embodied by the International Organization for Standardization (ISO) and International Electrotechnical Commission (IEC) as ISO/IEC 14496-10:2004. Whenever someone mentions MPEG-4 today they are almost certainly referring to MPEG-4 Part 10 AVC and not an earlier version of MPEG-4.

RealVideo10 and VC-1   While international standardization bodies were working on MPEG-4, several companies continued to release new versions of their proprietary audio/video compression systems. Real Networks created the RealVideo10 codec while Microsoft created Windows Media Video 9 (WMV9). While both companies initially focused on streaming video for use on computers, the quality of the latest codecs improved to match those of MPEG. The MPEG standard, however, continued to have a number of advantages for use with digital television and movies. Among these are a published standard (note this does not mean an open, or free, standard), widespread adoption, a focus on high quality movie and television content, and a fixed standard. The proprietary standards continued to evolve and change, making it difficult to include them in consumer electronics equipment that may not have the ability to download the latest codec software.

Microsoft decided to submit its WMV9 technology to the Society of Motion Picture and Television Engineers (SMPTE) standards body. Within this body, WMV9 is being considered as the standard VC-1. The proposed VC-1 standard differs slightly from WMV9 in that it includes provisions for interlaced video as displayed on television sets, versus the progressive video displayed on computer monitors. Microsoft was also able to get VC-1 approved as one of the codecs within both the HD-DVD and the Blu-ray Disc next generation high definition DVD player specifications. HD-DVD and Blue-ray Disc actually require decoders to support three codecs for content: MPEG-2, MPEG-4 AVC, and VC-1. Because

HD-DVD and Blue-ray Disc players are required to support all three, content creators are free to choose any of the three formats for their content and be guaranteed that the content will play back on the player.

Compression Gets Better with Time   When the MPEG-2 standard was first used in the early 1990s it required the development of fairly sophisticated algorithms to create the compressed bitstreams from digitized television and films. Over time, improvements were made to the algorithms for creating the resulting MPEG-2 bitstreams. One of the benefits of the MPEG standards is that they define the compressed bitstream but leave out the exact details of how to create them. This leaves room for innovation and improvement over time. While the measure of video quality in some ways is subjective, it is clear that over the years the number of bits required to produce the same resulting quality was reduced. More sophisticated algorithms and faster processors made the codec more efficient. Figure 4-35 illustrates the reduction in bitrate for the same quality over time for MPEG-2 and MPEG-4.

Some believe that the full potential of MPEG-2 has been reached and most of the major improvements have been exploited. Luckily, with MPEG-4 and the other advanced codecs, there is still room for this innovation to lower bitrates further. Already there are indications that

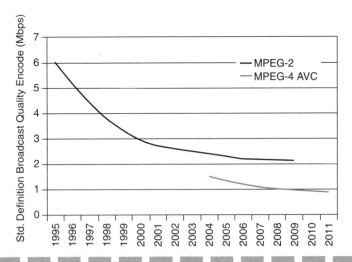

Figure 4-35
The compression efficiency of MPEG-2 and MPEG-4 improved over time as encoders learn the best way to utilize the many tools within the standards. Since MPEG-4 is in its early stage of deployment it may continue to see improvements in compression efficiency.

advanced codecs can produce the same quality image at half the bitrate of MPEG-2 and that factor may increase over time.

MPEG-7 and MPEG-21   While still bearing the MPEG name, MPEG-7 and MPEG-21 are not compression standards. MPEG-7, Multimedia Content Description Interface, is a metadata standard that defines in a common language how to describe digital audio/visual content. This descriptive metadata attached to digital files would make it easier to search for particular components of the file. For example, the MPEG-7 formatted data might include the name of the film's director, different sections or chapters of the film, and audio language options.

The MPEG-21 standard is a multimedia framework that applies business rules to digital media—for example, a DRM description language for use by copyright holders. It would provide a common language for the business rules associated with a piece of audio/visual content. As digital content becomes the norm, it is important to be able to monetize the inherent value of entertainment and information, especially in light of the fact that digital media can be copied indefinitely without loss of quality.

What Happened to MPEG-3, 5, and 6?   While the audio compression standard MP3 has become a common household word, it doesn't actually refer to a MPEG-3 standard. Instead is it shorthand for layer 3 of the audio codec within MPEG-1, or MPEG-1 Audio Codec Layer 3 (MP3). There is no MPEG-3 standard, nor an MPEG-5 or -6. Quoting from the MPEG-FAQ: "MPEG-3 existed once upon a time, but its goal, enabling HDTV, could be accomplished using the tools of MPEG-2, and hence the work item was abandoned. So after 1, 2 and 4, there was much speculation about the next number. Should it be 5 (the next) or 8 (creating an obvious binary pattern)? MPEG, however, decided not to follow either logical expansion of the sequence, but chose the number of 7 instead. So MPEG-5 and MPEG-6 are, just like MPEG-3, not defined." This quote is from http://www.chiariglione.org/mpeg/faq/mp7.htm.

▇▇▇ Chapter Summary

This large chapter is full of many technical details about digital television and compression standards. Hopefully you have come away with a number of facts that are relevant to other technical and nontechnical issues around IPTV—these, in particular:

- Digital television signals have many advantages over analog television signals including the ability to make perfect copies.

- Digital television signals must be compressed via algorithms such as MPEG-2 and MPEG-4 to be of manageable sizes and bitrates.

- The compression process can introduce artifacts that may degrade the image quality and be most noticeable on large television screens. The stronger the compression, the fewer the bits required, but the poorer the image quality.

- Variable bitrate (VBR) encoding and statistical multiplexing (stat-mux) are compression tools that enable more efficient encoding of multiple channels in a single broadcast.

- Compressed video bitstreams are fragile in that single bit errors can cause many pixels or even an entire frame to be corrupted or lost. Accurate transfer and copying of bits is important for good image quality.

- The MPEG compression process introduces temporal dependency such that the decoding process may need many previous and future frames to decode the present frame. This requires buffering on the decoding side and may introduce delays in presenting video to the user on the receiving end.

- MPEG-2 consists of three standards: audio compression, video compression, and system layer. The MPEG-2 system layer can be used to deliver digital television as well as other digital signals such as data services.

- Many digital video formats such as DVD video, ATSC and DVB digital television, digital cable, and digital satellite services are all based on the MPEG-2 standards.

- MPEG-4 and other advanced codecs continue to improve the compression efficiency and make it possible to deliver high quality digital television signals over lower bandwidth media such as DSL.

- As with the MPEG-2 compression standard, compression efficiencies for MPEG-4 and other advanced codecs will improve over time as experts find the best way to use the many tools available in the standards.

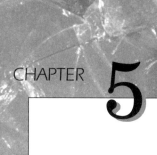

IPTV in the Home

Individuals (or at least techno nerds) get excited about all of the possibilities of home networking and the new equipment that can be purchased to do new and cool things. This chapter explores IP network client device architectures (both hardware and software), how computers factor into the equation, how content and data can be shared within the home, and advanced features within the home (such as triple play, video conferencing, and so on).

Digital Home Networking (DHN)

DHN has become more popular as a significant number of homes have acquired multiple computers and developed a strong desire to share information among them. Uses for a DHN include sharing an Internet connection, network gaming, file sharing, and hardware sharing (such as printers). With the latest advancements in digital video, consumers now want to include video distribution into the DHN. Some examples include IPTV, streaming video from one networked device to another, DVD library, and video conferencing.

As the use of DHN grows, the focus turns to the physical layer, the methods of connecting these devices to the network, and which DHN technology to use. The early approach was to string CAT5 Ethernet cable between two (or more) computers, assuming they were in close proximity. However, in the home, computers are not usually located near each other. In fact, most computers will likely be located in different rooms and quite possibly on different floors of the home. Thus, the DHN has to expand physically to different rooms, through walls and floors in the home. With a multiroom and multifloor network, the question becomes how one distributes the network through the home. Both the consumer and network operator want easy and simple installation solutions when connecting to or building up a DHN.

As technology advances and the market grows, we expect DHN installations to be customized toward each consumer's preference or ability to route the DHN within his or her unique physical home environment. The one common element of DHN will be IP, which plays out well for IPTV. Additionally, we expect many DHNs to be *hybrid* networks employing multiple transmission mediums and different technologies. For example, today a mix of CAT5 and wireless is commonly used to link computers within homes. As consumers add video data into the network, new solutions will be required because wireless technology used today is not suitable for video distribution due to issues such as insufficient bandwidth, no QoS, interference, and so on. We will explore DHN solutions in this section that address these and other network-related issues.

An example of a hybrid DHN is shown in Figure 5-1. This home has three computers and three televisions. At the heart of the DHN is the router/gateway connecting to a broadband service. An Ethernet to coax bridge device (in the study) connects two IP set-top boxes (STBs) to the network via coax cable. One is in the basement family room and the other is in an upstairs bedroom. Two devices connect to the network via

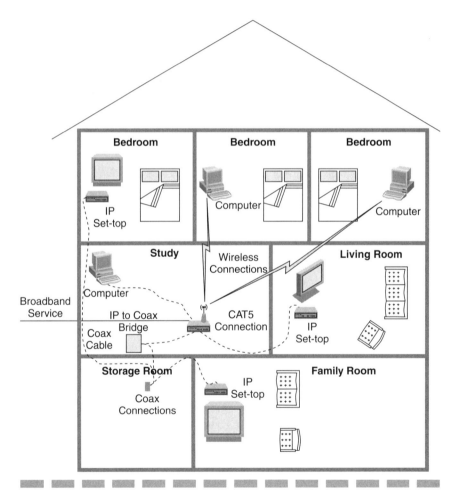

Figure 5-1
Example of a hybrid DHN.

CAT5 cabling—a computer in the study and an IP STB in the living room. Rounding out the network are two computers (upstairs bedrooms) connected wirelessly.

DHN Transmission Mediums

Routing new cables through homes can be a difficult and painful task. Therefore, a major goal of DHN is "no new wires." Wires or transmission mediums suitable for DHNs are listed here:

- **CAT5.** With the popularity of computers and home networking, many new homes include CAT5 runs for Ethernet connectivity. The number of these installations is currently low, but growing. What is nice about CAT5 is that most IP devices already have a connector (RJ-45) that provides a convenient interface. CAT5 also offers the best performing technology today.

- **Wireless.** Connecting IP devices in the home with wireless technology is one of the easiest approaches; no cables required. The computer industry has been providing wireless networking solutions for years. However, to date, wireless technologies have targeted data applications and do not truly support video distribution.

- **Powerline.** Power is distributed to just about every room in homes across the world. Furthermore, every room that has a television or computer must already have power accessible. Therefore, powerlines are ubiquitous, which makes powerline technology an attractive solution for digital home networks. Powerline adaptors bridge an IP network on CAT5 to the electrical outlet, where data then travels within the walls to another wall outlet somewhere else in the house, where it can be received with a similar powerline adapter and then distributed to the desired IP device (such as a computer, STB, and so on).

- **Telephone.** Most homes have a telephone connection, and many have telephone jacks in multiple rooms, which makes DHN technology based on telephone lines an attractive solution. However, not all rooms in consumer homes have telephone jacks. Also, even if a phone jack is located in the same room as a television, often the phone jack is located on the other side of the room, which also detracts (somewhat) from the use of telephone lines for distributing IP data.

- **Coax.** With the popularity of cable television, many new homes (constructed since cable introduction) have coax routed within them. Also, coax cables are installed where a television would normally be located. Coax cabling is available in many rooms (and in many homes), but not ubiquitously.

If a DHN approach is to have no new wires, then one of these transmission mediums will have to be utilized. In this section, we explore DHN technologies suitable for these transmission mediums and their associated solutions. Aside from the selection of a physical medium, other important DHN goals include the following:

- **Cost effective.** Any widely adopted DHN approach should have a relatively low cost associated with it.
- **Standards based.** Standards promote open competition, which naturally brings broad adoption and lower cost.
- **Robust.** Consumers will adopt technology only if the associated products function robustly within the home.
- **Ease of installation.** DHN technology should be easy to install and use; otherwise, consumers will not readily adopt it.
- **Bandwidth.** To support a significant number of devices and distribute video within the network, the DHN technology should provide adequate bandwidth to accommodate all the different device bandwidth requirements and profiles.
- **QoS.** Quality of service is especially important for audio and video traffic. This traffic cannot be lost or dropped; otherwise, the consumer experience will be poor.

Wireless Without a doubt, wireless is the easiest medium to connect devices within a DHN. No wires at all. The computer industry has led the way for mass adoption of wireless technology based on WiFi (also known as IEEE802.11x). Today, broadband router/gateway products have integrated WiFi into their product lines, making WiFi easily available to many homes with broadband service. When a consumer signs up for broadband service, she can receive a broadband modem with an integrated router plus WiFi; this is the heart of a DHN. It's usually best to connect devices with a CAT5 cable for performance and reliability, but if laying a new cable is not convenient, then (for data) WiFi is a proven technology that works well.

This section of wireless DHN technology will examine WiFi wireless solutions. Other wireless technologies exist (such as HiperLAN, Ultra

Wideband, proprietary, and so on), but we will focus our attention on 802.11. Not only does WiFi dominate today's marketplace, but it also has an aggressive roadmap with a huge engineering workforce to render other wireless technologies as "long shots." However, WiFi (and other wireless technologies) does have its own set of limitations and shortcomings. Table 5-1 shows the various 802.11x technologies and their associated features.

Table 5-1 Wireless Technology Parameters

Tech.	Freq.	Raw Data Rate	Video	Std.	Range	Cost	Avail.	Pene-tration
802.11a	5 GHz	54 Mbps	No	IEEE	Low	Low	Now	Low
802.11b	2.4 GHz	11 Mbps	No	IEEE	Low	Low	Now	Moderate
802.11g	2.4 GHz	54 Mbps	No	IEEE	Medium	Low	Now	High
802.11n	2.4 & 5 GHz	200+ Mbps	Yes	IEEE	Medium	Low	2007	No

802.11a is a WiFi technology that operates at 5 GHz and provides a relatively high data rate of 54 Mbps. It utilizes an OFDM (Orthogonal Frequency Division Multiplexing) modulation, which enables it to operate at 54 Mbps, but that rate can scale back as required: 48, 36, 24, 18, 12, 9, and 6 Mbps. Since 802.11a operates at 5 GHz, it does not experience the same interferences as that of 802.11b/g (discussed next). However, this higher frequency means that 802.11a cannot penetrate walls and floors as well as 802.11b because its energy gets absorbed more readily.

802.11b was the first widely adopted WiFi technology that operates at 2.4 GHz and provides a relatively low data rate of 11 Mbps. It utilizes CCK (Complementary Code Keying) modulation, which enables it to operate at 11 Mbps, but will scale back to 5.5, 2, and 1 Mbps by utilizing adaptive rate selection. Since 802.11b operates at the 2.4 GHz band, it has good propagation characteristics; however, microwave ovens, cordless phones, and Bluetooth devices can interfere with 802.11b.

802.11g is the current widely adopted WiFi technology, replacing 802.11b. It operates at the same 2.4 GHz frequency but delivers a higher data rate. It also utilizes an OFDM (like 802.11a) modulation, which enables the same data rates as 802.11a (54, 48, 36, 24, 18, 12, 9, and 6 Mbps) but also can support 802.11b CCK modulation for 11 and 5.5 Mbps. 802.11g has good propagation characteristics but is also affected by household devices (microwave ovens, cordless phones, and so on), much like 802.11b. Finally, the 802.11g technology is newer (and improved) over 802.11b and its popularity has made 802.11b obsolete for all practical purposes.

Note that none of these technologies (802.11a/b/g) is well suited for video distribution due to the following problems:

- Video distribution requires a high and constant bandwidth, but these wireless technologies experience a significant loss of data rate over distance. Therefore, as the WiFi receiver is positioned farther away from the transmitter (accruing additional losses through floors and walls), the data rate will scale down dramatically.

- Video distribution requires a constant reception of error-free data. These wireless technologies often experience transmission errors (such as signal interference), which leads to an unpleasant viewing experience.

None of these wireless technologies provides guaranteed QoS, only best effort. Therefore, the video reception will most likely experience video dropouts from time to time.

802.11n provides the possibility or hope to resolve many of these issues with respect to video distribution. As of this writing, the standard is expected to be completed in late 2006, which means initial product availability will be sometime in 2007. The 802.11n data rate is estimated to be 540 Mbps and incorporates QoS for video applications. 802.11n also incorporates multiple-input multiple-output (MIMO), which has multiple transmitter and receiver antennas. MIMO technology enables the 802.11n standard to achieve greater bandwidth and range through spatial multiplexing and diversity.

Consumers should ask some important questions when contemplating a wireless network:

- Will it perform adequately within my house's environment? Other questions such as what is the signal loss as the RF signal penetrates through walls and floors, and other RF interferences should be considered.

- How quickly does the performance and throughput drop off over distance?

- If video distribution is the desired application, what QoS is provided?

- Can my neighbors' 802.11 network interfere with mine?

Before deploying a wireless network, these issues should be evaluated because wireless technologies can sometimes fall short of a consumer's expectations.

Powerline Powerline communication (PLC) is another DHN technology that is easy to connect to. No new wires are required, and power outlets are usually located near televisions or any other DHN device. Therefore, from a DHN installation perspective, PLC is an attractive solution. Recent advancements in PLC have positioned it as a relevant competitor in this emerging marketplace, enabling PLC to compete with popular technologies such as WiFi, Ethernet, and coax. PLC technologies have incorporated OFDM, an efficient modulation scheme that enables a competitive bandwidth. Another interesting aspect regarding the current PLC solutions is that these solutions can also function on coax cable as well. Not only are PLC technologies interesting to consumers, but they also appeal to IPTV network operators who are interested in reducing installation costs. Table 5-2 shows the various PLC technologies and their associated features.

Table 5-2 Powerline Technology Parameters

Technology	Freq.	Raw Data Rate	Video	Std.	Cost	Avail.	Pene-tration
HomePlug 1.0	4.5–21 MHz	13.78 Mbps	No	Home Plug	Low	Now	Low
HomePlug AV	2–28 MHz	200 Mbps	Yes	Home Plug	Medium	Late 2006	N/A
Digital Home Standard (DHS) for powerline AV	1.6–30 MHz	200 Mbps	Yes	UPA	Medium	Now	Low
HD-PLC	4–28 MHz	190 Mbps	Yes	CEPCA	Medium	2006	N/A

The first two rows in Table 5-2 refer to HomePlug Powerline Alliance specifications and its suite of available products. The HomePlug Powerline Alliance was formed by several leading companies and their first generation specification, HomePlug 1.0, supports approximately 14 Mbps bandwidth, which is suitable for voice and data. Their next generation specification, HomePlug AV, is targeted for high-performance networks including the distribution of video. HomePlug AV adds secure connectivity and QoS. HomePlug AV also supports a raw data rate of 200 Mbps and an effective data rate of over 100 Mbps. This specification was finalized and approved in August 2005, and initial products started to enter the market in the middle of 2006.

The third row in Table 5-2 refers to the Universal Powerline Association (UPA) specification. In 2004 an interest group for UPA was formed and officially announced in January 2005. Much like HomePlug, the UPA has several leading companies as members; however, this list shares no commonality with HomePlug. This specification competes head-to-head with HomePlug AV, and as you can see (from the table), its feature set is nearly identical. Additionally, these technologies are not compatible with each other.

The final row in Table 5-2 references the Consumer Electronics Powerline Communication Alliance (CEPCA) specification and its class of products. Much like the UPA PLC solution, the CEPCA solution for Powerline is competitive with HomePlug and has a similar feature set. Additionally, these products are not compatible with UPA or HomePlug products.

Other leading PLC standards bodies follow:

- **IEEE.** The IEEE standards body has established four working groups aimed at standardizing PLC technology: IEEE BPL, Broadband over Powerline technologies; IEEE P1675, Broadband over Powerline hardware; IEEE P1775, PLC equipment electromagnetic compatibility (EMC) requirements, testing, and measurement methods; and IEEE P1901, Broadband over Powerline networks, with medium access control and physical layer specifications.

- **ETSI.** The European Telecommunication Standards Institute is officially responsible for standardization in telecommunications, broadcasting, and certain aspects of information technology within Europe.

- **OPERA.** The Open PLC European Research Alliance was launched by the European Commission in order to assist with the development and deployment of PLC products and services in Europe.

One drawback for PLC is the fact that competing standards and specifications (as well as proprietary solutions) add an element of confusion to the landscape. It is unclear which standard will win out, and this uncertainty will limit widespread PLC adoption. The result is a divergence within the PLC marketplace, with the leaders in the PLC industry aligning with separate standards bodies (such as HomePlug AV, UPA, and CEPCA). Even with this disparity, the various PLC technologies have impressive feature sets suitable for DHN and video distribution.

Following are some other issues related to PLC:

- Possible interference with neighbors, caused by data coupling through power meters or apartment walls.

- Possible radio interference because the power cables are not shielded or twisted. PLC on power cables has the ability to transmit energy over radio frequency, which interferes with other signals such as amateur radio signals.

- Performance issues (packet loss) due to various power-related issues such as power spikes, AC/DC switching noise, motors, and so on. These issues often require additional filtering and expense to resolve.

- Potentially a higher cost DHN than competing solutions.

Telephone or Phoneline   Regarding the "no new wires" category, phoneline technology partially meets this requirement. Most homes have telephone service, making phoneline a nearly ubiquitous medium similar to powerline. However, the positions of phone jacks within homes often do not lend themselves to computer or television connection. It is true that someone can install a DHN over phoneline through the house (in cases where phone jacks are in multiple rooms) without adding any new wires, but it is somewhat awkward to then stretch telephone cables across the room to reach either a computer or television.

The technology solution for DHN over phoneline is the Home Phoneline Networking Alliance (HomePNA), an incorporated, non-profit association of industry leading companies working together to help ensure adoption of a single, unified phoneline networking industry standard and rapidly bring to market a range of interoperable home networking solutions. There are no competing standards or approaches, simply HPNA. This makes for a clean approach to the mass market where multiple companies can provide phoneline HPNA solutions, which creates a competitive environment in the consumer marketplace, especially with respect to advanced feature set and cost.

Table 5-3 shows the three generations of HPNA specifications and their associated parameters. These specifications enable the DHN to connect computers in a fashion similar to typical Ethernet LANs. This allows for Internet access sharing, access to other home computers' peripherals, and multiplayer gaming. Additionally, HPNAv3 uses a different frequency for data than voice or fax calls. Finally, the raw data rate for HPNAv3 is 128 Mbps and effectively around 80 Mbps, suitable for video distribution.

Table 5-3 Telephone Line Technology Parameters

Tech.	Freq.	Raw Data Rate	Video	Std.	Range	Cost	Avail.	Pene- tration
HPNAv1	4–10 MHz	1 Mbps	No	HPNA	Medium	Low	Now	Medium
HPNAv2	4–10 MHz	10 Mbps	No	HPNA	Medium	Low	Now	Medium
HPNAv3	4–21 MHz	128 Mbps	Yes	HPNA	High	Low	Now	Low

Coax   Installing a DHN within a home over existing 75 Ohm coax is an attractive alternative because it falls into the "no new wires" category. Thanks to the popularity of cable television, today many homes have cable runs, especially newer homes. Even though coax cable is not nearly as ubiquitous as powerlines, coax cabling has reached critical mass and is one of the transmission mediums that require no new wires—though this claim can be debated, especially in countries where the percentage of new homes with coax installed is relatively low. Another nice aspect is that coax or cable outlets are located near the natural locations of televisions, which is convenient for IPTV devices.

Two leading technologies that compete for the DHN over coax market are Multimedia over Coax Alliance (MoCA), and Home Phoneline Networking Alliance or Home Phoneline Networking Adapter (HPNA) over coax which is also referred to as HCNA (HPNA Coax Network Adapter). Both approaches have the following design objectives:

- Design a modulated carrier for a 75 Ohm coax cable distribution system that may carry cable television or satellite services.

- Support for voice, data, and video services over coax networks.

- Designed to operate a bidirectional network over a coax network with splitters and unterminated stubs with reflections.

Table 5-4 shows the two main approaches, HCNA and MoCA, and their associated parameters. These technologies differ in modulation schemes and utilized frequency spectrum. HCNA employs QAM, where MoCA employs OFDM. MoCA operates in the frequency range between 860 MHz and 1.5 GHz, which has no conflicts with cable television or cable modem service. HCNA, on the other hand, operates between 4 MHz and 21 MHz, which does conflict with cable modem services. If a cable modem service is to be used alongside HCNA, a separate coax run is necessary, which will isolate the cable modem from the rest of the coax DHN.

Table 5-4 Coax Technology Parameters

Tech.	Freq.	Raw Data Rate	Video	Std.	Range	Cost	Avail.	Pene-tration
MoCA v1.0	>860 MHz	~250 Mbps	Yes	MoCA	Medium	Medium	Now	Low
HCNAv3	4–21 MHz	128 Mbps	Yes	HPNAv3	High	Medium	Now	Low

Because both technologies have different approaches to frequency spectrum, HCNA and MoCA also have different bandwidth and cable run (distances) characteristics. In general, the MoCA technology will achieve a higher available bandwidth, where the HCNA technology will support a much longer cable run.

Much like PLC, DHN over coax is faced with multiple standards and it is unclear which standard will win out. Also, cost is another possible issue with DHN over coax. With the two identified approaches, there is a single vendor (MoCA –Entropic; HPNA – Coppergate) which is currently dominating. This could inhibit competition and result in higher prices.

With new entries to the coax DHN field, it is too early to determine what impact they may or may not have. These include PLC technologies, which have shown the ability to operate on coax and proprietary solutions.

Emerging Trends with Computers

Rounding out our section on DHN, we include a short discussion on the latest trends within the computer industry. The bulk of homes equipped with DHNs today are primarily installed to network multiple computers in the home. Both Intel and Microsoft have commercially launched programs addressing home networking and entertainment, showing how consumers can enrich their entertainment experience with powerful networked computers or platforms within the living room and home.

Intel's approach is a combination of hardware and software technology, called Viiv Technology, targeted to deliver a great entertainment experience, ease of use, and installation of networked devices for the consumer. The Viiv Technology has combined the living room's user-friendly remote control (consumer electronics) functionality with PCs' networked access to content from within and outside the home (including the Internet). As part of this strategy, Intel verifies each PC and network media device for the market so consumers can visibly see the Viiv Technology brand and be assured that these devices will interoperate within the home network. Intel's Viiv Technology–based PCs include consumer electronics–like features for simplified usage, higher performance to support advanced features (such as high definition audio and video), and connectivity to online entertainment. The Viiv PC will be able to turn on and off instantly, be much smaller and quieter than typical PCs, and allow for simple user interface (UI) navigation via a remote control. Intel's latest dual-core, 65nm processors enable support for high definition video as well as 7.1 surround sound audio. The Viiv platform allows for content downloads, online gaming, and other online services. Additionally, Viiv allows for sharing of content within the home, such as home movies, music, and photos. Finally, this platform will provide support up to 1 Gbps Ethernet networking, which enables the Viiv platform to scale as the home networks migrate to Gigabit Ethernet.

Microsoft has approached the market with its Microsoft Windows XP Media Center Edition 2005. This software platform allows for the standard multimedia support including web browsing, gaming, e-mail, and so on. Media Center also provides support for digital entertainment including photos, music, TV, movies, home movies, and radio. Media Center allows the consumer this rich experience either in front of a desktop PC or with a remote control in front of a television in the living room. Media Center is targeted to be an all-in-one PC and home entertainment center.

These technologies may spur consumers to add video distribution to existing data home networks or increase overall DHN penetration. It is too early to know how well consumers will accept them, but these new capabilities may be compelling enough for consumers to add a networked computer into their living room.

IP Client Devices for the Home

Client devices are portals to the consumer's IPTV viewing experience. Because of this, a lot of emphasis is placed on how well they function, how quick the software responds to requests via an infrared remote control, and how good a picture it creates on the television or monitor. A typical configuration of a home network might consist of several client devices. For example, in Figure 5-2, two computers and two IP STBs (connected to televisions) are all connected via a local DHN.

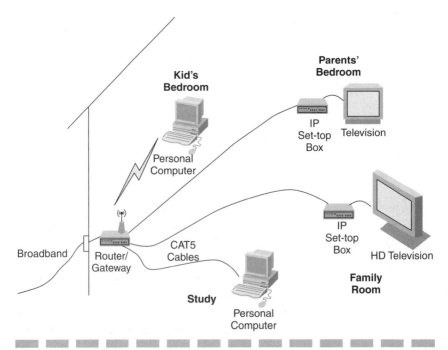

Figure 5-2
Broadband with IPTV services to the home.

In this section, we examine two types of client devices: the home router/gateway and the IP STB. The central point of the DHN is the home router/gateway device. It forms the boundary between the broadband IP service provider's network and the DHN. All other networked devices within the home receive IP traffic through the router/gateway. IP STBs receive the digital video services that were delivered over the IP delivery network and the home network and convert them into video signals for the television.

Routers/Gateways

The router/gateway is the entry point of the broadband and IPTV service within the home. Routers/gateways are IP network devices necessary for translating and distributing IP network traffic within the home as well as connecting the home network to the broadband service provider's network. They are a critical element for the consumer's DHN as well as enabling IPTV to the home. A typical router/gateway connects to an external network interface (such as DSL telephone line or cable's RF interface) and provides multiple interface connections for DHN IP devices (such as Ethernet jacks). Also, thanks to integration, many routers/gateways provide common wireless interfaces (such as IEEE802.11a/b/g). Because routers/gateways operate at the network layer, a router is able to transmit data packets from a local network to another network. Also, as the name suggests, a router manages the routing of the data to its proper destination. It will communicate with other routers via routing protocols to build internal route tables designed to optimize the routing of data.

IP STB Hardware Architectures

IP STBs come in various configurations with differing feature sets. It seems no two STBs have the same feature set, which from a consumer's (or network operator's) perspective can be both a blessing and a curse. We will cover a set or class of architectures but we will not try to encompass the entire spectrum of client device architectures. Our initial focus will be on IP STB architectures and how they stream audio and video services into the home.

At the center of any STB are integrated circuits (ICs) for audio and video decoding, the UI, and access control to the home network. These

ICs form the basis of an IP set-top architecture and play a significant role in the ultimate cost of the product. As we already discussed, the heritage or lineage of IP STBs comes from satellite and cable STBs. Furthermore, volume and profit from sales of ICs determine which requirements get added into the next generation ICs. As a consequence, these industries have driven the silicon vendor's products (ICs), architectures, and roadmaps for years. When designing an IP STB for an emerging indus-try such as IPTV, the original equipment manufacturers (OEMs) are able to utilize and leverage the cost advantages of these products and indus-tries. However, the flip side of the equation is that the ICs they will be designing with are not truly designed for IP networks but satellite or cable networks. The differences are subtle and the designers of IP STBs have to work around these issues.

In this section we review the first generation digital receivers targeted for the satellite and cable markets and progress to today's architectures targeted for the IP set-top market. We also cover hybrid products that are variants of the standard IP set-top products.

First Generation Digital Receivers   The first digital receivers were devices that bridged digital video to the analog television. These STBs received a digitally compressed signal via an RF interface and exe-cuted an MPEG-2 decode that eventually rendered pictures to a televi-sion. The decoding function was accomplished within a hardware-based decoder; the actual function and algorithm were designed and executed within a single integrated circuit (IC).

Figure 5-3 is a block diagram of a first generation digital receiver or decoder. This design consists of a combination of various IC components. The major components of this design are discussed next.

Tuner   The tuner selects the specific RF frequency of the channel desired by the user. Once the tuner tunes to the proper channel, cable frequency, or satellite transponder (satellite communications channels), the tuner will pass a valid intermediate RF signal onto the demod IC.

Demod   The demod IC will perform an analog to digital conversion (ADC, A/D, or A to D) and forward error correction (FEC). The output of the demod is a digital transport stream via a transport interface.

Transport   The transport IC is a key part of this design. The STB will perform a demux (short for de-multiplex) of the digital stream com-ing in from the transport interface within the transport IC. The demux

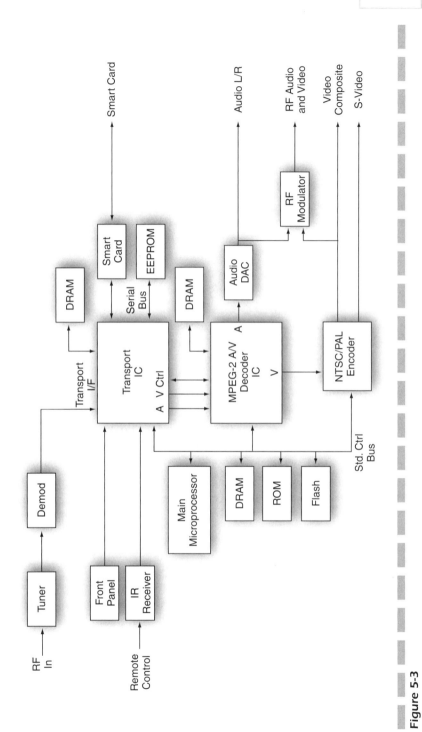

Figure 5-3
First generation digital receiver with a hardware-based decoder.

operation separates the audio packets from the video packets and then passes them on to the decoder. The demux also separates program specific information (PSI) packets from the transport stream that are intended for the general purpose microprocessor to utilize. The most useful PSI data would include Electronic Program Guide (EPG) data that tells the software how to tune to the right frequencies, get the right PIDs, and program metadata (such as event titles, event duration, and so on). The transport IC also provides glue for other important functions such as processing IR commands from the remote control, front panel interface, and smart card interface (for conditional access).

MPEG-2 A/V Decoder   The MPEG-2 A/V decoder IC is where all of the heavy lifting is done with respect to making pictures that get displayed on the TV. It receives the audio and video digital streams from the transport, does the actual decode or decompression of the bitstream, and creates pictures and sounds. Additionally, the MPEG-2 decoder contains the graphics functionality. The MPEG-2 decoder IC has a video plane and a graphics plane. The graphics plane is used for generating the UI and typically is displayed on top of the video plane. In more sophisticated decoder ICs, the graphics plane can be opaque or translucent. The consumer will see the video in the background and graphics covering part (opaque mode) of the video or blended (translucent or transparent mode) on a pixel-by-pixel basis with the video. The outputs of the MPEG-2 decoder are interfaces for the audio and video (to the NTSC/PALvideo encoder, and the audio DAC), which ultimately get converted to analog and sent to the television. The audio interface connects to an external audio Digital to Analog (DAC). The video signal comes out of the MPEG-2 decoder IC digitally and connects to the NTSC/PAL encoder for video processing.

General Purpose Microprocessor   The general purpose microprocessor (sometimes referred to as the main processor or main CPU, such as a 32 bit microprocessor) is where all of the system software (not including micro code within ICs) executes. Here the UI, middleware, operating system (OS), and low level drivers are executed. For example, the microprocessor will need to create UI screens and render those pictures to the TV via the graphics functionality within the MPEG decoder IC.

NTSC/PAL Video Encoder   The NTSC/PAL video encoder receives a digital interface (such as CCIR-656) and creates a standard video signal suitable for either NTSC or PAL televisions. Additionally, the video encoder handles other video-related functions such as Macrovision protection (VCR copy protection) and vertical blanking features such as closed captioning and CGMS-A (Copy Generation Management System-Analog).

Volatile Memory Volatile memory storage devices do not retain information when the system loses power or is reset/rebooted. The main microprocessor, transport, and MPEG-2 decoder all require dynamic random access memory (DRAM). The transport IC uses its memory for buffering MPEG packet data. The MPEG decoder also uses its memory for buffering data, and the actual decode of compressed bitstreams to the original audio and video data. The main microprocessor uses its memory for executing software (such as OS, device drivers, UI, and so on) from it.

Non-volatile Memory Non-volatile memory storage devices retain information when the system loses power or is reset/rebooted. The main microprocessor requires non-volatile memory. Figure 5-3 shows two different types of non-volatile memory: ROM (read only memory) and flash memory. The software required to boot the system would reside within the ROM. This bootup software is programmed at the factory and should be small and robust. The system also allows for software downloading (replacing old software within the STB with a new version of software) and the flash memory is where the bulk of the software resides. To minimize flash memory (which is much more expensive than dynamic memory), designers often employ compression of the software data (often called the software image) that gets stored in the flash. As part of the bootup process, the software operating from the ROM will decompress the image stored in flash and save it in dynamic memory. Then the full OS software will boot from this memory and start the IPTV application suite. The software in flash can get replaced with bug fixes or new software features, but the ROM cannot be replaced in the field. For this reason, the ROM must be robust and as bug-free as possible.

Another piece of small non-volatile memory within the system is the Electrically Erasable Programmable Read-Only Memory (EEPROM). The EEPROM is a slow (access speed) device with minimal memory storage capacity; however, it is also inexpensive. The EEPROM is connected to a slow serial bus such as an IIC bus (Inter-Integrated Circuit bus) coming off of the transport IC. The EEPROM usually holds consumer (or user) preferences such as preferred UI language, parental control settings, favorite channels, and so on. The architecture shown in Figure

5-3 uses a lot of memory. The next generation architecture (covered next in this chapter) reduces memory usage.

Smart Card Many STBs rely on a smart card as part of their conditional access system. A smart card device is approximately the size of a credit card and has an embedded microprocessor and memory. The smart card can provide decryption keys and assist in rights management. The transport IC has a smart card (ISO 7816) interface that connects to a smart card controller and socket. The STB chassis will often have a slot that enables the OEM or consumer to insert a smart card into the socket. Typically, the OEM will mate each STB with its associated commercial video service smart card at the factory. Some cable systems use a similar device called a CableCARD. Like a smart card, a Cable-CARD contains the conditional access system (CAS) components specific to the service network.

Second and Third Generation Digital Receivers Figure 5-4 shows a block diagram of the second and third generation digital receivers. The typical progression of consumer electronics is to reduce cost by integrating many of the device functions into a single IC. The outcome of this integration is called a System on a Chip (SoC). Figure 5-4 shows four of the ICs integrated into a single SoC IC: the main microprocessor, transport IC, MEPG-2 decoder, and NTSC/PAL video encoder. The second generation digital receiver has the same functionality as the first generation except it costs significantly less. The third generation augments the decoder to include advanced compression schemes such as AVC and VC-1, and the integration of other hardware features such as Ethernet (core for IPTV) interface, IDE interface (for a hard disk drive–PVR), USB, and so on. Advanced compression is important for IPTV because advanced compression reduces the required bandwidth while preserving the same video experience.

IPTV services emerged between the second and third generations of digital receivers. The satellite and cable industries had driven the cost reduction process, and the functionality, for the second generation of devices. The first IPTV STBs replaced the RF tuners with Ethernet controller ICs, thus enabling video to be streamed to it via an IP network instead of RF signals. The initial IPTV receivers were based on the MPEG-2 standard and were targeted for various field trials around the world.

Hardware and software engineers took these second generation designs and started to develop systems and products specifically for IPTV. The differences in functional requirements between a cable/satel-

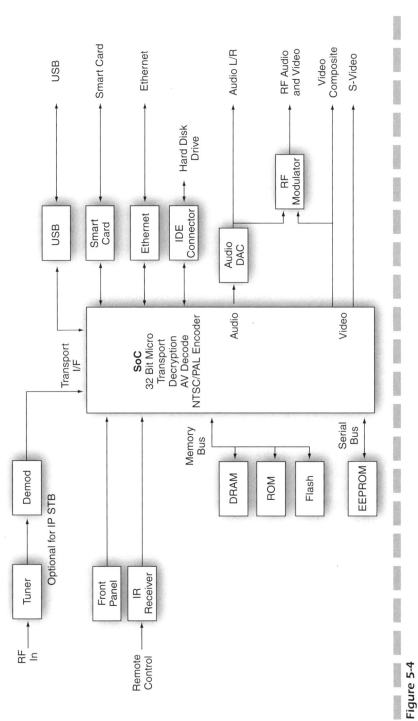

Figure 5-4
Second and third generation digital receivers with hardware-based decoder.

lite receiver and an IP receiver are subtle but significant. The most important difference is the flow of audio and video through the hardware. Cable and satellite receivers receive the digital audio and video from an RF interface and eventually route that data to the hardware decoder through a hardware transport interface. The transport hardware and the A/V decoder hardware of SoC ICs are designed (or wired) to function seamlessly with each other. An IP STB, on the other hand, does not receive the audio and video digital bitstream from an RF interface but from the Ethernet controller.

The first concern for the IP STB engineer was to ensure the architecture can sustain a transfer of the audio, video, and data from the Ethernet controller to system memory. Direct Memory Access (DMA, hardware-based logic that transfers blocks of data without requiring software to transfer it byte-by-byte) controllers usually get employed to accomplish this task. Every system or SoC has a limited number of DMA engines available and these engines must be discriminately used. Once the engineer knows he or she can transfer the incoming data from the Ethernet controller (or network interface) to system memory and satisfy the data speed or bandwidth requirement, the next task is to get this data into the transport or demux interface.

Many of the SoC solutions enable a DMA transfer from system memory to the hardware transport interface. If the SoC does not have this ability, a software demux would need to be implemented. A software demux might not be a good idea because it adds complexity and may create new problems (such as timing related) that would need to be addressed. The cable/satellite STB designer does not need to worry about routing the audio, video, and data from the network interface (RF input) to the hardware transport because all of this logic already exists within the SoCs. Once the audio and video data gets to the transport, then the SoC should easily be able to perform the decode function. Other problems the IP set-top designer needs to address include network jitter and clock recovery.

DSP Digital Receivers An alternative approach to a hardware-based digital set-top architecture is a Digital Signal Processor (DSP)–based architecture. A DSP is a specialized microprocessor that is designed (or optimized) to execute digital signal processing algorithms rapidly in real-time, such as those used in audio and video decoding. This approach maps itself well to a digital receiver or STB. Decoding multimedia (codec) algorithms (such as MPEG-2, AVC, and VC-1) is actually a DSP application. The significant difference between a DSP (based decoder) STB and a SoC (based decoder) STB is that the SoC approach has a finely tuned codec algorithm implemented in hardware (silicon blocks of logic), whereas the DSP approach has the same codec algorithm implemented purely in software.

Figure 5-5 shows a DSP-based digital receiver architecture that processes the audio and video decode in software within the DSP microprocessor. If you compare this architecture against the SoC hardware-based approach shown in Figure 5-4, both systems will perform the same basic functions.

The DSP approach has two major ICs: the main microprocessor and the DSP IC. The hardware-based approach has only one major IC: the SoC. When trying to compare an SoC solution to a DSP solution, three factors usually stand out:

- **Flexibility.** A DSP based design is usually more flexible than an SoC-based design because the codec is implemented in software. A software-based approach can be updated even after the STB has been deployed in the field—for example, to fix a problem in the codec. In addition, the software codec can be upgraded as more efficient algorithms are found or new services get rolled out. This may not be the case with an SoC solution. *Advantage: DSP*

- **Cost.** In general, two ICs will be more expensive than one. In addition to the cost of the ICs, having more ICs in the device increases the board size and power requirements. An optimized hardware-based design should always consume less silicon (which also relates to cost) than a software (flexible)–based solution. *Advantage: SoC*

- **Time-to-market.** Time-to-market can be a difficult parameter to measure because so many factors are related to a commercial service. Time-to-market should reflect when the final service is available to the consumer. Some issues that would hinder time-to-market can be related to the set-top development, others could be network or system related. Also, a lot depends on how many engineering resources the silicon vendor can apply to deploying its solution. But in the end, it is reasonable to assume that a DSP-based solution could be fielded before an SoC-based solution given the advantage in flexibility. *Slight advantage: DSP*

Often the lowest cost solution gets widely deployed; however, the current IP STB market includes a mix of SoC- and DSP-based solutions. This might be explained by the fact that not too many network operators

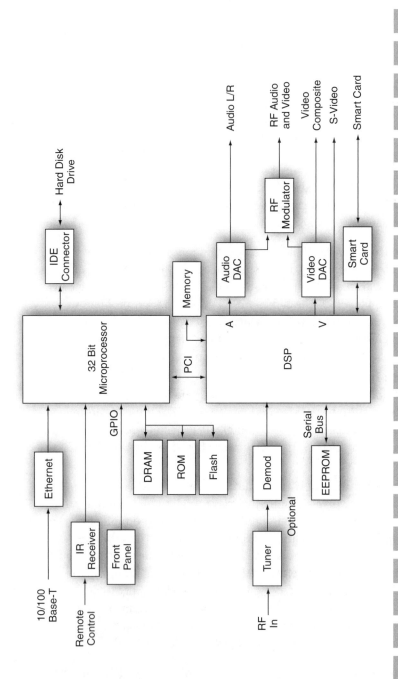

Figure 5-5
DSP digital receiver, software-based decoder.

have broad IPTV commercial deployments, but there are a lot of IPTV field trials. The network operators that have broad deployments primarily have launched with an MPEG-2 video service offering, which is well suited for SoC solutions because MPEG-2 has been cost-optimized into these devices. Other network operators want to deploy with advanced compression services so they can better utilize their network bandwidth. These network operators may tend to favor DSP-based solutions to leverage the flexibility DSPs offer. However, many of the silicon SoC vendors are pushing extremely hard to have deployable advanced compression solutions as soon as possible, which would reduce some of the advantage DSPs offer.

PC-Based Digital Receivers For years, set-top architects have kept a close eye on the PC market to see if a PC could become a viable alternative to a digital STB. Economics have always worked against any such approach. Not long ago, the cost of a PC was approximately $2,000, but over the years PC prices have steadily dropped, and today one can be acquired for a few hundred dollars (depending on the feature set). What makes the PC architecture interesting for IPTV is its ability to operate seamlessly within existing digital home networks. The PC-based solution is probably the most flexible option. Today, many companies prototype their set-top products on a PC platform because it's easy and inexpensive to do. In cases where time-to-market is critical, the PC's flexibility could prove useful in getting a product out to meet aggressive timeframes.

Furthermore, a growing segment of consumers are forgoing a separate television in favor of just a PC. The PC is becoming capable of supporting most video entertainment functions such as watching DVDs and television. Many PC "plug-in" solutions easily extend a computer to include digital television interfaces. Here are some examples:

- **NTSC Tuners.** PCI cards that connect to cable or antenna to receive analog television signals and make them available to the PC.

- **DVB-S (Digital Video Broadcasting–Satellite) Tuners.** PCI cards with software for receiving digital television signals compliant with the DVB-S standard.

- **DVB-T (Digital Video Broadcasting–Terrestrial) Tuners.** PCI cards with software.

- **ATSC-HD (Advanced Television Systems Committee–High Definition) Tuners.** PCI cards with software.

- **DHN (Digital Home Networking).** PCI or USB solutions that enable the PC to get IP data from home networks: powerline, wireless, coax, and so on.

Figure 5-6 shows a block diagram of a PC-based digital receiver architecture that will process the audio and video decode in software within the PC's microprocessor. If you compare this architecture against the SoC approach (Figure 5-4) and the DSP approach (Figure 5-5), you will see primarily the same system except with a third major IC. The three major ICs are the main microprocessor (X86), the north bridge IC, and the south bridge IC. One debatable argument would be that the overall performance (and cost) of the PC's microprocessor is extremely high in comparison to the other approaches and could be overkill for the intended function.

One challenge to deploying a PC-based digital STB is targeting it for the living room's television versus a PC monitor in the home office. Back in Chapter 2 we learned the differences between a television and a computer monitor. Care must be taken in both hardware and software to ensure the video outputs are consistent with interlaced television. On most analog televisions, the progressive frames of a PC will result in artifacts such as text flickering.

Let us compare the PC solution versus an SoC and a DSP solution using our three previously used factors:

- **Flexibility.** The PC-based design is usually more flexible than both the DSP- and SoC-based design. It shares the soft codec (a codec executed in software) approach; therefore, the software can be modified to resolve problems, and then get downloaded to the boxes in the field. The PC platform also has the advantage of being able to leverage the PC market for add-on features. *Advantage: PC, then DSP*

- **Cost.** In general, three ICs will be more expensive than either two or one. *Advantage: SoC, then DSP*

- **Time-to-market.** Again, time-to-market is difficult to measure because so many factors are related to it. But given the PC's flexibility, one could argue it could have the best time-to-market. *Slight advantage: PC, then DSP*

Hybrid Digital Receivers   An approach that is quickly becoming popular is hybrid video services, which combines IP-delivered television services with free or pay broadcast services. Worldwide, various "free-to-

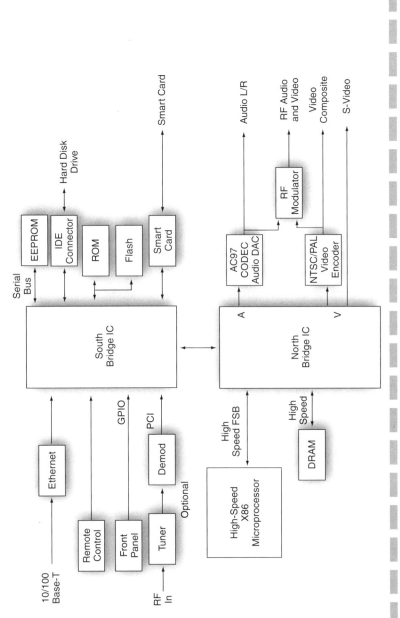

Figure 5-6

PC-based digital receiver, software-based decoder.

air" broadcast services, such as ATSC HD channels available via antenna tuner, exist in the US. Other popular approaches include DVB-S and DVB-T in Europe and parts of Asia, where all that is needed is either a satellite dish or an antenna along with the appropriate tuner and demod.

Figure 5-7 is a block diagram of an advanced STB architecture suitable for a hybrid system. It includes a dual ATSC tuner configuration where the outputs from the demod ICs are connected to the external transport input interfaces of an SoC IC. This device also has an IDE interface for a hard disk drive, which enables DVR (Digital Video Recording) features. Finally, the Ethernet interface receives streaming video programs from the IPTV video service.

When you put all of these modules together, the hybrid system provides a rich and compelling service offering. A significant amount of broadcast content (if not all broadcast content) could come from free-to-air modules (such as ATSC tuner + demod). It should be noted that Figure 5-7 shows two ATSC tuner + demod modules connecting to the transport interfaces of the SoC. These ATSC modules could easily be replaced with a DVB-T module, DVB-S module, or any other module that may be required to receive broadcast services.

In the hybrid scenario, the IP video channels would provide the VOD channels as well as any additional broadcast channels required to round out the video service. Finally, this product could include a dual tuner DVR. This is a powerful product that enables watch-and-record, and the network operator can leverage free-to-air content in the process.

IP Set-top Software Architectures

In all emerging markets, each company that provides system components tries to broaden its own position and offerings. Needless to say, the IPTV market will eventually consolidate and some companies will become winners while others become losers. With respect to IPTV software, this is true as many companies with software solutions are trying to find their niche or piece of the client software stack. To give you an idea of the kinds of companies and solutions that are available, the following list is broken into broad categories.

Hardware Set-top manufacturers (OEMs) provide the hardware and core software that manages the platform as well as integrating in other third-party software components (such as OS, CA, and so on).

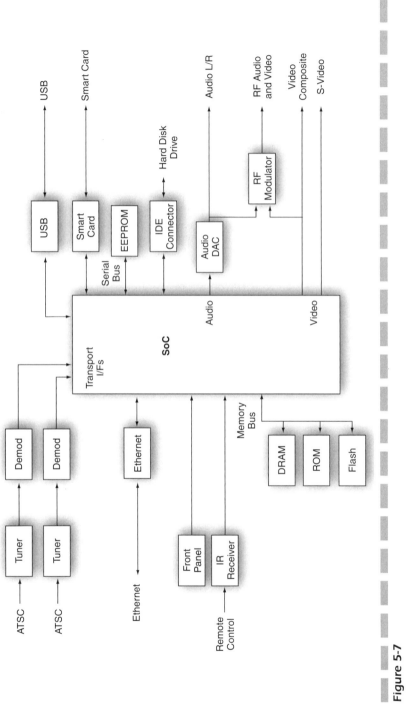

Figure 5-7
Hybrid IP + ATSC + DVR advanced STB.

Drivers   Drivers originate with the IC vendors, get integrated by the OEM, and are made robust within the product's intended operational environment.

Operating System (OS)   Various OS solutions are available from software companies.

CA or DRM   Various CA/DRM software solutions are available from security companies. These solutions are becoming more important within the software stack as this emerging market takes off.

Specialized Web Components   Numerous software companies provide software modules that perform web-related functions that are integral or required for an IP set-top product. Examples include web browsers, virtual machines (such as Java, Macromedia Flash), and networking solutions.

Middleware   Traditionally, middleware software modules reside within a software stack and have two predominant interfaces, one for higher level software to communicate with it, and another for lower level software. Middleware software typically sits between the higher level user interface and lower level hardware abstraction layers. In IPTV, middleware is a vague and poorly used term that has taken on a much larger role that includes traditional middleware functionality plus all IPTV applications for the end user (consumer), and software that interfaces to the back-office equipment in the headend (such as billing, EPG, and so on).

Application   Application software presents the visible user interface, allowing the user to access the various services provided by the set-top. Ideally, the application software is the only component the customer has to interact with.

The various software components on top of the hardware are shown in Figure 5-8.

The following sections explore these software functions and provide insight into how a client device's software gets architected.

IPTV Software Layered Architecture   The hardware architectures for IP STBs are based on satellite or cable STB architectures, and the differences in hardware can simply be the network input: RF interface for cable or satellite versus an IP interface (such as Ethernet, WiFi, and so on) for IPTV. This fact is not necessarily the same for software architectures. The low level drivers in the software stack are primarily the same because the silicon vendors provide the same basic driver to

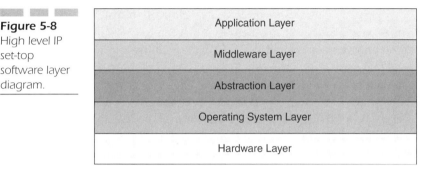

Figure 5-8
High level IP
set-top
software layer
diagram.

OEMs that design either satellite/cable STBs or IP STBs. Also, the OS can be the same between the two. However, this is where the software stacks start to deviate. Because IP STBs are IP network devices, the software architectures include a full suite of IP protocols and web-centric modules and applications.

One way to conceptualize the entire software stack for an IP client device is to break it down into four software layers, as shown in Figure 5-8.

Figure 5-9 expands the simplified software stack to form a complete working IPTV system. We explain these layers in more detail in this section.

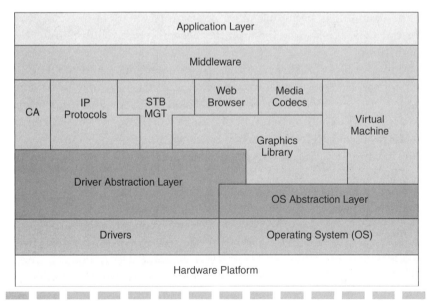

Figure 5-9
Typical IPTV client device software layer diagram.

OS Layer   The OS layer consists primarily of the OS and the low-level drivers. STB architectures typically employ real-time OSs to be able to play (transport + decode + display) audio and video in real-time to the television. Consumers will not accept a product that does not play content flawlessly. If the OS prevents the system from presenting stutter-free audio and video playback, the software architecture would be severely flawed. One example of such a problem is interrupt latency—the time it takes to respond to inputs such as remote control presses. If the interrupt latency of the system is too long for the interrupts to be fielded within the required timeframe, it could interfere with the overall timing of the decode process. Such a design would not meet the requirements nor be adequate. The transport and decode system have to respond to interrupts in a short period of time to keep the decode process performing properly.

Originally, set-top vendors utilized small, fast, and low-cost OSs. In some cases, proprietary solutions were used; however, over the years, set-top architects have primarily used commercial products to provide continuing support for numerous required IP protocols and networking modules. Choosing a proprietary, feature-limited OS could become a trap for software architects, which could render their platform obsolete later down the road because IPTV network operators expect the OEM to keep its software up to date with the latest version of these protocols. Because of this trend, it is becoming more important for OEMs to utilize commercial OSs; otherwise, their platforms will quickly fall behind their competition.

For example, the Internet Group Management Protocol (IGMP—critical for IPTV) evolved in a way that could have excluded some manufacturers. IGMP started with version 0 and has migrated to version 3 (IGMPv3). If a customer requires IGMPv3, but the platform's IGMP protocol is IGMPv1, the software architect needs to find a quick solution to get to IGMPv3; otherwise, their solution would lose the business.

When selecting an OS for an IPTV platform, the OS requirements should be compared against each OS's feature list. Also, all OS feature lists are not equivalent, and complete solution packages should be part of the selection process. In other words, try to compare apples with apples. For example, an expensive OS may come with a complete list of features including a feature-rich graphics library, where a less expensive OS may not include any graphics library and additional software would need to be developed or bought.

The following list of features can be typical of commercial OSs:

- Real-time embedded OS (RTOS), which provides features or support that enables real-time applications to be executed that meet critical timelines, deterministically. These features are specialized task scheduling algorithms, low interrupt latency, and fast thread/task context switching.

- IP networking feature set, such as web browsers, Universal Plug and Play (UPnP), Digital Living Network Alliance (DLNA), virtual machines, and so on. It should be noted that some OSs do not include these features (such as web browsers) while others do.

- Latest IP protocols (such as DHCP, UDP, TCP, and so on) supported.

- Relatively small memory footprint. For embedded systems that are cost sensitive, minimizing memory usage is critical to the success of the product.

- Memory Management Unit (MMU), which provides the translation of virtual memory to physical memory, memory protection, and memory caching. Often microprocessors have built-in hardware that performs the MMU function, but the OS needs to take advantage of these hardware features.

- Multitasking support—all STBs implement either a multitasking or multithreaded system. Multitasking occurs when the system has separate tasks (two or more) or programs running at nearly the same time, and each task has its own memory space. Multithreading occurs when a single program is divided into separate threads of execution, each performing its own job.

- Application(s) support, such as rich graphics libraries that greatly aid in the development of applications.

Software Drivers   Software drivers also lie within the OS layer. Drivers are the software modules that interface directly to the hardware (such as ICs) and provide a common interface with which higher level software can interface. Typically, drivers are the only software that should access the hardware directly (such as for setting registers, setting tuning frequencies, and so on). Drivers should ultimately be supported and maintained by the silicon vendor, which should also provide any bug fixes or new low-level features, because they are best suited to manage, maintain, and match the driver software along with different versions of the ICs. As an example, assume a software patch exists for a driver to get around a limitation in an IC, and the next revision of the IC resolves this limitation. Then the next version of the driver is required to remove the patch, and of course this new driver needs to be mated with the new version of the IC. The OEM is responsible for integrating drivers into the platform software along with managing the different hardware and software versions, assuring in all cases that the software functions flawlessly with the hardware.

Therefore, the OEM and the silicon vendor need to coordinate product development closely with respect to software drivers and hardware. An OEM takes multiple drivers from the various silicon vendors and integrates them along with the hardware, creating a platform.

Following is a list of typical drivers:

- Network interface (Ethernet driver, WiFi, and so on)
- Audio driver
- Video driver
- Graphics driver
- Transport driver
- NTSC/PAL driver
- IR driver
- Front panel driver
- Smart card driver

Abstraction Layer   Platforms evolve for a number of reasons, and architects need to be able to change the hardware quickly and efficiently to meet customer requirements, feature sets, and cost pressures. An abstraction layer is a software technique that enables someone to swap out an underlying architecture (either hardware or software) easily without dramatically impacting remaining software (usually the bulk of their software). An abstraction layer done well is a relatively thin layer, and all of the upper layer software utilizes the abstraction layer API entirely to utilize components beneath it (such as drivers and OS). Abstraction layers are typically thin to minimize the time required to swap out the underlying component and to minimize the latency of the runtime software (or optimize efficiency). The abstraction layer shown back in Figure 5-8 is a platform abstraction layer in which the major components being abstracted are the hardware platform with the associated drivers and the OS. OSs come under similar pressures but to a lesser degree. Also, it should be noted that abstraction layers can be implemented anywhere within the software stack. In the IPTV market, many of the major vendors (OEMs, middleware, OS, CA, and silicon) implement abstraction layers or API interfaces to position themselves to be able to partner with various companies so they can quickly provide solutions to the end customer (such as IPTV network operators).

Middleware Layer Currently there is no common middleware standard for IPTV as the market is still in its infancy. The middleware layer consists of numerous functional modules from potentially multiple companies, and frequently these modules are partitioned so they perform work for a single purpose or discipline. Good examples of middleware modules include graphics, conditional access, and electronic program guides. Often, middleware is complex in nature and provides a large API or set of external function calls that an application would utilize. Middleware sits in the middle of the application layer and the OS layer. Like an abstraction layer, effective middleware allows the application layer to remain the same if various lower level functional modules are modified or replaced. Shown in Figure 5-9, the typical middleware modules are as follows:

- **CA or DRM.** Conditional access or digital rights management solutions are usually selected by the customer or IPTV network operator. As the name implies, the primary purpose is to protect content from potential pirates or thieves, and to allow paying customers to view the content seamlessly.

- **IP protocols.** IP protocols provide the necessary standards-based functionality for network-based applications.

- **STB MGT.** STB management is the module (usually provided by the OEM) that enables the middleware to control the platform in a robust fashion.

- **Web browser.** Within an IPTV STB, a web browser can be utilized as a standalone web browser (used for browsing the Internet) or as a tool used to render the UI to the television. When the web browser is used in the UI, it no longer looks and feels like a traditional web browser. It processes web pages (HTML) to render widgets, buttons, text, and so on that make up a standard UI. In this capacity, the browser is invisible and only the UI is visible to the consumer.

- **Graphics library.** Every computer or STB has a graphics library. Some graphics libraries can be extremely complex, such as those used in game platforms such as the Microsoft X-box or the Sony PlayStation. In a typical IPTV STB, the graphics library is not nearly as sophisticated and typically provides 2-D graphics functionality.

- **Media codecs.** The media codecs are the software-based decoders. For STBs that have a hardware-based decoder, these software codecs are not included in the software stack.

- **Virtual machine (VM).** A VM is a software module that provides a virtual execution environment that behaves like a standalone computer system but is executed by software. These modules isolate or abstract the application software from the platform's OS and hardware. VMs are commonly ported to various platforms allowing software applications hardware independence. Virtual machines expand an STB's capability for providing rich and compelling applications to the user. Customer requirements sometimes include a web-centric virtual machine (such as Macromedia Flash or Java) to be included in the IPTV product's software stack. However, it should be noted that these virtual machines come with a price; additional computing resources (memory, microprocessor throughput) are required as well as royalties.

- **Middleware.** Rounding out the middleware layer is the middleware abstraction layer itself. As mentioned previously, middleware companies in the IPTV space provide much more than just libraries or modules that get integrated into a software stack. IPTV middleware provides a rich and common API for their IPTV applications.

OCAP and DVB-MHP The Open Cable Application Platform (OCAP) is a middleware specification created by Cable Television Laboratories for the cable industry. It provides a common set of APIs and a runtime environment for applications that run on cable STBs. By defining a common middleware for cable operators, application developers can design to a single middleware and have their product run on any cable system regardless of the underlying OS and hardware. Having a common specification across cable systems should enable economies of scale both in terms of development and in access to subscribers. In particular, if an application is tied to an advertisement, it can reach many consumers quickly via a common middleware across cable.

Much of OCAP is based on the DVB-MHP (Multimedia Home Platform) specification for European cable operators. Both use Java as the runtime environment and share many APIs. DVB-MHP adds a presentation component (a browser) as well. The many common elements between OCAP and DVB-MHP could make cable television applications international in scope.

Application Layer The application layer is where the suite of IPTV applications resides. Since an IP STB is an IP networked device, the software stack easily supports web application development. Traditionally, UI design has been accomplished with native C code development. Now, UI designers can leverage numerous and flexible web interfaces: HTML/XHTML, CSS, Java script, XML, Java applets and applications, Macromedia Flash, ActiveX controls, SVG and SMIL, and so on. These technologies potentially simplify IPTV application development and provide cost savings opportunities as well. Some possible IPTV applications or features are listed here:

- Typical STB menus (such as user preferences, setup, and so on)
- Electronic program guide, or EPG (grid guide, Mosaic)
- E-mail
- Video on demand, or VOD
- Video conferencing
- Collaboration
- Content sharing
- Portable media interface
- Weather and news
- Multiple stream decode, picture-in-picture (PIP)
- Picture in graphics (PIG) with real-time metadata (such as sporting statistics)
- Home security

IPTV networks create a vast array of application possibilities due to point-to-point network, high-speed bidirectional communications, natural integration to a digital home network, integrated client-server interface, and a natural bridge to the Internet.

Thin versus Thick Client The system architect (such as an IPTV network operator) has numerous choices in middleware from which to select. One important question to answer is whether they want to employ a thin or thick client within the consumer's home. This selection will ultimately impact the overall system (headend servers, network bandwidth/traffic, cost, and customer satisfaction) and the STB in the consumer's home.

Thin client architecture requires little set-top resources other than an embedded web browser, minimal memory, and minimal microprocessor performance. It is called a *thin* client because of the limited amount of local processing. A thin client offloads processing power from the UI to the network and requires dedicated servers within the network to manage each client's environment and state. Think of the UI as being executed in the network server and not in the STB within the home. The STB simply passes IR button press information to a server, and the server returns HTML web pages (to the STB) of what to render to the television.

Figure 5-10 walks through a typical process required for a thin client to display an EPG grid guide screen to the consumer's television. The start of the process occurs when the consumer selects the GUIDE button on the IR remote control. The STB receives this key and sends an IP-based message (GUIDE BUTTON) to an application server within the IPTV network. These application servers run an instance of each set-top active within the system, and the GUIDE BUTTON message gets processed by one of these instances. The application server knows everything with respect to the client's machine (what channels or content it can view, selected preferences, and so on) and creates the requested screen in HTML. This HTML web page is then sent to the thin client STB over the IPTV network. The thin client application receives the web page, processes it with the embedded web browser, and renders it (EPG grid guide screen) to the television.

Thick client architecture, on the other hand, requires sufficient set-top resources to manage and process the user experience locally. This

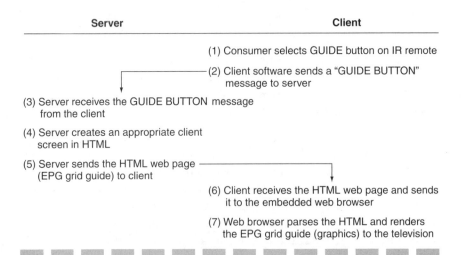

Figure 5-10
How a thin client processes an EPG grid guide for the television.

means more memory (or storage) and more microprocessor performance is required than from that of a thin client. For the most part, the thick client manages the user experience locally, without assistance from an application server within the network. It does require server support; however, only to provide system-related data (guide data, CA data, and so on) instead of application support. Whenever the consumer selects keys on the IR remote, the thick client processes them locally and provides the UI to the television. The thick client network traffic is primarily system data and not UI screens. Also, the complexity and cost of the servers is minimized.

Figure 5-11 walks through the process required for a thick client to display an EPG grid guide screen to the consumer's television. Before the consumer ever requests the guide, the thick client (typically) requests EPG data from an EPG server within the IPTV network. It will also receive guide updates on a periodic basis as the data changes over time. This background task is always running to keep its guide information up to date. When the consumer selects the GUIDE button on the IR remote control, the thick client application receives a (local) GUIDE BUTTON message and starts to formulate an appropriate screen based on its internal EPG database, consumer preferences, and associated rights. Once the screen is ready, the thick client will render it graphically to the television.

Table 5-5 shows pros and cons of thin and thick clients.

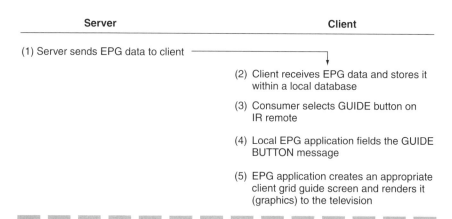

Figure 5-11
How a thick client processes an EPG grid guide for the television.

Table 5-5 Comparison of Thin Client vs. Thick Client Architectures

	Pros	Cons
Thin client	Lowest hardware (STB) cost	Slower response time for the consumer
	Simple client architecture	More servers required
	Easily field updatable	More server complexity
		Most network traffic
Thick client	Fastest response for the consumer	Higher hardware (STB) cost
	Less network traffic required	Complex client architecture
	Less servers required	

In summary, a thick client will provide the quickest response for the consumer, but the STB could be more expensive. Also, the thin client approach will have a more complex and expensive headend design than a thick client approach. Some systems will have a hybrid architecture where some applications are local to the set-top and others are served from the network.

Personal Computers

There is no denying the fact that PCs have played a major role within the consumer's home as well as how people access and utilize data, especially with regard to the Internet. In fact, PCs have been the primary portal into the Internet for millions of people. Computers have been streaming audio and video for a while now, and many companies are expanding the role of the computer in the living room or family room zones (such as Microsoft's Media Center PC). As such, the PC should be considered the ultimate IP client device. But most of the interaction consumers have had with computers has been in the study/den or with a laptop. This is often called "the two foot experience" and is an extremely interactive session. Watching television has been traditionally from a much farther distance—"the ten foot experience"—and much more passive with little interaction.

Also, many homes today have multiple computers all connected via a DHN to share data or resources (printers, hard disk drives, and so on). IPTV is a natural extension of DHN and it is expected that computers and IPTV client devices will coexist seamlessly within the DHN. Since computers have the ability to drive NTSC/PAL televisions, quite possibly, the IPTV client device in the living room could be a computer. Security may be an issue as computers have not always been the securest platform, with hackers and pirates traditionally using computers for their primary development.

Advanced Features for Client Devices

We cover some advanced features for IPTV client devices. Figure 5-12 shows a possible IPTV configuration within the home—three IPTV STBs; two are the standard version and simply provide television services to the locally attached TV, while the other is an advanced high-end device. The standard version would be a basic IP streaming device with an Ethernet interface and the usual audio and video output jacks for a

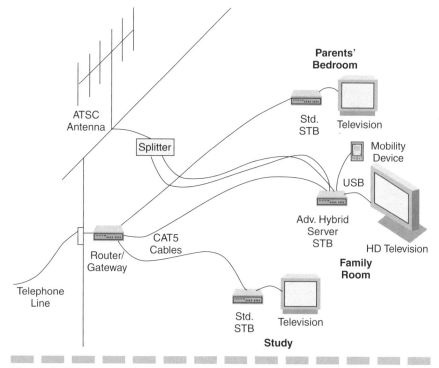

Figure 5-12
Advanced IP STB that performs server functionality within the home.

standard definition television. The advanced hybrid server STB has add-on features such as dual tuners for terrestrial or satellite reception, hard disk drive for DVR capabilities, USB and wireless IP interface, and all standard and high definition output jacks (including HD decoder). An antenna provides two signals to the dual tuners so the device can provide a "watch one channel and record another channel" (simultaneously) feature. Also, the broadband service enters the home and gets distributed via the home router/gateway, including the wireless option. All IPTV devices connect through the gateway.

This specific topology could support the following list of advanced features:

Personal Video Recording (PVR)   The advanced set-top can record multiple channels of content to the hard disk drive in the advanced set-top. These channels of content can come from the tuner cards or the broadband IPTV service. Depending on the available bandwidth to the home (broadband service), the PVR unit can record as many digital channels as are available from both the off-air and IPTV network.

Video Gateway   The advanced set-top can act as a server and stream content from its hard disk drive to any authorized standard IP STB in the home, including mobile devices such as portable media players.

Host Data Services for Devices within the DHN   The advanced set-top can act as a server providing data for local devices. Examples might include EPG data, software downloading, and cached system data. This feature can reduce the amount of external network traffic as well as reduce the latency for devices requesting the information.

External Access   External access allows someone to log into the set-top from outside the home to configure events or parameters. Examples of this might include setting up timed recordings from the office, or changing preferences such as a password or parental control ratings limits.

Multiple Decode   An advanced set-top could perform multiple digital decodes if it has sufficient decode resources. Each decode could be targeted for a specific television within the home and distributed over existing coax. The advanced set-top would modulate the decoded audio and video channels over well-defined NTSC/PAL channels (such as channel 3 or 4) for the remote televisions (such as in bedrooms). The remote televisions would not require any STB, but simply connect the coax to the televisions' input tuner. With this configuration, the remote television user would tune to the desired channel (3 or 4) and receive programming from the advanced set-top. Also, users of the television in other rooms would require RF remotes to tell the advanced set-top (in the living room) via RF signaling to which channel they want it to tune and decode. This feature would enable a Telco operator to match a cable installation, which provides analog channels over the existing coax cables to multiple TVs in the home without additional digital receivers.

Advanced Services

So far, we have reviewed client device architectures and digital home networking. The more advanced hardware platforms, software architectures, and DHNs become, the more likely new and advanced services can be developed and deployed. IPTV network operators can launch these advanced services to enrich the consumer's entertainment experience. In this section, we briefly explore some of the possible advanced services an IPTV network operator could deploy to increase their revenue or increase customer loyalty.

Triple Play

The concept of a triple play service has been around for a while, but only the cable companies have been able to deploy triple play services commercially in recent times. A triple play service comprises the following:

- **Voice.** A telephony service that could replace the consumer's traditional land-line telephone service. The technology that enables this is VoIP (Voice over IP). There are various levels of VoIP service, from full service (QoS + full emergency 911 + service while experiencing power loss) to a simple "best effort" service.

- **Data.** The data service is a broadband service enabling standard web functionality (web browsing, e-mail, and so on) with much faster performance than dial-up speed and an "always on" functionality.

- **Video.** Video service is similar to traditional cable or satellite broadcast video services. Much like voice, video services can come with various differentiating features including VOD, NVOD, HDTV, and PVR.

To deploy a viable triple play service, the operator must be able to provide video and broadband. Broadband enables voice and data. Providing the broadband network is designed to support video; an IPTV broadband network can handle all three (voice, data, and video) services. This allows Telco network operators to compete with cable companies in the triple play market. The satellite industry is trying to catch up to these competitors, but an effective return channel or alternative broadband approach is required.

Mobility

Mobility is quickly becoming a hot market, especially with the popularity of cell phones and the success Apple Computer has had with its iPod product line. With the battles quickly approaching for triple play, network operators are searching for unique service offerings that they can add to their bundled service, and mobility is high on their list. A natural extension of a video broadcast service (cable, satellite, and Telco) would be to enable the digital STB to download or transcode audio and video content, or audio only (music) content to a portable format suitable for portable A/V players or audio (MP3) players. Not only will the STB have to transcode, but it may have to re-encrypt the content with a content protection system and possibly store (even temporarily) it on an embedded hard disk drive. Finally, the STB would need to transfer the content to a portable device over a high-speed interface such as USB 2.0. Portable devices can include proprietary devices compatible with the network operator's system, commercially available audio players, commercially available audio and video players, and possibly even cell phones.

Network Gaming

Playing computer games in the home is extremely popular and today it is a multibillion dollar industry. Multiplayer or networked gaming is popular as many people enjoy playing games with or against friends. The gaming market can be thought of as having two separate segments: home computers (PCs and Apple computers) gaming platforms (Xbox,

PlayStation, and Nintendo). Both segments have powerful platforms that enable rich and compelling gaming applications. IPTV devices are a different class of machine from these gaming platforms as they lack the microprocessor horsepower and cutting-edge graphics capability. However, many IPTV set-top platforms are able to run less computationally intensive applications (such as card games and board games). An IPTV network operator could generate incremental revenue with a network gaming strategy and business model based on this class of applications. These games could be multiplayer or single player, and these applications can be downloaded over the network that would eliminate the need to have a hard disk drive. Network gaming could be a growth area for IPTV in years to come.

Video Conferencing

Many people have often considered video conferencing a "killer app" for IPTV, especially since IPTV devices are IP network enabled and leverage many web-based protocols. Progress in the field of video conferencing is occurring—for example, the ITU (International Telecommunication Union) standards body has been generating a series of "recommendations" (non-binding standards) for video conferencing: H.3xx. These recommendations reference well-defined standards, protocols, and audio and video codecs. H.323 covers narrow-band video conferencing over non-guaranteed QoS networks (LAN, Internet, and so on). This effort plus a vast amount of energy in web-based communications (webcams, web meetings, and so on) brings us closer than ever to being able to link IPTV with video conferencing. Some questions regarding video conferencing over IPTV might include these:

- Shouldn't an effective home video conferencing strategy include a ubiquitous deployment over multiple networks so nearly everyone has access to the video conferencing network?
- Are consumers willing to pay for home video conferencing?
- Is video conferencing useful given current web capabilities?

It will be interesting to see if some IPTV network operator(s) can create a business model that includes video conferencing over IPTV. This feature is the one many people have been dreaming about for years, but it has not yet materialized.

Remote Control

As the home environment grows and has multiple devices, the consumer may wish to access devices remotely (away from home). Some usage cases for this might include the following:

- While at work, someone may want to set up a recording of an upcoming event or program on a home IPTV PVR STB.
- While at a second home or cottage, someone may want to access content from a home IPTV network.
- A consumer may want to monitor home security devices remotely.

As STBs become more advanced and as the DHN grows in size, the consumer could find more reasons to access IPTV devices and content remotely.

Remote Diagnostics

Remote diagnostics is not a new feature for networked devices, but we want to touch on this topic because it is a critical element for an IPTV network operator, and companies are constantly coming up with new elements of IPTV that require remote monitoring. Two prominent approaches for remote diagnostics are SNMP (Simple Network Management Protocol) and TR-069—Technical Report 69 (DSL Forum) on CPE WAN Management Protocol. Some useful applications of remote diagnostics include these:

- Monitor the health of hardware (STBs, router/gateway, and so on) devices. Advanced notification of a failing device could prevent an expensive "truck roll."
- Trigger new software downloads to IPTV devices.
- Manage user preferences or security elements (password, entitlements, and so on).
- Monitor network traffic to isolate network equipment failures, including lost packets, decoder underflows, decoder overflows, and so on.
- Embedded hard disk drive management.

Remote diagnostics enable the network operator to manage the network and remote devices from a central location (headend) and is a critical building block for a commercial service.

Copy Protection and Digital Rights Management

The technology behind digital media makes it easy to create, and widely distribute, many copies of digital content. With a personal computer and an Internet connection, a single "pirate" can send thousands of copies of a movie or television program throughout the world. As a result, content owners and their distributors must implement security measures to prevent unauthorized copies of digital content.

A Digital Rights Management (DRM) system makes it possible for a distributor to securely deliver digital content to subscribers while also protecting the rights of the content owners. Using various digital encryption technologies, a DRM system enables subscribers to view and enjoy content but not to make unauthorized copies that could be distributed to others. In this chapter we look at the need for copy protection control, the basics of digital encryption used to protect content, and other components of a full DRM system.

The Need for Security

Unlike previous analog media such as videotapes, from which it was difficult or expensive to mass-produce quality copies, digital media makes it easy to create many perfect copies of content. Analog signals degrade with every copy, making the images softer and sounds noisier with every copy. And creating many copies of a movie, for example, was time consuming and required expensive duplication equipment. Digital copies, however, reproduce the 1s and 0s of binary bits, which do not degrade with multiple copies. Digital equipment such as computers and hard drive storage components are built to make millions of copies of 1s and 0s without making mistakes. In addition, the equipment for mass-producing digital copies is less expensive than analog equipment.

The fact that millions of PCs are connected throughout the world via the Internet makes the need for security even more critical. While an analog medium such as videotape requires physically delivering the tapes, the Internet can be used to deliver thousands of copies of digital content anywhere in the world in a matter of minutes. Napster proved that when a digital medium, in this case music CDs, does not contain a security system, the Internet can be used to share that content and therefore change the business model. While there remains some debate on the exact financial impact on the music business, there is no doubt that it was a major concern to content owners and resulted in a flurry of legal activity. As a consequence, copy protection and the associated

Napster

Napster pioneered Peer-to-Peer (P2P) file sharing technology when Shawn Fanning and Sean Parker first released the original version of Napster in 1999.

Napster made it easy to share large files between computers, in particular digital music files. Users could create large libraries of digital music copied from other Napster users. This naturally drew the attention of lawyers from major record studios who feared a loss in retail music sales. Napster has gone through many transformations after the initial lawsuits forced it to shut down, including being a free popular music file sharing service, a subscription online music service, and ultimately falling into bankruptcy. Nevertheless this widely popular P2P music sharing service has had a dramatic effect on how people use the Internet and access data, and has made content owners leery of Internet distribution.

rights management systems have been at the forefront of IPTV business models. Video content owners want to make sure that their content is not "Napsterized" via the Internet, while at the same time taking advantage of broadband and IP technology to create new delivery methods such as IPTV. Only when the security of an IPTV DRM system has been proven will content owners feel secure about making their valuable merchandise available to IPTV service providers. Just as Apple's iTunes store demonstrated that consumers are willing to pay for IP-delivered content and accept DRM restrictions if the model is convenient and attractive, IPTV business models must also create service models that enable consumers to enjoy their content while at the same time keeping the content secure.

The content industry has historically been conservative in its adoption of new technologies. Existing business models and their associated revenues to artists and distributors are lucrative, and it may be understandable that the industry wants to preserve them. In the 1970s, the Motion Picture Association of America (MPAA) tried to stop the distribution of VCRs through legal means. They saw VHS tapes as a threat to their industry and its distribution system of movie theatres. Decades later, when the DVD technology was developed, some studios refused to release movies onto DVD until they were satisfied with the security of the copy protection system. Paradoxically, both VHS tapes and DVDs have been extremely lucrative for the movie industry. We expect the same outcome for IPTV: As the new business models prove themselves, the content industry stands to gain by the increased competition in distributors. And like VHS and DVD, IPTV can create new ways for consumers to purchase and enjoy television and movie content, creating potentially new revenue streams for the industry. Of course, the key to this is effective and secure DRM systems.

A Layer Model for DRM

A complete DRM system consists of multiple layers that protect the content from unauthorized copying and ensure the rights of both the user and the content owner. Figure 6-1 shows the various elements of a DRM system. At the core is digital encryption, which is used to scramble the bits that make up the digital media content and make it very difficult to use them without the necessary digital keys to unscramble (decrypt) them. The rights access system, or Conditional Access System (CAS), ensures that only authorized devices receive the keys they need to decrypt the content. Authentication verifies users and devices within the system and secures communication among various elements carrying the secret conditional access information. Perhaps the most important part of any digital security system is the rights management system, which defines both the content provider's and the consumer's rights with respect to content usage. A rights management system uses a rights expression language that defines the types of business models that can be developed for purchasing, renting, or storing digital content.

Not all DRM systems contain every element of our model. Some may have a limited implementation of a component. For example, in the Digital Transmission Content Protection (DTCP) system, the rights expression language is limited to a few bits of copy control information. These bits define only a few distinct actions that can be performed by the receiving device. In particular, content can be labeled as "copy never," indicating that the content should never be copied, or as "copy once," in which the content can be copied and delivered to another device, but then it must be labeled as "copy never." Conversely, the Extensible Rights Markup Language (XrML) used in some DRM systems is extremely flexible and can define a number of complicated agreements between content owners and consumers.

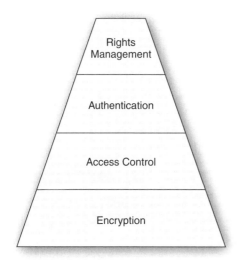

- Defining the terms (price, time period, number of copies allowed, etc.) for gaining access to the content.

- Authenticating the device/user requesting keys and verifying their rights to access content.

- Controlling who gets access to the keys necessary to unscramble the content.

- Encryption/scrambling of the bits that make up the digital content using secret keys.

Figure 6-1
A DRM system consists of a number of elements, from encryption to rights management.

Encryption

Digital encryption is the process of changing a series of digital bits so that they appear random and the information that they contain is obscured. A unique key, itself a series of digital bits, is needed to undo the encryption process and retrieve the original information. A typical encryption algorithm, or *cipher*, takes the original unscrambled bits (also called *cleartext*) and a key and produces a series of seemingly random bits. This process is shown in Figure 6-2. In a symmetric cipher, the decryption key is the same as the encryption key.

Many books on encryption describe the numerous ciphers and their relative strengths and weaknesses. For our purposes, it is sufficient to list what makes a particular cipher good for digital encryption. A strong cipher is difficult to "crack" to determine the original data from the ciphertext. The strongest, ideal cipher is one for which the only way to retrieve the cleartext without knowing the decryption key is to try every possible key until you discover it. Someone attempting to retrieve the original digital information must therefore perform an exhaustive search over every possible key. The number of possible keys can be very large. If the key size is n-bits long, there are 2^n possible keys. A very small key

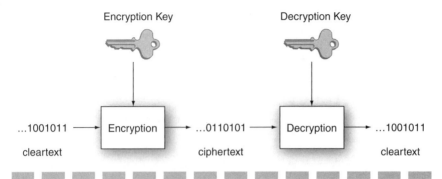

Figure 6-2
Encryption uses an encryption key to scramble cleartext bits and produce seemingly random ciphertext; cleartext is recovered using the associated decryption key.

size of 32 bits, for example, contains more than 4 billion possible keys. Symmetric cipher key sizes are typically 64 to 512 bits in length, resulting in a huge number of possible keys.

Of course, the large number of possible keys that need to be tried to find the decryption key is offset by the ever-increasing computation power of computers. Specialized code-cracking computers can try billions of keys in a matter of seconds. As computational resources continue to improve, ciphers need to become more sophisticated and the key lengths need to become longer to prevent would-be digital media pirates from finding the keys and gaining access to the content.

Ciphers can also be attacked by using various sophisticated mathematical algorithms to reduce the number of keys that must be attempted in guessing the key. A cipher's relative strength lies in how difficult it is to reduce the number of keys that must be searched to find the decryption key. Brute-force attacks, where every possible key is tried, can be attempted by people using specialized computers, while algorithmic attacks that seek to find fundamental weaknesses in the cipher itself are attempted by mathematicians.

Common Block Ciphers   The Data Encryption Standard (DES) cipher has been used extensively for encryption since the 1970s. DES was developed by IBM in response to a request for proposals from the US government for a secure cipher. It was made available to the public in 1975. A curious, paradoxical theory of encryption states that the more open and publicly available a cipher is, the more secure it can be. Theoretically, if thousands of mathematicians and hackers are attempting to find weaknesses in the cipher and fail, it is considered secure. Attempting to hide the details of a cipher, also called *security through obscurity*, may actually backfire in that glaring weaknesses of the cipher may be found by a few in secret and not published in the open forum of academia. The exact sequence of operations in the DES cipher has been published for years, and, despite this, no one has found a way to recover cleartext after it has gone through the DES cipher without knowledge of the decryption key.

DES is a *block cipher* in that it takes in a fixed number of bits (a block) with a fixed (56 bit) key and produces the same number of encrypted bits as it took in. For DES, the block size is 64 bits. A digital message longer than 64 bits must be broken up into a series of 64 bit blocks and fed individually into the cipher algorithm. DES block mode is illustrated in Figure 6-3. Every possible cleartext block (there are 2^{64} or 1.8×10^{19} possible input blocks) produces a unique 64 bit ciphertext block. There is a unique one-to-one mapping between input blocks and output blocks for each key.

While a block cipher such as DES operates on a fixed length of bits at a time, a *stream cipher* takes a continuous stream of bits and produces a continuous stream of encrypted bits. For digital media such as MPEG-2 bitstreams, the cleartext might consist of millions of consecutive bits. It would seem that a stream cipher would make more sense, but typically a block cipher such as DES is used. Another problem with a block cipher for compressed video streams is the one-to-one mapping of blocks of cleartext to ciphertext. For a digital message that has a commonly repeating 64 bit sequence (for example, the unique packet header in MPEG-2), the resulting ciphertext will also have a repeating (but different) 64 bit sequence. This could be used to help discover the key that was used.

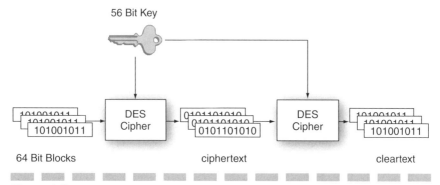

Figure 6-3
The symmetric key, DES block cipher operates on 64 bit blocks of digital data.

Luckily, DES and other block ciphers can be used in a block-chain mode that simulates a stream cipher. In particular, the cipher-block chaining (CBC) mode of DES takes the output of a single block and feeds it back into the input. A binary exclusive OR (XOR) is performed between the next input block and the previous output block, effectively creating a chain of dependent blocks. For decryption, the input is fed forward to the output of the DES cipher. The XOR is repeated on the output block, reproducing the original plaintext (recall that two consecutive XOR operations on a binary number return the original number). DES in CBC mode is illustrated in Figure 6-4.

DES has been an extremely effective cipher that has protected secret digital information against brute-force attacks from computers since the 1970s. However, with improvements in computational power, DES became susceptible to attacks by relatively inexpensive computers. It is estimated that a 56 bit DES key can be found within weeks using commercial computers. A variant called *triple DES* uses the same basic algorithm as DES but makes use of three different keys, theoretically increasing the key size to 168 bits. The increased key length makes it much more difficult to mount a brute-force attack and find the keys.

DES and triple DES are being phased out in favor of a new block cipher called the *Advanced Encryption Standard (AES)*. AES operates on 128 bit blocks and uses 128 bit keys. After some theoretical flaws in DES were found, the National Institute of Standards and Technology (NIST) now recommends AES instead of DES for security systems. IPTV services providers will probably be required by content owners to use AES or other newer ciphers to protect their content.

Many other block ciphers are in use in modern DRM systems for IPTV and other security purposes. Blowfish, C2, and IDEA are just a

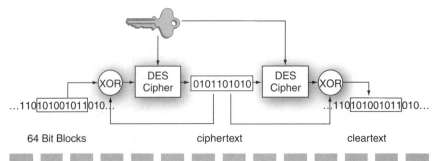

64 Bit Blocks   ciphertext   cleartext

Figure 6-4
DES in CBC mode is used on continuous streams of bits to simulate a stream cipher.

few of the many alternatives. As stated earlier, the true strength of a cipher is in its ability to force someone attempting to crack it to try every possible key. Then the length of the key determines how difficult that attack will be. The best ciphers have few or no practical ways of reducing the number of keys required in a brute-force attack. Therefore, DRM systems are usually attacked at different levels, such as at the access control level, to attempt to find the keys. Often it is easier to break the system that delivers the keys than to break the encryption cipher. Ultimately, the cipher used is only as secure as the DRM system's ability to keep keys secret.

Encryption of MPEG Bitstreams   As you learned in an earlier chapter, the digital bitstreams within an IPTV service comprise an elementary stream layer and a system layer. The elementary streams contain the compressed audio and video elements that make up the programs in the service. The system layer contains information on the various programs within the service and how to extract them from the whole multiplex. When encrypting an MPEG-2 transport stream, only the elements of the bitstream containing elementary stream data are encrypted. Elements important for parsing the multiplex such as header information and system information components are not encrypted. Those elements must remain in the clear so that receiving devices can parse the bitstream and identify program elements.

Access Control

Once the audio and video bitstreams of an IPTV service have been encrypted, the secret keys used to encrypt the content must somehow be delivered potentially to millions of devices within consumers' homes. Each device will get a different set of keys, depending on the services for which it is authorized. Finally, the authorizations may change from day to day as consumers change their subscription packages. Managing this complex, dynamic system of key distribution is the purview of the CAS, which must control all of these keys while at the same time keeping them secret.

While encryption ciphers are generally published and open for all to examine and attempt to break, CAS suppliers tend to be extremely secretive in how their products work. A good cipher is completely open and the only way to break it is to learn and use the key. Because CAS delivers the keys used by the cipher, it is typically the focus of attack. In a broadcast-only network, such as a satellite video system, the keys are broadcast potentially to every home in North America. The true value of a CAS system is its ability to broadcast this information to millions of devices and yet keep the essential information secret. CAS vendors are in a constant battle with individuals who are attempting to find the secrets of the key management system and thereby gain access to the keys.

Key Hierarchy Thousands of different encryption keys can be used in a digital television service. The access control element of the DRM system manages all of these keys and controls who receives them. An access control system also typically uses a hierarchy of keys to reduce the number of discrete keys that need to be managed. In the hierarchy, higher level keys are used to encrypt groups of other lower level keys. The encrypted groups of keys are sent to all subscribers in bulk. A single higher level key can then be delivered to individual customers depending on their authorization. The higher level key can be used to decrypt the proper group of lower level keys. This hierarchical approach is particularly effective when television services are themselves offered in groups, such as a basic tier of channels and premium tiers that include an additional set. All of the keys associated with a particular tier can then be encrypted by a single tier key.

The key hierarchy begins at the keys used to encrypt the elementary streams. For security reasons, these keys frequently change, on the order of seconds or minutes depending on the system. If one of the keys were to be discovered, it would be useful only for a limited time period. Once the key changes, the new key would have to be discovered to decrypt the rest of the content. Instead of having to deliver a new key every time period, the keys are encrypted and inserted into the bitstream itself. This concept is shown in Figure 6-5. Thus, the keys to decrypt the elementary stream are immediately available to the receiving device.

A single key, here called the *session key*, is delivered to the device separately. It can then be used to decrypt the *content keys*. The content keys may change frequently but the session key can remain the same. To keep it more secure than the individual content keys, the session key is valid for a longer time and it may have a longer key length.

Continuing the hierarchy, the session keys themselves may be encrypted by other keys, and so on. In our example, a session key would perhaps apply only to a single program. For a multichannel video service, the session keys associated with groups of channels might be encrypted by another key higher up in the hierarchy. This "tier" key would be delivered only to those customers authorized to receive a certain set of channels or tier of service. The receiving device in each cus-

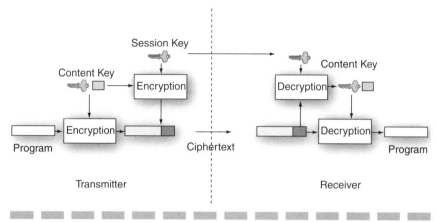

Figure 6-5

Because individual content keys change frequently, they are encrypted and inserted into the program directly; only the session key needs to be delivered to the receiver.

tomer's home would use the single tier key to decrypt the various session keys for the programs it is authorized to receive. The session keys could then be encrypted and sent along with the program information, leaving only the tier key that has to be delivered individually to the various users in the system. This concept is illustrated in Figure 6-6.

Entitlement Control Messages and Entitlement Management Messages   In a key hierarchy structure, we see that some key information is sent along with the content, typically within the MPEG-2 transport stream. The MPEG-2 transport stream is delivered to the receiving device via a method called the *in-band channel*. A separate *out-of-band* communication channel is used to deliver non-time -ritical communications. These terms come from cable television, where the two communication channels were established on two different frequency bands on the cable plant. While IP networks do not use frequencies and channels, the concept still applies to IPTV. In-band information is sent along with the digitally compressed bitstreams containing the audio and video data, typically in a User Datagram Protocol/Internet Protocol (UDP/IP) session, while out-of-band information is sent separately, typically on a Transmission Control Protocol/IP (TCP/IP) session. UDP/IP is more appropriate for time-critical data delivery while TCP/IP is better suited for command and control communications.

The in-band key information such as content and session keys are sent in what are called Entitlement Control Messages (ECMs). The cor-

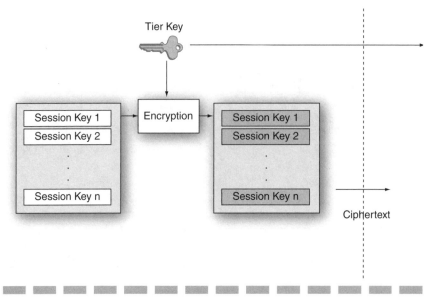

Figure 6-6
Session keys for individual programs may be grouped and encrypted by a single tier key; a subscriber with a tier key could decrypt the session keys and access programs within that group.

responding out-of-band information is contained in Entitlement Management Messages (EMMs). The ECMs contain important key information needed to decrypt the content they are sent with, while the EMMs contain information about which devices are authorized to decrypt the content. The concept is shown in Figure 6-7.

Authentication

The access control element of a DRM system manages the multitude of encryption keys used in encrypting digital content. Ultimately some secret information must be delivered to the receiving device in an IPTV system. Authentication is used to verify both the validity of messages containing secret information and the identity of the sender. Before delivering keys to a particular device, the DRM system must authenticate the receiver to make sure it is authorized to receive the keys. Conversely, the receiver must make sure that messages delivered to it came from the proper sender. This can be accomplished by using a shared secret that both the sender and receiver know or by establishing a

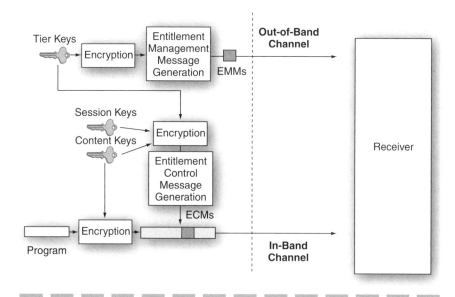

Figure 6-7
Key management systems often use two communication channels, in-band and out-of-band, to deliver entitlement messages containing encryption key information.

secure, trusted communication path between the sender and receiver. We will look at both approaches in this section.

Shared Secrets   Many DRM systems are used in one-way, broadcast-only networks. Key information in these systems is broadcast to all receivers. Because communication is only one-way, there is no way to authenticate the receiving device before sending it information. These systems instead rely upon common shared secrets between sender and receiver. These global secrets are embedded into all of the receiving devices at the time of manufacture and are known only by the DRM system. For example, the secrets might be embedded into a special chip on the STB receiver or in a security card inserted into the device. The access control system then encrypts tier keys and other important messages from the DRM system with the global secret key and broadcasts the encrypted messages to all devices. Since each receiving device has a copy of the secret key, it can decrypt those keys and messages.

If, however, a hacker or content pirate were to discover the global secret key, the pirate would also be able to decrypt messages from the DRM system. The system would have no way of automatically detecting that the secret was no longer secret. Multiple copies of the secret key might be created and sold to people wanting to receive digital television services for free. Such one-way DRM systems periodically have to create new secret keys and get those keys into all of the receiving devices in consumers' homes. This can be an expensive proposition for the service provider. Therefore, it is extremely important to keep these shared keys secret.

Public Key Encryption and Digital Signatures   In two-way networks, a more sophisticated security system can be used that does not require global secrets that are known by all receiving devices. Two-way network systems can make use of public key encryption (PKE) and digital signatures to create secure communication paths between sender and receiver. PKE establishes a way to encrypt messages between two devices, and digital signatures ensure that a message is authentic. The DRM system can use these tools to send information securely and directly to individual receiving devices instead of broadcasting it to all receivers.

PKE uses two different keys in the process of encrypting and decrypting digital information (also known as *asymmetric cryptography*). A digital message is encrypted via a cipher using a *private* key. The message can be decrypted only by using a different, matching *public* key. The process is shown in Figure 6-8. Very complex mathematical processes are used to create the matching public-private pairs of keys. In an effective PKE system, the original message can be decrypted only by the particular public key. In addition, knowledge of the public key does not grant one knowledge of the private key. In fact, the public key is made public for anyone to see. By recovering the message using the public key, the receiver knows that the secret private key was used to create it. As long as the sender keeps the private key secret, the message is known to be authentic.

A digital signature is used to verify that a message was created by the sender and not someone pretending to be the sender. Digital signatures can be created using PKE. To create a signature for a digital message, the sender creates a summary digest of the message called a *hash*. The hash is usually significantly smaller than the message itself. The hash is created in such a manner that if the message is altered, the hash of the altered message will change and will no longer match. The sender encrypts the hash using the sender's private key. This encrypted hash is the message's *signature*: it can be created only by the private key of the sender. The message, signature, and public key are sent to the receiver. The receiver uses the public key to decrypt the signature. The receiver reads the message, creates the same hash of the message, and compares

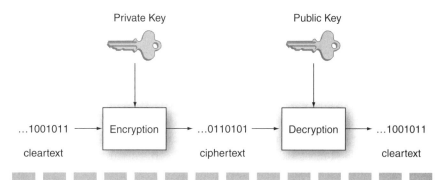

Figure 6-8
In public key encryption, a private key encrypts the digital data that can be decrypted only by a special matching public key.

that with the decrypted signature. If they match, the receiver knows that the message is authentic. If the two hashes do not match, the receiver knows the message was altered somewhere in delivery. Only the public key can produce a signature that matches. The digital signature process is shown in Figure 6-9.

Certificates and Certificate Authorities   With PKE, anyone can create a public-private key pair and use the private key to sign messages. The receiver can verify that the message was not tampered with by using the public key and verifying the signature. However, although

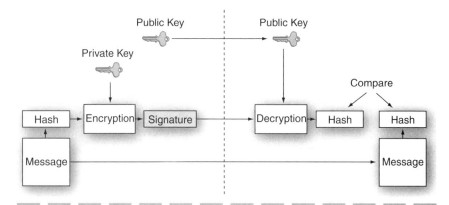

Figure 6-9
To digitally sign a message, a summary digest of the message is encrypted with a private key and the receiver decrypts it with the sender's public key, comparing it to the digest of the received message.

the signature has been verified, how does the receiver know it can trust the sender? How does the receiver know that the person who claims to be the sender is in fact who he or she claims to be? PKE can also be used to solve this question through the use of digital certificates and a trusted certificate authority.

A *digital certificate* is a message containing the sender's public key and information about the sender, such as the sender's name and similar unique information. The sender creates a signature across this information and also places it into the certificate. This signature proves that the sender created these parts of the certificate. To create a *trusted* certificate, the sender's information is sent to a trusted third party, called a *certificate authority* (CA). (Certificate authorities are discussed in more detail shortly.) The CA adds information to the message about itself and signs the message with the CA's private key to create the trusted certificate. This certificate is sent back to the sender who can use it to ensure his or her identity.

When the sender signs a message, the trusted certificate is sent to the receiver. The receiver of a trusted certificate can read the information about the sender and use the public key in the certificate to verify the signature. The receiver also reads the information about the certificate authority. If the receiver trusts that particular CA, the receiver can use the CA's public key to verify the signature of the certificate. In this way, the receiver knows that the sender (and the sender's public key) are authentic. The receiver would also have a copy of the CA's self-certificate, which includes the CA's public key and a signature verifying it. This process is shown in Figure 6-10. As long as the CA keeps its private key secret, both sender and receiver can use the CA to trust messages sent between them because they can trust the public key information.

In addition to issuing certificates, a CA may also maintain a certificate revocation list (CRL), a list of certificates once issued by the CA but now revoked. A certificate might be revoked because the corresponding private key of the sender became known and is no longer secret, or the sender no longer has the CA's trust. When a receiver checks the validity of a sender's certificate, it also checks the CRL from the trusted CA to make sure the certificate is still valid.

Certificates (and CRLs) are usually formatted using the International Telecommunication Union (ITU-T) X.509 standard. X.509 defines a uniform standard for including information on the sender and the certificate authority, as well as the technical information on the encryption methods used for the digital signatures. The X.509 format includes information on the period of validity of the certificate. CAs typically

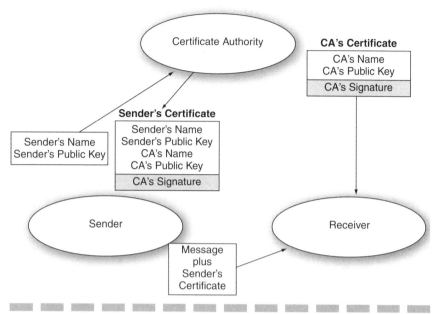

Figure 6-10
A Certificate Authority can be used by both sender and receiver to verify each other.

issue certificates only for a finite time period, requiring the sender to request new certificates periodically. Since the certificate is signed, if the validity period information is tampered with, the signature will no longer match the message.

A CA might handle hundreds of thousands or even millions of certificates to maintain the public key infrastructure (PKI) used by senders and receivers. A DRM system will either maintain its own PKI or use a third party such as Verisign to create and maintain databases of certificates. In a DRM system, the PKI is used to create certificates for every device in the system. The trusted authority usually places strict requirements on the device manufacturers to keep the private keys associated with the public keys in the certificates secret. If the private key becomes known, the CA needs to add the corresponding certificate to its CRL. Maintaining a large PKI can be a difficult process.

In PKE, each device has a unique secret key. If one of these keys is compromised, only that device is affected. This gives a two-way network DRM system a great advantage over a broadcast-only one that uses global secret keys. If a global secret key becomes compromised, it can affect the whole network.

Rights Management

After encrypting digital audio/video content, managing the various keys used to create tiers of service, and authenticating receiving devices, the DRM system must convey what the client device is allowed to do with the content it can decrypt. For a simple STB, the number of things it can do with the content is limited; typically it simply decodes the television program and sends it to the TV. However, if the STB has other capabilities—such as internal storage for recording, or other outputs that let it share the content with other devices such as a PC or portable media device—the DRM system must define what is allowed. For example, the subscriber might have purchased the rights only to view the content, but not to store it for viewing later, or may have a rental window of one week, after which time the content can no longer be viewed. A rights expression language defines the various rights a particular client device has with respect to content.

The rights management system can include usage controls, constraints, and associated financial information. Some of the usage controls include the right to decrypt and display content, the ability to store a local copy securely, the right to make copies (for example, on a writeable DVD), and the ability to share content with other trusted devices. Constraints on usage controls may include time intervals when certain controls are valid, such as a window for the right to decrypt and view content, and numerical limits on certain actions such as the number of copies that can be made.

The rights management system can be generic, allowing a vast array of transaction options. For an IPTV system, a flexible rights system could define business models such as "pick any two premium channels for $29.99 per month" or "watch any two movies for $4.99 per weekday, $5.99 per weekend." Such flexibility is important for a DRM system, as it can be used to create many different business models. Existing multi-channel pay TV system operators such as cable and digital broadcast satellite (DBS) may not have legacy DRM systems with such flexibility. As IPTV business models develop, the ability of the DRM system to create unique pay models may be a competitive advantage.

Content owners and copyright holders are concerned about unauthorized copies of their content. Client devices such as STBs and PCs might have several different outputs for content. For example, an STB might have a digital connector to a digital television and an analog output that could connect to a VCR. A rights management system might have selectable output controls that state which outputs can be used with which content. A content owner might require that an analog output not be used since it could connect to a VCR, or that a digital output use a lower resolution if that output is not encrypted. As for spatial distribution control, a DRM system might use its authorization component to limit transfers of content among a finite set of trusted devices. For example, a user may have the right to share content between STBs within his or her home, but not with a neighbor. The more flexible the rights expression language (REL), the more use cases are possible for the content.

A well-defined REL is abstracted from any particulars about enforcement or policy. Enforcing the rights expressed in the REL is the duty of other components within the full DRM system. The REL should only be able to express the possible rights and business models, and it should not be constrained by what those models might be. However, any effective DRM system depends on legal arrangements between manufacturers and system operators to ensure secrets and comply with hardware output control. Typically, only licensed equipment that meets strict requirements can participate in the DRM system.

Some Rights Expression Languages Many proprietary DRM systems have RELs built in. These languages are typically not in a standard, open format and are instead held secret like the key management system. However, some open RELs are available for the public to examine. Many companies participate in the development of open standard DRM systems to promote interoperability and to offset the monopoly power of a single proprietary system. An open DRM system supported by many manufacturers could theoretically increase the reach of a distribution system based on that DRM, and therefore increase the attractiveness of the distribution channel to content owners. (Note that an open standard does not necessarily mean *free*. Usage rights may still be associated with a standard that requires a license for commercial use.)

XrML XrML is an REL that was created at Xerox Palo Alto Research Center and is now governed and licensed by ContentGuard, Inc. It describes a generic rights model, enabling many different business models. Like many RELs, XrML is defined using extensible markup language (XML). XML defines the syntax of documents written in XML. An XML schema is used to define a grammar for content within the XML syntax. The XrML schema therefore defines the required elements of the REL, along with which elements are optional, and how they must be grouped together. Because XML defines a fixed, computer-readable syntax, it is possible for software applications to extract the necessary information from the rights management messages and apply them to content. The XrML schema tells the software which elements to expect when parsing the file.

The XrML rights model consists of the following elements: principals, rights, resources, conditions, grants, issuers, and licenses. In this generic model, rights to a resource are granted to principals under certain conditions through a grant from an issuer via a license. A resource can be a piece of content contained in an MPEG-2 file or a whole tier of channels in the television service. Rights can include the right to play video content or make a copy for personal use. A principal is an entity that is authenticated within the DRM system, either through a shared secret key or the use of PKE. Conditions are limits or parameters associated with rights, such as the number of times a video can be played or the number of copies that can be made. These elements together constitute a grant. Multiple grants together with the identity of the issuers are called a license. The relationship among the model elements is shown in Figure 6-11.

The XrML model is used to create an XML schema that places requirements on how each element of the model is defined. An XML file

Figure 6-11

The XrML rights model, where a license identifies the grants from an issuer, giving a principal rights to a resource under certain conditions.

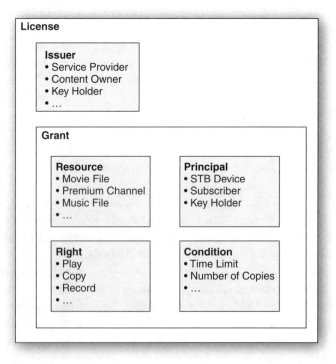

written to the XrML schema contains these elements in the grammar defined by the schema. The following example of an XML file written under the XrML schema identifies a license that grants a principal (in this case, anyone) a right (in this case to play) a resource (an MPEG-2 file) for 12 hours (a condition). For anyone not accustomed to XML, the syntax may seem a little strange. However, the methodical syntax makes it easy for a computer algorithm to read.

```
<license>
  <grant>
    <principal varRef="anyone"/>
    <resource>
      <cx:digitalWork>
        <cx:locator>
          <nonSecureIndirect URI="http://ficticiousIPTV.com/
          movie.mpg">
        </cx:locator>
      </cx:digitalWork>
    </resource>
    <right>
      <cx:play/>
    </right>
    <condition>
      <duration>12H</duration>
    </condition>
  </grant>
</license>
```

An REL is just one component of a full DRM system. XrML is used by a number of DRM systems as the REL, including Microsoft's Windows Media DRM system. XrML is also contained within parts of the MPEG-21 standard, which has an REL component.

MPEG-21 The Moving Picture Experts Group (MPEG) has defined the "MPEG-21 Part 5: Rights Expression Language" and corresponding "MPEG-21 Part 6: Rights Data Dictionary" as part of the larger MPEG-21 Multimedia Framework initiative. As with MPEG-2 and MPEG-4, MPEG is creating a standard that can be used across many devices in many contexts. MPEG-21 is designed to enable interoperability among different devices from different manufacturers via a common REL.

The MPEG-21 REL is based on XrML but it has been extended. In addition, MPEG-21 separates the REL from a complementary rights data dictionary (RDD) that defines the terms that are used within the REL. MPEG-21 also adds a multimedia extension to the core XrML that increases the flexibility (and complexity) of the REL by adding actions such as *modify* and *Move* to the list of rights. Because of the work on MPEG-21, ContentGuard has frozen XrML at version 2.0 and expects standards bodies such as MPEG-21 to be the source of more development.

ODRL   The Open Digital Rights Language (ODRL) is another open standard REL. Like MPEG-21, ODRL defines two XML schemas—one for the REL, and the other for the associated RDD. ODRL is supported by the Open Mobile Alliance (OMA), a group of wireless services operators and device manufacturers. The OMA DRM 2.0 is based on ODRL. While OMA is concerned primarily with mobile devices (cellular phones), it has extended its rights model to include video content to enable IPTV services.

Similar to the XrML model, the ODRL rights model consists of elements called assets, rights, parties, offers, and agreements. Rights can contain permissions, which identify constraints, requirements, and conditions. While not a direct one-to-one mapping, many of the model elements in XrML and ODRL have similar functions as shown in Table 6-1.

Table 6-1   Corresponding Elements of XrML and ORDL Rights Models

ODRL	XrML
Assets	Resources
Rights	Rights
Parties	Principals
Offers	Grants
Agreements	Licenses
Permissions	Conditions

▮▮▮ DRM System Implementations

A DRM system for an IPTV service would include each of the components in our DRM model. The functions of the DRM system are illustrated in Figure 6-12. The digital video channels, in the form of compressed MPEG-2 or MPEG-4 bitstreams, for example, are encrypted using digital ciphers and encryption keys. The access control system manages the many keys used to encrypt content, key information, and

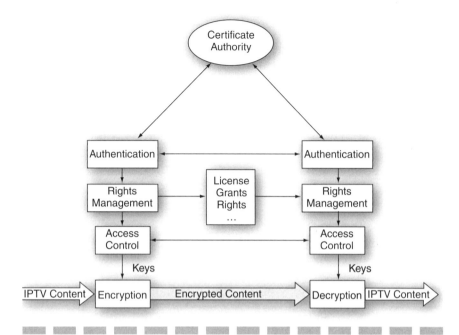

Figure 6-12

The components of an IPTV service's DRM system: encryption, access control, rights management, and authentication.

service tier information, and securely communicates that information to the receiving device. The rights management system defines what rights to use the content are granted to receiving devices in the form of license information expressed in the REL. And the authentication system verifies that only authorized devices are able to participate in the system, typically using a third-party certificate authority and digital certificates.

The various components of a DRM system can be implemented in a number of different ways. Next we look at some of the options and the consequences of each with respect to the IPTV service that uses them.

Hardware, Software, and Renewability

The encryption and access control elements of a DRM system are critical to the security of the content. The digital encryption ciphers need to be sophisticated enough to make brute-force attacks—where every key combination is attempted—impractical. The more sophisticated the cipher, the more computation resources are required to encrypt content with the cipher. Likewise the access control system needs to be able to keep digital keys secure. When a private key is used to create a digital signature, for example, the key must not be accessible outside of the system.

The encryption and key management functions can be performed in dedicated hardware such as Application Specific Integrated Circuits (ASICs), or performed in software on general-purpose central processing units (CPUs). Hardware approaches have several advantages. First, they can accelerate computationally expensive ciphers. Second, they offload processing from the CPU, which may be performing other tasks and features such as the graphical user interface (GUI) or video decoding. Third, hardware implementations can make it easier to keep keys secret.

Security ASICs can be built with tamper-resistant features that foil attempts to gain access to secrets within the chip, such as special circuits that will erase the secret keys if they detect tampering. Such features are typically not found on general purpose CPUs because they are expensive to implement on the larger integrated circuits of CPUs. Security ASICs embed secret keys within special internal memory circuits. Software processing of these keys on a general purpose CPU could expose secret keys because a CPU communicates with its memory via an external, accessible bus. In an implementation of a software encryption system, the information for the secret keys must cross the memory interface where it could potentially be intercepted.

In some ways, the distinction *software DRM* is a misnomer because ultimately some form of integrated circuit performs the required computations. The difference comes in how hard-wired the solution is. A software solution uses code that can be changed, while hardware solutions are often implemented in circuit logic that cannot be changed. As a result, while hardware implementations may be able to manage keys better than software implementations, software implementations can be more flexible. If a flaw is found in the cipher or key management algorithms, or the system is compromised because critical secrets have become known, software systems can be changed. New software can be downloaded to devices to correct the flaw or install new secrets. Such a downloadable Conditional Access System (DCAS) can be renewed in the field almost instantly via a software download. With a hardware system, the physical circuits have to be replaced if the system is compromised. Renewability becomes a more expensive proposition in the hardware approach as STBs need to be modified and the hardware security components replaced.

Hardware-based systems can be further differentiated by their renewability. A system that has all of its hardware components built into the STB would not be economically renewable: changing the DRM system would require replacing the entire STB. Instead, some hardware elements are contained in separate cards or modules that can be inserted and removed from the STB. If the component in the card is compromised or needs to be updated, it can be removed from the STB and replaced with a new one. This is important for an IPTV service provider because renewing the DRM system means replacing only the separable component. This could be mailed to the subscriber who could perform the operation. If the entire STB needs to be replaced, the service provider may have to roll a truck to the subscriber's home and switch out the unit. This can be an expensive proposition when the service provider has millions of customers.

Some DBS and cable systems use smart card–based DRM systems. Smart cards are credit card–sized devices containing security Application Specific Integrated Circuits (ASICs). In DRM systems based on smart cards, key management functions are implemented in separable hardware, while the encryption cipher remains inside the STB. The smart card provides the decryption keys to ciphers within the STB. If secret keys are discovered or the key management algorithms are found to be flawed, the smart cards can be updated and sent to consumers via postal mail. Smart cards are based on the ISO/IEC 7816 and 7810 international standards. Because these standards are widely used in many security applications, smart cards are relatively inexpensive.

Some security systems incorporate both the key management and the encryption cipher components in a separable module. The OpenCable CableCARD, for example, defines such a system for digital cable services. The encrypted digital content is delivered to the card and is returned to the STB unencrypted (but copy protected). To accomplish both of these tasks, the CableCARD is significantly larger, consumes more power, and is more expensive to manufacturer than a traditional smart card. Because the digital video bitstreams are transported across the interface between the STB and the CableCARD, significant bandwidth on the order of tens of megabits per second is required on the interface as well. The two different approaches are illustrated in Figure 6-13.

Legal Agreements   Another aspect of the security of a DRM system is the set of legal documents behind it. DRM manufacturers typically require a set of license agreements before a device manufacturer can implement the system. Among these are compliance rules that require the manufacturer to comply with specific standards in its handling of sensitive materials such as secret keys. The manufacturer is also

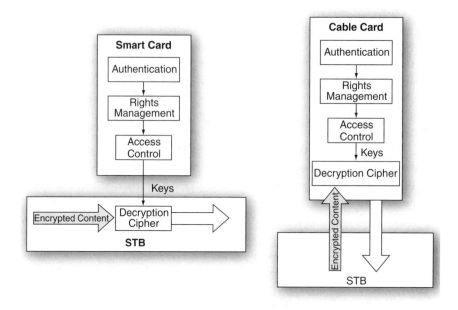

Figure 6-13
Two different approaches to separable hardware security.

required to comply with robustness rules that guarantee the resulting product is manufactured in such a way as to frustrate attempts at extracting secrets.

At the other end, customers who use IPTV services may be required to accept terms of usage or an end user license agreement (EULA) in which they agree not to attempt to thwart the DRM system. This could make the end user liable for any attempts at theft of service. Together, this chain of license agreements serves to protect the secrets of the DRM system and the integrity of the service.

DRM Vendors

The traditional vendors of DRM systems for cable and satellite television service providers in North America include Motorola, Scientific-Atlanta (recently acquired by Cisco), NagraStar, and NDS Ltd. Motorola's MediaCipher CAS is used in its digital cable products and has been licensed to other STB manufacturers as well. Scientific-Atlanta's PowerVu CAS is used in its digital cable products. NagraStar

(NDS) is a joint venture between Echostar, owner of the Dish satellite television service, and the Kudelski Group. NDS offers the VideoGuard system, which is used by digital cable and satellite pay-TV service operators worldwide; customers include DBS providers DirecTV in the US and BSkyB in the UK. All of these systems are being adapted for IPTV services as well.

Microsoft's Windows Media DRM (MS-DRM) originated as a system for controlling content on the PC, but it has become a key element in Microsoft's IPTV product as well. The MS-DRM uses XrML for its REL, giving it flexibility in the business models that can be defined. MS-DRM has also been adapted for portable media devices, which may make it easier for an IPTV service provider to offer portability of the content it delivers—that is, a consumer could view content outside of the home. MS-DRM also includes provisions for a digital content subscription service, where subscribers get access to a library of content as long as they continue to subscribe to the service.

Other vendors participating in the emerging IPTV space include Widevine, Verimatrix, and Nagravision, just to name a few. Widevine is a proponent of downloadable, software-based DRM systems. The Widevine Virtual SmartCard is used in place of a physical smart card for key management. Verimatrix also has a software solution; its DRM includes provisions to identify content that was copied from a network using its solution. Nagravision's DRM and CAS have been adapted for IPTV as well.

Protecting Analog and Digital Outputs

While an IPTV service provider's DRM system protects content within the service provider's network, eventually the content is handed off to other consumer electronics products such as TVs and video recorders. An IPTV service provider must ensure that content is protected over these interfaces as well. If the content is protected in the IPTV system down to the client device, but "escapes" after that, the service provider will be unable to secure rights from the content owners to distribute content. Typical service contracts from content owners will require that the IPTV service provider enable output content protection measures on the end devices of their service.

As part of the end-to-end content protection system, the client devices such as the STB employ copy protection measures on the outputs that connect to other consumer devices. As shown in Figure 6-14, these outputs can include analog or digital outputs directly to TVs, analog outputs to VCRs, or connections to local networks that deliver content to other consumer electronics components. The IP STB may also have an integrated DVD burner for copying the content onto recordable DVDs. This also is a form of digital output to a recording medium. We will look at some of the copy protection systems for all of these outputs in this section.

Redistribution Control: The Broadcast Flag   The ATSC standard used for digital television (DTV) broadcasts in North America does not include provisions for encrypting the content. As a result, TV shows and movies broadcast on DTV are vulnerable to being copied and/or distributed over the Internet. In an attempt to protect content owners and to encourage them to continue to make high definition, quality content available for DTV broadcasts, the Federal Communica-

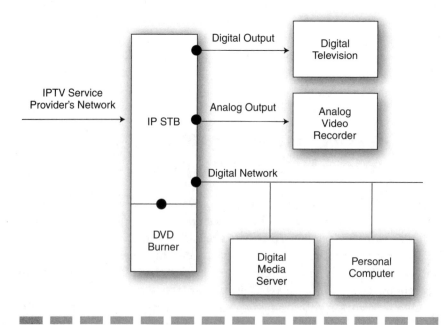

Figure 6-14
Some of the various content outputs from an IP STB that must employ copy protection mechanisms to protect content from unauthorized copying.

tions Commission (FCC) drafted a proposal to address digital broadcast content protection. Also called the *broadcast flag*, the FCC's proposal would require any TV or other device that receives and decodes ATSC signals to look for a single bit flag within the MPEG-2 bitstream. If this flag is present, the device is to take measures to prevent the content from being rebroadcast onto the Internet. This means any digital output on the receiving device has to be enabled with an approved form of copy protection; otherwise the content could not be presented on that output. Copy protection systems could be proposed to the FCC to be added to the approved list.

While the FCC's proposal was thrown out after a court challenge spearheaded by the Electronic Frontier Foundation (EFF), it is possible that similar legislation could reappear in the future. IPTV client devices may be subject to such a flag and therefore be required to include provisions for detecting the flag and asserting copy protection methods on its outputs. Content owners themselves might introduce similar flags in their content and include recognition of those flags in negotiations with IPTV service providers.

Digital Output Copy Protection

Digital outputs from IPTV client devices preserve the quality of DTV signals. Converting to analog could introduce artifacts not present in the original content. While most TVs and video recorders only have analog inputs, more and more devices are incorporating digital inputs. The digital inputs not only preserve the quality of the digital signal, but make it easier to add digital copy protection methods across the interface. We look at three types of digital interfaces: direct, point-to-point outputs such as high definition multimedia interface (HDMI); recording interfaces to digital recording media devices such as DVD burners; and digital networks such as Firewire/1394.

HDCP on HDMI HDMI is a consumer electronics–friendly upgrade of the digital visual interface (DVI). Like DVI, HDMI is used to convey uncompressed digital video signals from a source (a PC, DVD player, or a STB, for example) to a monitor or television. HDMI carries both digital audio and video signals and is in a smaller form factor than DVI, making it more suitable for consumer electronics equipment. An all-digital interface, HDMI preserves the picture quality of DTV signals as they are transferred from the STB to the TV.

Because HDMI transports the raw, uncompressed DTV signal, it makes that digital information available for potential copying. Therefore, HDMI includes support for the High-bandwidth Digital Content Protection (HDCP) system. Both the source (the STB) and the sink (the DTV) must support HDMI to transmit information securely. Some content owners may require that DVI or HDMI interfaces without HDCP support must lower the resolution of the video images (also called down-res) before transmitting across the interface. The thinking is that the down-res version is less valuable if it is copied on the unprotected interface.

HDCP is actually a full DRM system as defined by the DRM model earlier in this chapter: it employs encryption of the content via a symmetric cipher, key management through exchange of keys using public-private key encryption, authentication of the receiver, and a rights management system. In the case of HDCP, the REL is limited to one bit of information: either the two devices are authenticated and they share information, or they are not, and the data will be not delivered. The secret keys are administered by Digital Content Protection, LLC, which acts as the certificate authority.

HDCP employs a "black list" in its authentication component. If a device becomes compromised, its unique identifier is added to a list of revoked devices. This revocation list contains the identities of all devices that should not be allowed to participate in the exchange of encrypted information. During the authentication process, the transmitter device is required to check the identifier of the receiving device against the revocation list. System renewability messages (SRMs) are sent periodically within digital content to HDMI transmitters, which use these messages to update the black list. Service providers may be required to include SRMs in content they distribute to their client devices.

DTCP on Firewire/1394   Firewire, also known as 1394 or i.Link, is a networking technology for digital devices. The Firewire digital interface is capable of supporting HDTV signals and is used by many camcorders, PCs, digital VHS recorders (D-VHS), and some TVs. The Firewire standard defines how MPEG-2 transport streams are delivered over the network to other devices. The Digital Transmission Content Protection (DTCP) system encrypts the MPEG video content as it is transmitted over 1394. DTCP is also called *5C copy protection* for the five companies involved in its definition (Hitachi, Intel, Matsushita, Toshiba, and Sony). Like HDCP, DTCP involves an encryption cipher, key management, authentication via certificates, and a limited rights management component. Secret keys are administered by the Digital Transmission Licensing Administrator (DTLA).

The rights management component of DTCP consists of several bits of copy control information (CCI). The CCI bits are embedded in the MPEG-2 transport stream in a descriptor specific to DTCP. The CCI bits define the REL for DTCP. It consists of five components:

- **Copy generation management information (2 bits).** Describes how the receiving device can, or cannot, create copies of the content. The four possible copy management states are 00 Copy freely; 01 No more copies; 10 Copy one generation; 11 Copy never.

- **Image constraint token (1 bit).** When set, requires the device to produce a lower resolution image for any analog high definition output. Analog high definition outputs typically do not have any copy protection mechanism associated with them, and therefore it is possible to use those outputs to create copies of the content. By constraining the resolution of the analog outputs, the resulting copy would be of lower resolution than the full, original digital signal.

- **Analog copy protection information (2 bits).** Dictates how content is to be protected if sent across an analog output. This information is used to assert the Macrovision copy protection mechanism on analog outputs.

- **Encryption plus non-assertion (EPN) (1 bit).** When this bit is set, content is encrypted and can be passed only between licensed 5C products. However, it can be copied as many times as the user wants.

- **Retention state (3 bits).** Determine how long content can be retained by digital recording devices. The three bits of information provide only eight possible states. This is in contrast with a more flexible REL such as XrML, where almost any possible time frame can be expressed.

Table 6-2 shows retention time associated with each CCI retention state.

DTCP is also renewable via a black list approach. Each device stores a CRL of disabled devices in non-volatile memory. CRLs are also delivered by digital content and recognized by the DTCP hardware.

DTCP on IP   While originally defined for a Firewire-based network, DTCP has been extended for use over IP networks such as Ethernet. This allows it to be used as the copy protection system for most home

Table 6-2 Defined Retention Time for Each CCI Retention State

CCI Retention State	Retention Time
000	Forever
001	One week
010	Two days
011	One day
100	Twelve hours
101	Six hours
110	Three hours
111	Ninety minutes

networks in addition to Firewire, making it easier for an IPTV service provider to distribute content over an existing home network. Since content is already formatted for IP delivery by the service provider's network, it can continue across the home network protected with DTCP. DTCP over IP has also increased the number of bits in its rights expression language, providing more flexibility in the uses of the content by the receiving device.

Removable Media Copy Protection   Digital recording media such as DVD-R are also digital outputs in that content sourced from an IPTV service might be recorded for personal use by the subscriber. An IPTV service provider may want to make arrangements with content owners to allow subscribers to make personal copies, while the content owners would want copy protection measures to limit the number of copies made. Two content protection technologies are available for removable media that allow consumers to make copies of digital content for personal use while protecting the content from unauthorized copying.

Content Protection for Recordable Media   Content Protection for Recordable Media (CPRM) was developed by four companies (Intel, IBM, MEI, and Toshiba) as a copy protection method for recordable media such as DVD-R and Flash memory cards. CPRM allows a single copy to be made but prevents the recordable media from being used for further copies. The digital content is encrypted using a cipher and a randomly generated content key. The content key is encrypted and placed on the recordable media along with the encrypted content. Only authorized devices with CPRM secrets are able to decrypt the encrypted content key and therefore able to decrypt the content as well. CPRM-enabled devices are required by legal agreements not to create further copies.

Like HDCP and DTCP, CPRM uses encryption ciphers, key management, authentication, and rights management, in this case as a set of CCI bits. CPRM also has a revocation list that contains devices that have been compromised and are no longer allowed to decrypt content. The revocation information is carried in the blank recordable media. If a device is found to have been compromised, it is added to the list and imprinted on future blank media. Over time, the compromised device will only find media that will no longer work with it.

Video Content Protection System   Hewlett-Packard and Philips Electronics developed another recordable media copy protection system called the Video Content Protection System (VCPS). VCPS can be used for DVD+R and DVD+RW recordable media. Like CPRM, the digital content is encrypted on the recordable media and only CPRM-authorized playing devices can decrypt the content.

Analog Output Copy Protection

Even though IPTV services will deliver only digital information, the majority of TVs and video recorders in subscribers' homes are analog. Therefore, IPTV STBs will include analog outputs to present content to analog devices. Content owners are concerned about their content being copied as it is sent across these analog outputs. They will require the IPTV service provider to enable copy protection measures on analog outputs before making content available. We look at some of the analog copy protection systems here.

Macrovision   To discourage copying of analog television signals, the Macrovision system was developed to prevent recording on VCRs, without affecting viewing on televisions. Certain pulses are inserted into the NTSC signal that affect video recording devices but not TVs. An IPTV STB would insert the Macrovision pulses onto its analog outputs, allowing the subscriber to watch the video on the analog television but not be able to record it. Modern digital VCRs and DVRs are required to detect the Macrovision pulses and refuse to record the content or make sure the Macrovision is reapplied on any of their analog outputs.

CGMS–A The Copy Generation Management System–Analog (CGMS–A) is similar to Macrovision. It modifies the analog NTSC signal to disrupt VCRs. CGMS–A also inserts data into the VBI of the NTSC signal. Two bits of this data describe the copy control information and indicate whether the content can be labeled "copy freely," "copy once," or "copy never," similar to the CCI information in DTCP.

Watermarks Watermarking is another technology for marking analog content. However, instead of preventing copies, watermarks insert a message into the media (either video or audio). The message usually identifies the source of the content and can therefore be used to track the source of illegal copies. Watermarks can be visible or invisible: invisible watermarks alter the signal to insert the message but without creating visible artifacts. Robust watermarks are designed to preserve the message despite repeated copies or attempts to remove the watermark.

Some content owners are working with IPTV service providers to include watermarks in the content they make available to the service. This would be used in addition to other analog copy protection mechanisms.

IPTV Standard- ization Efforts

To boost the popularity and widespread acceptance of this new technology, the overall IPTV industry needs help from standardization efforts. In this chapter, we look at some of the standardization bodies and efforts currently underway for IPTV technology.

As you saw in the previous chapters, the core technologies behind IPTV are based on mature, open standards, such as MPEG-2 for audio/video compression and transport, and Internet protocols such as TCP, UDP, and IP for networking and communications. Emerging IPTV service offerings can take advantage of open standards throughout, from the basic transport layer for delivering content, to the user interface, to back office customer management software. Internet and MPEG standards theoretically create a platform that can promote rapid innovation while taking advantage of decreasing cost trends. The layered approach of Internet protocols makes it potentially easier for a service provider to mix and match IPTV vendor equipment, and the large base of existing IP infrastructure provides a ready platform for new services.

Despite all of the existing open standards, additional standardization within the IPTV community is necessary to ensure interoperability. The Internet Engineering Task Force (IETF) protocols intentionally define an isolated component of a system. Complete solutions are formed by combining and constraining different protocols. These specification efforts typically do not define new protocols but instead define subsets and usage models of existing protocols. For example, if one broadcaster used one subset of these formats and another broadcaster a different set, television manufacturers could not be sure their devices could receive those broadcasts unless they implemented all possible formats. So the standards body for the Advanced Television Systems Committee (ATSC) created requirements for HDTV broadcasts in the US that bounded the potentially hundreds of video formats possible (within MPEG-2) to just 18 specific digital TV formats, making it easier to build and test devices for compliance. In addition to interoperability, economies of scale are created when manufacturers can produce equipment that can be used by several different IPTV services with a larger aggregate customer base.

Significant effort has been made to create standards at the consumer device level for digital video content. Standards bodies such as the Consumer Electronics Association (CEA) and the Universal Plug and Play (UPnP) Forum are working on interoperability of consumer devices for finding and moving digital video between devices. This could potentially make it easier to create innovative products that can distribute content within, or beyond, the subscriber's home. However, IPTV services still need to get the content to the subscriber's home and to the consumer devices within the home. This standardization effort is still in its infancy. In a recent survey sponsored by the Internet Streaming Media Alliance (ISMA), all but one of the IPTV technology companies surveyed indicated a strong interest in open IPTV standards, with about half agreeing that standards to ensure quality of service are necessary for IPTV to be successful.

The Internet Streaming Media Alliance

ISMA was formed to create standards for the distribution of media content over the Internet. ISMA integrates a number of the open-standard Internet-related (for example, IETF) protocols described in previous chapters. The ISMA specifications also place requirements on content receiving devices such as set-top boxes (STBs) and PCs. Defining the required capabilities of the receiving device increases the potential number of devices that are guaranteed to be able to decode the content and interoperate with other networked devices. The founding members of ISMA (Apple, Sun Microsystems, Philips, IBM, and Cisco Systems) all have strong track records in creating consumer and Internet-based standards. ISMA was created in response to early efforts of streaming media to PCs that relied on a mix of proprietary and open solutions. Membership in ISMA has grown significantly since its founding, indicating the growing popularity and interest in this technology, which puts a greater emphasis and importance on standards for delivering video over the Internet.

ISMA version 1.0, released in August 2001, used the original MPEG-4 video codec specification—the only advanced codec available at the time. Version 2.0 of the ISMA specifications was released in April 2005. Version 2.0 added the MPEG-4 AVC video codec and High Efficiency AAC (HE-AAC) audio codec, as well as high definition video profiles. Figure 7-1 shows the architectural overview of the ISMA version 2.0 specification.

As can be seen from the architectural overview in Figure 7-1, ISMA has used existing standards from MPEG and IETF but has placed requirements on how they are used. The group's approach was to create requirements for four functional areas: media formats, media storage, media transport, and media description/control.

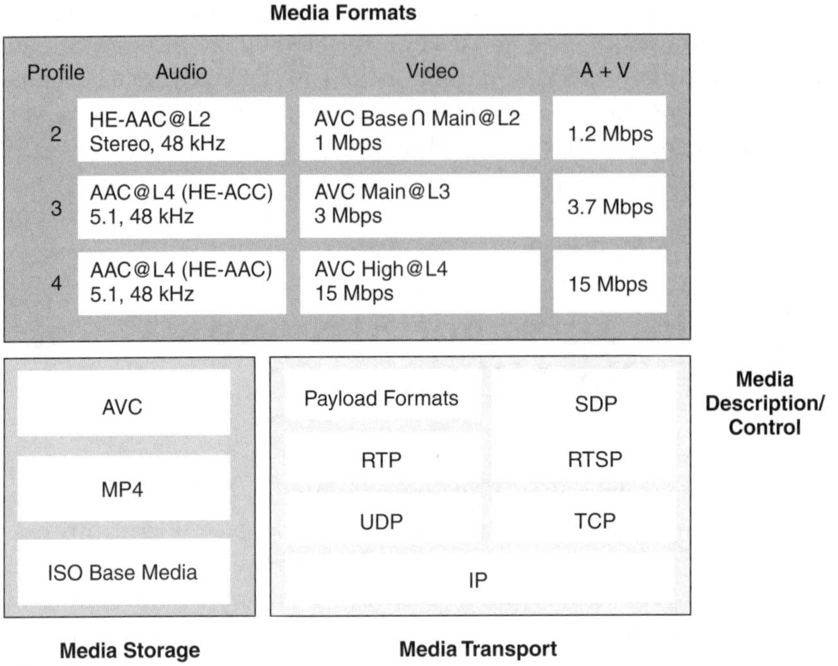

Media Formats

Profile	Audio	Video	A + V
2	HE-AAC@L2 Stereo, 48 kHz	AVC Base ∩ Main@L2 1 Mbps	1.2 Mbps
3	AAC@L4 (HE-ACC) 5.1, 48 kHz	AVC Main@L3 3 Mbps	3.7 Mbps
4	AAC@L4 (HE-AAC) 5.1, 48 kHz	AVC High@L4 15 Mbps	15 Mbps

Media Storage		Media Transport		Media Description/Control
AVC		Payload Formats	SDP	
MP4		RTP	RTSP	
		UDP	TCP	
ISO Base Media		IP		

Figure 7-1

The ISMA architecture overview, taken from Internet Streaming Media Alliance Implementation Specification version 2.0, April 2005.

Within the media formats functional area, the various profiles identify subsets of the MPEG-4 Advanced Video Codec (AVC) codec. This provides manufacturers with guidelines on what formats they must support to meet various profile requirements. The original Profile 0 from version 1.0, for example, required only low resolution Quarter Common Intermediate Format (Q-CIF) images of 176 × 120 pixels. Profiles 2, 3, and 4 progressively increase the image resolution and compressed bitstream data rates. Profile 4 includes high definition video resolutions (MPEG-4 High Profile Level 4) consisting of 1280 × 720 pixels at 60 frames per second (fps), and 1920 × 1080 pixels at 30 fps. Compressed bitstream data rates can be as high as 15 Mbps.

In the media transport and description/control functional area, ISMA version 2.0 requires the usage of the Real-time Transport Protocol (RTP), Real-Time Control Protocol (RTCP), Real-Time Streaming Protocol (RTSP), and Session Description Protocol (SDP) for streaming, encapsulating, and describing media content. Devices implementing these protocols should be able to discover, control, and view ISMA-compatible content from IPTV service providers. In the media storage functional area, ISMA version 2.0 requires the usage of the MPEG-4 and AVC file format (a.k.a. MP4FF and AVCFF).

In the IMSA home reference model shown in Figure 7-2, IPTV services are delivered from the IPTV service network to a delivery gateway device. For example, a DSL modem/gateway for IPTV services from telephone operators would act as a delivery network gateway device. The home network bridges the gateway to home network end devices such as IPTV STBs and digital TVs (DTVs). The home network could be as simple as an Ethernet cable connecting the gateway to the DTV.

The Digital Video Broadcasting Project

DVB has created a series of specifications for digital video services delivered over cable, satellite, and terrestrial broadcast. Traditionally DVB activities focused on the European market, with specification efforts led by European companies. The goal of DVB's Internet Protocol (DVB-IP) group is to specify the interface between an IP service network and in-

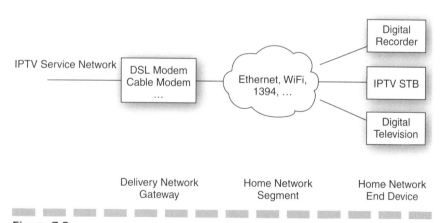

Figure 7-2
The components of the ISMA home reference model. The ISMA standards deal with the interfaces between the various components in the model.

home receivers, enabling the end user to buy a DVB-IP receiver at retail and receive DVB services over IP-based networks.

The DVB-IP set of standards defines an architectural framework for the delivery of DVB services over IP-based networks, and within home networks to end devices. Consistent with the IMSA home reference model (shown in Figure 7-2), DVB-IP has based this framework on a similar reference model. The goal of DVB-IP is to standardize the protocols on the interfaces between the different elements of the model.

DVB-IP identifies the IETF protocol stack for transport of IPTV services, as shown in Figure 7-3 (we reviewed most of these protocols in earlier chapters). Basic transport of services is built upon TCP and UDP over IP. Media is delivered over RTP in MPEG-2 transport streams, using IGMP for IP multicast management. RTSP is used for on-demand content control (for example, pause, play, and so on); while RTCP provides feedback with control information to assist RTP flow (for example, broadcast TV and audio content). Other critical networking support comes from such protocols as HTTP/HTTPS (Hypertext Transfer Protocol is the method used to transfer information to/from the Internet; HTTPS is like HTTP but includes security), DNS (used to translate domain names into IP addresses), DHCP (client receives critical configuration information to participate on an IP network), and NTP and SNTP (to synchronize clocks or time). DVB also defines service discovery and selection protocols (DVB SDS) delivered over DVB Service Transport Protocol (DVB-STP). These protocols describe how an IPTV service

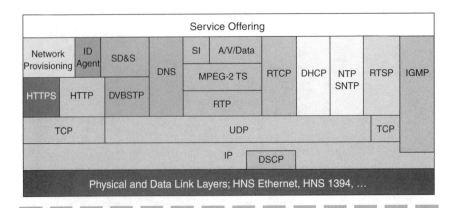

Figure 7-3
The protocol stack for DVB-IP services, taken from ETSI TS 102 034, Digital Video Broadcasting (DVB); Transport of MPEG-2 Based DVB Services over IP Based Networks, March 2005.

provider identifies the available services as well as domain names and resource locators.

Part of the DVB-IP effort includes adding support for IPTV services within the DVB Multimedia Home Platform (DVB-MHP). DVB-MHP is a middleware specification for DVB STBs. It should be noted that the US cable OpenCable Application Platform (OCAP) middleware is based on DVB-MHP. The DVB-MHP for IP effort defines how networked client devices receive programming and applications from the Internet as well as from cable or satellite broadcasts. It addresses such things as service information, application signaling, and control of IP-sourced programming.

The Consumer Electronics Association

In 2005, the CEA created the IPTV Interface Discovery Group to examine the need for standards to support the delivery of commercial video content to the home over the Internet. In particular, the CEA is interested in interfaces between the Internet service, the home network, and various consumer electronics in the home. This discovery group will make recommendations on any required specification activity and assign it to existing standards committees within the CEA.

The CEA has a long history of creating interoperability standards between consumer electronics and service providers. For example, it worked with the cable television industry to create standards for digital cable receiving devices and the CableCARD separable conditional access interface. It has engaged early with IPTV service providers to ensure consumer electronics devices, most notably digital televisions, can interoperate with IPTV services. In 2006, the CEA along with AT&T, BellSouth, and Verizon announced a set of principles to ensure commercial availability of consumer electronics devices that can receive content from IPTV networks. The organizations agreed in principle to work toward nationwide compatibility between consumer electronics and IPTV provider platforms, using open standards agreed upon in industry forums. Some of the other topics discussed in the joint statement included the goals of reasonable licensing terms for intellectual property behind IPTV technologies, and testing and certification procedures for compatible equipment.

The Alliance for Telecommunications Industry Solutions

The ATIS is an organization that helps develop and promote technical and operations standards for the communications and related information technologies industry using a sensible, flexible, and open approach. The ATIS recognized the need of standards for IPTV services from telephone and broadband companies. The ATIS board thus created the IPTV Interoperability Forum (IIF) to work with its members in meeting that need.

The ATIS IIF goal is to create an industry-wide reference architecture for IPTV, including defining interfaces between devices. Other tasks include digital rights management, interoperability and testing activities, and quality of service metrics for IPTV services. In May 2006, the ATIS released requirement overview documents for IPTV architecture and DRM. The "IPTV Architecture Requirements" document defines high-level requirements for IPTV services, including the functions necessary for content owners to deliver content to service providers, network service provider requirements, and home network requirements to support IPTV services. The IPTV "DRM Interoperability Requirements" defines requirements for interoperability among IPTV DRM and security elements.

ATIS membership comes from major telecom companies in North America and equipment suppliers to the telecom industry. The emphasis for the IIF is on IPTV services delivered by facilities-based operators such as telephone operators. This is in contrast to the CEA's emphasis on the consumer electronics component, and ISMA's emphasis on IPTV delivered over the generic Internet. As such, the IIF is targeting security, quality of service, and network performance to ensure a quality viewing experience that promotes the business requirements of its members.

Digital Living Network Alliance

The DLNA is an organization consisting of companies that provide products in the consumer electronics, computer, and mobile device markets. Its vision consists of a wired and wireless interoperable network of PCs, consumer electronics, and mobile devices to enable a seamless environment for sharing and growing digital content services. The DLNA has recognized the fact that today, within consumer's homes, three separate areas of entertainment and communications exist, which do not broadly share information or content with each other: computers and Internet-centric devices, consumer electronics (such as broadcast TV, radios, and so on), and mobile technology (such as cell phones).

To accomplish its vision, the DLNA is focused on delivering interoperability guidelines based on open industry standards to complete the convergence (of PCs, consumer electronics devices, and mobility). These guidelines specify the interoperable building blocks that are readily available today based on existing technology. Also, their initial focus is on interoperability between networked devices in support of areas such as digital entertainment (for example, digital broadcast, VOD, streaming Internet video, and so on), personal media (for example, e-mail, Internet, home movies, and so on), and static media (for example, digital cameras and home photographs, and so on). Over time, the DLNA expects to revise its guidelines to support new technology and standards as they become available.

Table 7-1 shows an overview of the functional components and their associated required technology covered by the DLNA guidelines.

The DLNA also has created three device categories along with twelve separate device classes divided among these categories. For a product or device to achieve the DLNA certification, it must fall into one of the following defined classes and categories listed on the next page:

Table 7-1 DLNA Interoperability Guideline Components and Technology

Functional Components	Technology
Connectivity	Ethernet, 802.11, and Bluetooth
Networking	IPv4
Device discovery and control	UPnP device architecture v1.0
Media management and control	UPnP AV v1 and UPnP printer:1
Media formats	JPEG, LPCM, and MPEG-2
Media transport	HTTP (mandatory) and RTP (optional)

- **Home Network Device (HND) Category.** Consists of five device classes that connect to the home network:
  - **Digital Media Server (DMS).** An HND device that performs server functionality, including acquisition, recording, storage, and sourcing capabilities; also including content protection enforcement.
  - **Digital Media Player (DMP).** An HND device that performs playback and rendering of content from the network.
  - **Digital Media Renderer (DMR).** An HND device that plays content after being set up by another network device.
  - **Digital Media Controller (DMC).** An HND device that finds content on DMS devices and matches it to appropriate DMR devices.
  - **Digital Media Printer (DMPr).** An HND device that performs network printing capability.
- **Mobile Handheld Device (MHD) Category.** Consists of five device classes that have similar functionality as those in the HND category, but are targeted for mobility:
  - **Mobile Digital Media Server (M-DMS).** An MHD device that provides mobile content to the network.
  - **Mobile Digital Media Player (M-DMP).** An MHD device that finds mobile content and plays it.
  - **Mobile Digital Media Uploader (M-DMU).** An MHD device that sends mobile content to an M-DMS device.
  - **Mobile Digital Media Downloader (M-DMD).** An MHD device that can find and download mobile content from an M-DMS, and then play it.
  - **Mobile Digital Media Controller (M-DMC).** An MHD device that can find content residing on an M-DMS and match it to a DMR device.
- **Home Infrastructure Device (HID) Category.** Consists of two class devices:
  - **Mobile Network Connectivity Function (M-NCF).** An HID device that provides bridging functionality between MHD and HND.
  - **Media Interoperability Unit (MIU).** An HID device that is able to transform content between HND and MHD for supported formats.

DLNA first published its "Home Networked Device Interoperability Guidelines" one year after DLNA was founded, in June 2004. In January 2005, DLNA released the "Optional Media Format Addendum Guidelines," which provided support for additional media formats that were common to many CE, mobile, and PC devices. Finally, in March 2006, it released the 2006 "Home Networked Device Interoperability Guidelines," which rounded the guidelines out to the full range of class devices and categories.

Products designed to the "DLNA Interoperability Guidelines" are granted use of the DLNA CERTIFIED logo after meeting all DLNA certification and testing requirements.

DSL Forum

The DSL Forum is an international industry consortium with more than 200 service providers, equipment, and component manufacturers and other interested parties that focuses on developing the potential of broadband DSL. Established in 1994, the forum's mission is to develop technical specifications that enable the delivery and support of broadband DSL products and services.

The DSL Forum develops specifications that set the stage for effective deployments and continuing global DSL growth. By developing these new standards and embracing new applications, the DSL Forum is tailoring DSL to meet the needs of the next generation of multimedia services and the online community.

The DSL Forum develops technical reports on the capabilities, testing, management, and network architecture for deployment and operation of DSL from the network to the home. Through these technical reports, the forum contributes to global industry standards and global standards bodies such as ANSI, ETSI, ATIS, and ITU.

Internet Standards Organizations

Other pertinent Internet standards bodies include the following:

- **World Wide Web Consortium (W3C).** An important standards body for web-related material.

- **Internet Engineering Task Force (IETF).** Manages and tracks many of the fundamental protocols on the Internet.

- **European Telecommunications Standards Institute (ETSI).** A non-profit organization whose mission is to produce the telecommunications standards that will be used for decades to come throughout Europe and beyond.

- **International Telecommunication Union (ITU).** An international organization within the United Nations system where governments and the private sector coordinate global telecom networks and services.

- **Internet Society (ISOC).** Provides leadership in addressing issues that confront the future of the Internet and is the home for groups responsible for Internet infrastructure standards, including the IETF and the IAB.

- **Internet Architecture Board (IAB).** A committee of the IETF and a technical advisory group of the ISOC.

- **Internet Research Task Force (IRTF).** Research groups work on topics related to Internet protocols, applications, architecture, and technology.

- **RFC Editor.** Publisher of RFCs (Requests for Comments) and is responsible for the final editorial review.

The End of TV as We Know It or Business as Usual?

This final chapter offers thoughts on how IPTV will, or will not, change the business of television. Technically, IPTV represents a new approach for delivering digital TV (DTV) signals to consumers' homes. Will the introduction of IPTV services necessarily translate into a fundamental shift in the business of television? We believe that the IPTV technology does not in itself represent a new type of television service; the method of digital data delivery does not fundamentally change how users enjoy television. Instead, IPTV has the *potential* for changing how people access, share, and consume television services. The two-way, networked capabilities at the core of the Internet Protocol will bring about new services and new models for pay services. However, these new models have yet to be proven as profitable or capable of changing the current television industry.

IPTV does have the proven capability of enabling telephone companies (Telcos) to create competitive television services to incumbent cable and satellite service providers. While these new services may only be direct substitutes for existing services, they will definitely change the competitive landscape of the industry. However, it is yet to be seen if IPTV will lead to unique and differentiated services.

Ultimately, the ability of a new IPTV-enabled service to succeed and challenge existing business models lies in its ability to obtain and deliver compelling content. The on-demand, interactive nature of over-the-top IPTV services enables delivery of niche and user-generated content by multiple players, from new startups to industry giants. This may prove to be the new model that changes the television industry.

New Delivery Protocol, Same Old TV?

At the technical level, IPTV is about the delivery of digital audio and video over IP—the same technology used throughout the Internet's architecture. Both existing and new service providers can use IPTV to deliver pay television services. But does the consumer really care whether his or her television service is delivered over IP packets or by one of the traditional methods used in cable or satellite services today? Is there something unique about the underlying method of delivery that differentiates an IPTV service from a traditional one? We believe early deployments of IPTV, in particular from facilities-based operators such as Telcos and cable operators, will mostly be undifferentiated from existing DTV services. The Telcos will be new entrants into an existing market, not a new paradigm for pay television.

Early IPTV deployments from major Telcos seem to support this conclusion. They appear to offer packages almost identical to those of cable and broadcast satellite; the consumer can choose from various bundles of the same broadcast, cable channels, and premium channels (for example Gold, Silver, or Bronze packages). Only the underlying transport protocol is different. While the service package may look very similar, IPTV has clearly changed the business landscape by making it possible for new entrants, the Telcos, to provide television services. And IPTV is enabling other new distribution models such as downloading TV shows over the Internet as well.

But does IPTV represent a fundamental shift in the business of delivering TV services, or does it also create a fundamental shift in the user experience of watching TV? Will IPTV deliver on its potential of disrupting not only the distribution industry but also the entire business model end-to-end: from content creation to the way consumers enjoy it in the home? We believe the interactive nature of IP will lead to more customized, web-centric, and on-demand content for TV services. For cable, digital broadcast satellite (DBS), and Telcos, this will be a gradual shift from existing services to more web and on-demand services, but it will not pose a radical change in the basic TV experience.

At its core, IP is an interactive, bidirectional, on-demand medium. Despite initially deploying only a duplicate TV service, Telcos have begun touting the interactive nature of IPTV as a differentiated advantage over cable and satellite services. The on-demand nature could permeate the service, shifting all TV from a passive broadcast medium to a preference-based targeted medium. This would represent a change in the underlying TV service model beyond the underlying technical changes. As TV services become increasingly available via the PC and other Internet-enabled devices, we will also see a change in where we watch TV. IPTV and the adaptability to mobility could mean a shift from viewing exclusively in the living room to the office, to cars, and potentially anywhere via portable players and wireless networked devices (such as WiFi, WiMAX, and so on).

But what are some of the additional features that IPTV may deliver? IP is the basis for much of what we do online, including web surfing, e-commerce, and other interactive applications. Will these capabilities become part of the TV viewing experience as well? To date, interactive TV has met with limited success since its introduction in the 1980s. Hundreds of thousands of consumers have had access to various interactive TV trial deployments—cable subscribers in Hawaii ordering pizza through their TV, subscribers in Philadelphia participating in video dating, and so on. Consumers have had the ability to surf the Web on their TV for years, but there appears to be limited demand for this capability. Additionally, interactive games, e-commerce, and novel interactive program guides have also been deployed. Yet none of these has resulted in clear customer demand. We believe it isn't apparent yet how the interactivity of the web experience will transfer to the TV experience.

At a minimum, IPTV provides Telcos the ability to offer service bundles on par with cable operators, namely the "quadruple play" of television, telephone, broadband, and mobility (wireless) services. When services are bundled, the service provider not only enjoys an increase in ARPU (average revenue per unit) but also a reduction in subscriber churn. When customers receive a single, discounted bill for a bundle of services they are less likely to switch all of those services to another provider (or various providers). The service provider also has the ability to cross-promote across those services, such as the recent wireless phone advertisements linked to theatrical releases.

Will the Telcos Succeed?

It is too early to predict whether the Telcos will be successful in launching IPTV services over their broadband networks to millions of paying customers and reaping sufficient profit to recoup their investment. Ultimately, the consumer will determine the outcome either by dropping current service providers and signing up with these new Telco offerings or by staying with their current providers. We believe that consumers will choose only on the basis of content and price, and not the underlying technology or new interactive features.

Most likely, the business model for a new Telco IPTV service offering will be quite complex with several discounts across services when purchased in a bundle. To date, Telcos have been successful at bundling a lower cost broadband data service (DSL) with landline phone service. A Telco quadruple play with IPTV may become a lower cost alternative to cable TV services and attract a significant market share. However, it may be difficult for a Telco to show profitability while providing customers with more on-demand and interactive features while providing a significantly lower cost video service. Additionally, content providers usually charge more money for access to their content to service operators with fewer subscribers. Therefore, to attract customers, Telcos will initially have to offer TV services at a lower price (and lower profit) while paying more for content than the incumbent cable or DBS providers.

Not Just for Telcos

Other companies can exploit the transition to IP delivery for TV services. Cable companies may also be able to enjoy any of the benefits that IPTV distribution provides. The cable HFC (Hybrid Fiber Coax) network was a natural evolution of the analog cable infrastructure. As DTV became economically feasible, cable operators migrated their cable infrastructure to one that could accommodate digital broadcasts. The HFC network was the least costly (but in no way inexpensive) way to leverage existing analog cable to provide new digital signals. Most cable operators have stated that they can deliver IPTV over their HFC networks if the need arises. In fact, more and more of the HFC plant's components are using IP technology. High-speed connections between content ingest and RF modulation locations in the cable plant use Gigabit Ethernet; today these fiber backbones carry broadcast and on-demand channels over IP. Just as the original transformation of cable plants to HFC was a gradual migration of optical technologies closer to the subscriber's home, IP technology continues to be utilized deeper into the cable plant toward the subscriber, replacing older radio frequency (RF) technologies. Over time, the cable HFC plant will evolve into an IP-based network and thus become an IPTV service provider.

Significant bandwidth on the RF cable plant is already dedicated to DOCSIS, which carries IP packets for broadband services. While IP-based delivery of video content typically terminates at the content network part of the cable plant, eventually it will reach all the way into the consumer's home. Time Warner Cable, for example, launched a trial in San Diego where broadcast TV channels are simulcast over IPTV to a subscriber's PC. While currently an experimental service, it demonstrates the versatility of the cable plant and its ability to deliver IPTV services if necessary.

The cable operators' telephony services are also based on IP technology and serve millions of customers over HFC networks. Cable telephony is a facilities-based Voice over IP (VoIP) offering that presents a compelling alternative to traditional telephone landlines and promises to increase the rate at which traditional telephone operators lose their traditional landline phone customers. Also, since the voice service is deployed over their network, the cable operator (like the telephone operator) can guarantee better quality of service than competing over-the-top services.

Short of the "IPTV-only killer app," many of the promises of IPTV are nonetheless available today in cable networks, in particular making content available on-demand. In fact, Comcast has served billions of programs on-demand to its customers without a single IPTV packet reaching the consumer's home. Other IPTV services such as interactive TV, purchasing goods via the remote control, targeted advertising, and surfing the Web are all possible on modern cable systems. As cable operators migrate to the next generation of DOCSIS, they will enable their networks to deliver higher bandwidth IP connections. If and when IPTV services resonate with customers (thereby requiring cable operators to offer IPTV services), it appears the HFC cable plant may be in a position to allow the operator to launch these services as well.

When the time is right, or more importantly when the economic model becomes apparent, cable operators will be able to deliver IP-based services to customers. However, the motivation doesn't exist today since operators would need to see significant cost or bandwidth savings in making the transition, or some new service that can be delivered only by IPTV. That "killer app" has not yet appeared.

New Over-the-Top Approaches

IPTV enables over-the-top service providers that are not facilities-based, but instead rely on the open Internet to deliver services. Will these services be able to change the business of television significantly? Currently, the greatest concern with an over-the-top service is in obtaining enough bandwidth to deliver the service in a timely manner. Today, over-the-top services do not have the ability to provide a built-in Quality of Service (QoS) with guaranteed bandwidth and must instead rely on a best-effort approach. As such, increasing the available downstream bandwidth is the best solution to this problem as more bandwidth reduces the probability of packets getting lost or dropped. Therefore, the over-the-top approach relies on continued advancements in broadband (continued increases in available bandwidth and in consumer penetration) to the home. We believe that if these services are able to obtain sufficient bandwidth to maintain adequate QoS, via network neutrality or other means, then they will offer the greatest potential for changing the landscape of the TV industry.

While initially offering only niche or user-generated content, over-the-top services are already delivering premium content from the major broadcast networks and some studios. We believe this trend will continue as traditional content providers test new outlets for their content. It's easy to imagine how over-the-top IPTV services may one day compete head-to-head with cable, satellite, and Telco distributors. It will also be interesting to see if traditional service providers start to offer niche content to minimize the popularity of over-the-top services. The biggest advantage of the over-the-top service provider lies in not having to fund the deployment and management of a facilities-based network. Many of the over-the-top companies can trace their origins to the early Internet era and are quite adept at deploying, managing, and marketing Internet services to consumers on a broad scale, without having to build the pipes to deliver those services to the customer's home.

Because the expected quality of service of an over-the-top TV service will be much lower than that of cable, satellite, and Telco services, one approach may be to build the business model on an advertisement-based approach similar to Google and Yahoo!. Such a service could post ads within web pages, play streaming advertisements before playing the desired content, or include ad insertion for live events. These targeted, dynamic advertisements have the potential of demanding a higher premium to advertisers than existing static broadcast advertisements. ABC, for example, has created a web service that offers episodes of its hit series "Lost" for free with the commercials intact, in addition to other promotions for other ABC shows and major advertisers.

The advantages of an over-the-top approach are as follows:

- Greatly reduces capital expenses since it does not require building a new delivery network.
- Decreases time-to-market by using existing standards-based web services.
- Reduces operating expenses by relying on broadband service providers to maintain their networks.
- Internet TV plays well to the strengths of Internet companies: web servers and customer access (that is, web portals) in the home.

The disadvantages of an over-the-top approach are as follows:

- The quality of the video service may be low and make it difficult to charge consumers for it. Alternative business models may be required.
- Not managing the network puts the service at the mercy of the owners of the broadband networks.

- Inconsistent bandwidth to the homes complicates the video sources.
- Unproven business models.

A topic currently being debated in Washington D.C. is "net neutrality," which is studying regulating access to the Internet. The network operator of a private network (broadcast) IPTV service may want to prioritize its own services to ensure quality of service. If it cannot prioritize its service data over Internet TV data, then it could lose competitive advantage over networks it built and funded itself. On the other hand, if network traffic for Internet TV services is not prioritized, the quality of the Internet TV service for all service providers could suffer greatly. Net neutrality could relegate the DSL and cable operators as commodity data services (dumb bit pipes). The outcome of this debate could have a dramatic effect on the future of over-the-top services and their ability to create an alternative service to facilities-based incumbents.

Content Is King

Ultimately, the quality of the content and the perceived value of the service drive subscriber growth. When DBS debuted in the 1990s, it offered a service that was not very different from what cable TV was already providing. Subscribers were offered virtually the same channel lineup as cable. For some, particularly in rural areas, DBS was the only choice for multi-channel services. But for others, the decision to switch from cable was based on the ability to get particular content. The exclusive NFL Sunday ticket drew millions of customers, many of them leaving cable for DBS. As with DBS, will IPTV ultimately be driven by the content instead of the delivery technology? As long as IPTV's only distinction is in how bits of digital video or content are delivered to the home, we believe that content will continue to be a major differentiating factor between services.

What the Future Holds for IPTV

We believe that IPTV holds the potential to be a "Schumpeter-like" event for the TV services industry—that is, a process of creative destruction in

Schumpeter's Ideas on Business Cycles and Economic Development

Joseph Alois Schumpeter (born February 8, 1883–died January 8, 1950) was a famous early 20th century economist from Austria who moved to the United States in 1932. Schumpeter wrote of business cycles driven by creative destruction where new businesses would outpace older ones until they themselves became the old businesses.

which entrepreneurs and new technology will disrupt and eventually replace established business models. As IPTV opens up new distribution and consumption models, the ways in which consumers receive and enjoy TV content will change. How that process will unfold is not clear, as we are in the early stages of the transformation from conventional analog and digital TV services to IPTV. Smaller, faster, more innovative companies may be able to exploit the technology to create that new model. As of the writing of this book, the handful of people at one-year-old startup YouTube managed to grab more visitors to its IPTV video website than Google did to its site. Today's startup has outpaced yesterday's startup. If that doesn't epitomize Schumpeter's theory, we don't know what does.

Further Details on Channel Change Delays

Despite the many advantages of digital television (DTV), it is possible that with IPTV changing channels may take longer than with analog TV. IPTV, like digital cable and digital broadcast satellite (DBS), uses compressed digital video that requires some extra time to decode. But IPTV also introduces additional protocol layers that enable new service options but could also make the simple operation of changing channels more computationally complex. In general, three sources of channel change delay exist in DTV systems: network, transport, and compression based. Transport and compression-based delays are inherent in any DTV distribution system. Network-based delays are introduced in any on-demand switched network model where TV channels are delivered when requested instead of continuously being broadcast. In this appendix we look at the components of channel change delay in digital and IPTV systems.

Compression Delays

Any temporal reference–based compression system, such as MPEG-2, MPEG-4, and VC-1, will have inherent delays between reception of digital data and when decode and display of video can begin. Decoding cannot start until one or several reference frames such as MPEG-2 I-frames have been received. As discussed in Chapter 4, compressed bitstreams are typically sent at rates such that one frame of data is received every 33 ms (one frame interval). Waiting for the reference frames to arrive will take several frame intervals or possibly hundreds of milliseconds. Most MPEG-2 systems transmit two I-frames per second, or once every 15 frames. Typically this is the biggest contributor to channel change delay. Once the bits have been received, it takes time for the processor to decode the image and present it to the graphics buffer, where other delays might occur because of post-processing, such as image scaling or graphics overlay.

Variable Bits Per Frame

While the original analog TV signal consisted of discrete frames that arrived at a fixed time interval of once every 33 ms, compressed video bitstreams arrive at different time intervals. The analog frames are digitized into a fixed number of bits per frame. However, the compressed digital frame units are typically a variable number of bits depending on the frame type. In a broadcast DTV environment the bits of compressed digitized frame units are transmitted at a rate such that one frame unit worth of bits is received *on average* once per frame unit time interval. Because some compressed frames are larger than others, however, they may take more or less time than one frame time interval to arrive.

Dependent and Reference Frames

As part of the compression process, the compressed digitized frame units come in two flavors: reference frames (RF), such as I-frames in MPEG-2, which can be converted back into uncompressed digitized frame units using the bits contained in the RF alone; and dependent frames (DF), such B- and P-frames in MPEG-2, which can be built only from RFs (and possibly other DFs), and the motion vector information for that DF. As a result, to start decoding a stream of frames, it is necessary to wait until at least one RF and possibly multiple DFs are received by the decoder.

Figure A-1 shows how the analog media (TV) signal is digitized into uniform-sized digital frames, which are then compressed into variable-sized frames, and how the resulting frames may be dependent on other frames.

When an IPTV set-top box (STB) tunes to a particular stream (channel), the unit starts receiving the compressed digitized frame units. It may start receiving frames anywhere in the stream, most likely in the

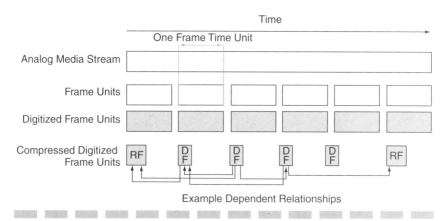

Figure A-1
In compressed video streams, most frames are dependent on other frames to be fully decoded.

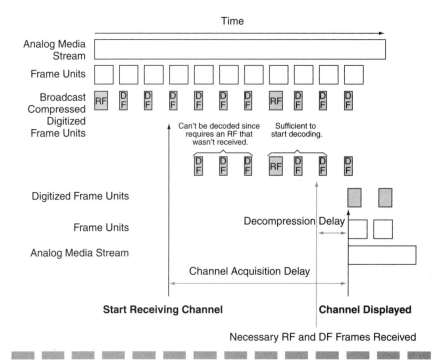

Figure A-2

A summary of the various elements of video compression that introduce a delay between receiving a channel and when it can be displayed.

middle of a frame unit. It must wait until the necessary RF and DF frames have been received before it can decode the frames and display the original analog media stream. This is the *channel acquisition delay* that occurs whenever acquisition and decoding of a new channel is initiated, such as during a channel change. Another time interval, the *decompress delay*, occurs between when the necessary RF and DF frames have been received and when they are decompressed and converted back into uncompressed digital frame units. The combined delays can result in a time interval of several frame time units, as illustrated in Figure A-2.

Transport Delays

The transport of compressed video data within IP packets requires the use of various encapsulation protocols such as MPEG-2, RTP, IP, and networking frames. These protocol layers introduce delay in channel changing because at the receiving STB the video data must be extracted from the various transport protocols.

The MPEG-2 transport stream protocol, for example, encapsulates the various audio and video components that make up a digital program into 188-byte transport stream packets. The protocol also introduces system information (SI) and other packets that must be examined in order to extract the media components. When switching to a new program, the digital decoder looks up the elements that are required from the SI. It then instructs the transport stream demultiplex layer to locate and remove those elements from the multiprogram transport stream.

IP transport of real-time data introduces Real-Time Protocol (RTP) encapsulation, on top of the standard IP/User Datagram Protocol (UDP) encapsulation of IP packets. Each encapsulation introduces its own packet header information. These must be read and removed to re-create the underlying bitstream. Also, the packet-based underpinning of IP networks will introduce jitter in the arrival time of packets. The buffers used to overcome jitter must fill before they are delivered to the transport demultiplex component, introducing another delay.

Figure A-3 illustrates how digital video delivered over Ethernet is encapsulated in multiple transport protocols. Most unwrapping from these protocols is done very quickly in specialized hardware within the STB, but ultimately some delay occurs as the media data is unpacked.

Figure A-3
Transporting compressed audio and video data over Ethernet/IP requires encapsulation of the data within several different protocols.

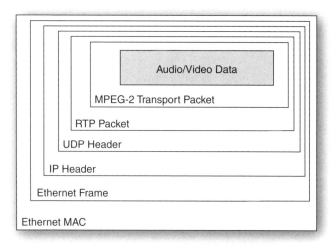

Encryption

The conditional access system of the IPTV service will encrypt the content before it is delivered over the network. When the encrypted service is received at the STB, it must be decrypted before it can be decoded for display. Decryption of the content involves extracting keys from the conditional access system and performing the decryption algorithm on the content data. While most STB devices have dedicated integrated circuits for rapid decryption, it can still lead to some additional delays in the channel changing process.

Network Delays

In any switched video network, requests to change channels must be propagated upstream from the subscriber's home into the access network. The channel change is managed by a server (or other device) outside the subscriber's home. This communication introduces more delay than conventional channel change requests that take place only within the television or STB. Because the requested channel on a switched network typically is not already being delivered to the subscriber, the access network must arrange for the program to be sent down the access network to the particular subscriber's home. In some cases, a system may be designed to preemptively send adjacent channels on the assumption that channel changes are typically up or down a single channel in the lineup. This may speed things up for adjacent channel changes.

For IPTV over DSL, almost every channel change will need to propagate into the access network because of the bandwidth restrictions of DSL. The switched model used in IPTV systems will most likely be based on the IP multicast protocol as well. This requires multicast group join requests to propagate upstream into the network to multicast routers. For premium video services on a switched network, a channel change request might have to travel farther up the network for authorization. This could add more delay.

A delay between the output of the STB and the TV display could also occur, as the TV takes time to synchronize with the STB output signal. This could add around 100 ms to the delay. Finally, an inherent delay is experienced in the use of any remote control. IR codes are usually received and decoded in no less than 10 ms. However, these two factors would occur in any TV system (analog or digital) and are minimal.

The causes of delay in changing a digital channel for a switched broadcast system are summarized in Table A-1.

Table A-1 Causes for Delay in Channel Change for a Switched Broadcast System

Layer	Cause	Delay	Notes	Mitigation
Network	Authorization	100–1500 ms	Requests on a switched network may need to propagate to an authorization server deeper in the network.	Integrate authorization into the client.
	Switched channel request	100–500 ms	Round-trip time for channel request to reach multicast network equipment and initiate new stream. Applies to switched and IP delivery systems, but not MPEG/QAM broadcast.	Increase network bandwidth. Pre-send a low-bandwidth version of the channel first in anticipation of the channel change.
	Total network	**200–2000 ms**		
Transport	Remote control	10 ms	IR protocol and key debounce.	None.
	Transport buffering	33–50 ms	Any jitter in the transport layer will require buffering. IP packets may also arrive out of order.	QoS or extra bandwidth.
	Total transport	**53–70 ms**		
Compression	Reference frame arrival	0–500 ms	Receiver must wait for a reference frame (I-frame) to be received.	More frequent I-frames, which requires more bandwidth.
	Decode buffer	25–500 ms	At least one frame must be received and buffered before decode can begin. A 100 Kbit frame at 4 Mbps takes 25 ms to receive (this is a lower bound in the delay).	Increase network bandwidth.
	Decode	~1–10 ms	Creation of the video frame from compressed data.	Faster decoder circuits.
	Frame buffer	35 ms	Encoding the digital picture into an NTSC (analog) or DVI (digital) signal for transport to television.	Digital connections between the STB and TV.
	Synchronization	~1 ms	Audio and video data arrive at different times requiring buffering. Both must arrive and be decoded before display.	None.
	Total compression	**60–1050 ms**		
	Total delay	**315–3500 ms**		

Mitigation

Operators that roll out IPTV services with long channel change delays need to dissuade users from channel surfing. Alternatively, the STB may need to "distract" the user during the waiting period. One way to accomplish this is to use the electronic program guide (EPG) to post information on the channel that has been tuned to. The user will read that information and therefore be distracted from the fact that the video has not yet appeared. Because the EPG information is local to the STB, it is immediately available and can be displayed while the user waits for the images. Ultimately, IPTV may be a significantly different viewing experience, with most content on demand, so users will not channel surf anyway.

Some IPTV vendors are developing ways to deliver reference frames of the compressed bitstream very quickly when a channel change is requested. This would reduce the delay associated with waiting for reference frames to arrive in the stream. When the subscriber changes the channel, a message is sent upstream requesting reference frames immediately. At the same time, the regular bitstream begins to be streamed to the STB. The STB receives the reference frames and some of the dependent frames quickly and can start decoding faster.

Another approach is to continuously broadcast a low-bandwidth version of channels. Upon a channel change, the STB can immediately decode the low-bandwidth version while it is waiting for the full bandwidth version to arrive. While the consumer might notice the change in image quality as the STB switches from the low-bandwidth to the full bandwidth version, it may be more acceptable than simply waiting and seeing nothing.

Delivering reference frames on request, or continuously broadcasting low-bandwidth versions of channels, requires additional bandwidth from the network, and expensive high-speed servers may be required in the network to handle many requests during peak viewing times. An IPTV service provider needs to look at the feasibility of scaling such a system during peak usage.

IPTV
Company
References
and
Information
Sources

Content Aggregators

3Vision—http://www.3vision.tv

Akimbo Systems Inc.—http://www.akimbo.com

Backspace Communications—http://www.backspace.tv

Brightcove—http://www.brightcove.com

CinemaNow—http://www.cinemanow.com

Comcast Media Center—http://comcastmediacenter.com

GlobeCast—http://www.globecast.com

Gotuit Media—http://www.gotuit.com

iN DEMAND Networks—http://www.indemand.com

Movielink—http://www.movielink.com

National Cable Television Cooperative (NCTC)—
http://www.cabletvcoop.com

Starz Entertainment Group—http://www.starz.com

TiVo—http://www.tivo.com

TVN Entertainment—http://www.tvn.com

VBrick Systems—http://www.vbrick.com

Content Creation Tools

Adobe—http://www.adobe.com

Apple Computer—http://www.apple.com

Avid—http://www.avid.com

Desk Share—http://www.deskshare.com

Pinnacle—http://www.pinnaclesys.com

Digital Rights Management and Conditional Access System

Conax—http://www.conax.com

Irdeto—http://www.irdeto.com

Latens—http://www.latens.com

Microsoft—http://microsoft.com

Motorola—http://www.motorola.com

Nagra—http://www.nagravision.com

NDS—http://www.nds.com

Scientific Atlanta—http://www.sciatl.com

Secure Media—http://www.securemedia.com

Verimatrix—http://www.verimatrix.com

Viaccess—http://www.viaccess.com

Widevine Technologies—http://www.widevine.com

Headend and Networking Equipment Manufacturers

Alcatel—http://www.alcatel.com

Bigband Networks—http://www.bigbandnet.com

Calix—http://www.calix.com

C-COR—http://www.c-cor.com

Cicso—http://www.cisco.com

Entone—http://www.entone.com

Envivio—http://www.envivio.com

Harmonic—http:/www.harmonicinc.com

Lucent—http://www.lucent.com

Minerva Networks—http://www.minervanetworks.com

Modulus Video—http://www.modulusvideo.com

Motorola—http://broadband.motorola.com

Occam Networks—http://www.occamnetworks.com

Optibase—http://www.optibase.com

Pannaway—http://www.pannaway.com

RGB Networks—http://www.rgbmedia.net

Scientific Atlanta—http://www.sciatl.com

Siemens—http://www.siemens.com

Skystream Networks—http://www.skystream.com

Tandberg Television—http://www.tandberg.net

Thomson/Grass Valley Group—http://www.grassvalley.com

Tut Systems—http://tutsystems.com

Zhone Technologies—http://www.zhone.com

IPTV Set-Top Box Manufacturers

2Wire—http://www.2wire.com

Advanced Digital Broadcast (ADB)—http://adbglobal.com

Amino Communications—http://www.aminocom.com

Entone—http://www.entone.com

Helius—http://www.helius.com

Humax—http://www.humaxdigital.com/global

I3 Micro Technology—http://www.i3micro.com

Kreatel—http://www.kreatel.com

LG Electronics—http://www.lge.com

Motorola—http://www.motorola.com

Pace Micro Technology—http://www.pacemicro.com

Sagem—http://www.sagem.com

Samsung—http://www.samsung.com

Scientific Atlanta—http://www.sciatl.com

Siemens—http://www.siemens.com

Tatungtel Telecom—http://www.tatungtel.com

Thomson—http://www.thomson.net

TiVo—http://www.tivo.com

IPTV STB IC Manufacturers

ATI—http://www.ati.com

Broadcom—http://www.broadcom.com

BroadLogic—http://www.broadlogic.com

Intel—http://www.intel.com

LSI Logic—http://www.lsilogic.com

Philips—http://www.semiconductors.philips.com

Sigma Designs—http://www.sigmadesigns.com

ST Microelectronics—http://www.st.com/stonline

Texas Instruments—http://www.ti.com

Zoran—http://www.zoran.com

Media Servers

Allegro—http://www.allegrosoft.com/ams.html

Apple Computer—http://www.apple.com

Axis Communications—http://www.axis.com

BitBand—http://www.bitband.com

Broadbus Technologies—http://www.broadbus.com

C-COR—www.c-cor.com

Cisco—http://www.cisco.com

Concurrent—http://ccur.com

Dell—http://www.dell.com

Dylogic—http://www.dylogic.com

HP—http://www.hp.com/

Kasenna—http://www.kasenna.com

Keene Software Corporation—http://www.keenesoftware.com

Microsoft—http://www.microsoft.com

Real—http://www.realnetworks.com

SeaChange International—http://www.seachange.com

Sun—http://www.sun.com

Unreal Streaming Technologies—http://www.umediaserver.net

Vital Stream—http://www.vitalstream.com

Media Software

Apple—http://www.apple.com

Macromedia—http://www.adobe.com

Media Excel—http://www.mediaexcel.com

Microsoft—http://www.microsoft.com

Real—http://www.real.com

Tut Systems—http://tutsystems.com

Middleware

Alcatel—http://www.alcatel.com

Alticast—http://alticast.com

Ant Limited—http://www.antplc.com/index.htm

Aptiv Digital—http://www.aptivdigital.com

Broadstream—http://www.broadstream.com

Microsoft—http://microsoft.com

Minerva Networks—http://www.minervanetworks.com

Myrio—http://www.myrio.com

OpenTV—http://www.opentv.com

Opera—http://www.opera.com

Orca Interactive—http://www.orcainteractive.com

Osmosys—http://www.osmosys.tv

Thomson/Thales Broadcast & Multimedia
http://www.thales-bm.com

Tut Systems—http://tutsystems.com

Vidiom Systems—http://www.vidiom.com

Network Operators

Aliant—http://www.aliant.com

AT&T—http://att.sbc.com

Belgacom—http://www.belgacom.com

Bell Canada—http://www.bell.ca

Bell ExpressVu—http://www.bell.ca/satellite

BellSouth—http://www.bellsouth.com

British Telecom—http://www.bt.com

Cablevision—http://www.cablevision.com

Charter Communications—http://www.chartercom.com

Chunghwa Telecom—http://www.cht.com.tw

Comcast—http://www.comcast.com

Cox Communications—http://www.cox.com

DirecTV—http://www.directv.com

Dish Network—http://www.dishnetwork.com

France Telecom—http://www.francetelecom.com

Free (Iliad)—http://www.free.fr

Insight Communications—http://www.insight-com.com

Neuf Cegetel Group—http://www.groupeneufcegetel.fr

Reliance Infocomm—http://www.relianceinfo.com

Ringgold Telephone—http://www.rtctel.com

Rogers Cable—http://www.rogers.com

Sasktel—http://www.sasktel.com

Shaw Communications—http://www.shaw.ca

Sky—http://www.sky.com

Surewest—http://www.surewest.com

Swisscom—http://www.swisscom.ch

T-Online—http://www.t-online.com

Telecom Italia—http://www.telecomitalia.com

Telefonica—http://www.telefonica.com

Telenor—http://www.telenor.com

Telus—http://www.telus.com

Time Warner Cable—http://www.timewarnercable.com

Verizon—http://www.verizon.com

Links to Standards Organizations

ANSI—http://www.ansi.org

ATIS—http://www.atis.org

ATSC—http://www.atsc.org

CableLabs—http://www.cablelabs.com

CEA—http://www.ce.org

DLNA—http://www.dlna.org/home

DSL Forum—http://www.dslforum.org/index.shtml

DVB—http://www.dvb.org

ETSI—http://www.etsi.org

IAB—http://www.iab.org

IETF—http://www.ietf.org

IRTF—http://www.irtf.org

ISMA—http://www.isma.tv

ISO—http://www.iso.org

ISOC—http://www.isoc.org

ITU—http://www.itu.int

MPEG—http://www.chiariglione.org/mpeg

RFCs (IETF)—http://www.ietf.org/rfc

RFC Editor—http://www.rfc-editor.org

TV Anytime Forum—http://www.tv-anytime.org

UPnP—http://www.upnp.org

World Wide Web Consortium—http://www.w3.org

Links to Additional Internet-Related Sites

American National Standards Institute (ANSI)—
  http://www.ansi.org

Internet Assigned Numbers Authority (IANA)—
  http://www.iana.org

InterNIC (Internet domain name registration services)—
  http://www.internic.net

US Domain Name Service (NIC)—http://www.nic.us

Glossary

10/100Base-T

10 or 100 Mbps Ethernet over twisted-pair cabling (e.g., CAT5).

1080i

A video mode for high definition TV with 1080 lines of interlaced video, an overall resolution of 1920×1080 pixels, and an aspect ratio of 16:9.

1080p

A video mode for high definition TV with 1080 lines of progressive video, an overall resolution of 1920×1080 pixels, and an aspect ratio of 16:9.

16:9

Aspect ratio of 16 (horizontal) by 9 (vertical) or 1.78:1; also considered widescreen television.

4:3

Aspect ratio of 4 (horizontal) by 3 (vertical), or 1.33:1.

480i

A video mode for standard definition TV, with 480 lines of interlaced video, an overall resolution of 720×480 pixels, and an aspect ratio of 4:3.

480p

A video mode that has 480 lines of progressive video, an overall resolution of 720×480 pixels, and an aspect ratio of 4:3.

4Cs

A group of four companies (Intel, IBM, MEI, and Toshiba) that have developed content protection technology (e.g., CPRM/CPPM).

5Cs

A group of five companies (Hitachi, Intel, MEI, Toshiba, and Sony) that have developed content protection technology (e.g., DTCP).

720p

A video mode for high definition TV, with 720 lines of progressive video, an overall resolution of 1280×720 pixels, and an aspect ratio of 16:9.

A

AAC

Advanced Audio Coding is an audio encoding format (MPEG-2 part 7) designed to be an improved format over MP3.

AC-3

A lossy audio codec developed (and marketed) by Dolby Laboratories that is now called Dolby Digital. This audio codec provides up to six channels of audio sound: front left, front right, center, rear left, rear right, and subwoofer.

ADSL

Asymmetric Digital Subscriber Line is a data communications technology designed to provide fast data transfer speeds (e.g., broadband) over telephone twisted-pair copper lines.

advanced compression

Refers to video compression formats (e.g., MPEG-4 AVC and VC-1) that provide similar video quality to the MPEG-2 compression format with a significantly less amount of required bandwidth.

AES

Audio Engineering Society (http://www.aes.org) is a professional group organized to advance audio technologies.

ANSI

American National Standards Institute (http://www.ansi.org) is a nonprofit organization that coordinates the development (and use) of industry standards or specifications within the United States.

API

Application Programming Interface is a software interface between two (or more) software modules that helps them exchange information.

application layer

The application layer is layer 7 in the OSI reference model and is where data is managed and manipulated to perform network tasks or services. See Chapter 3 for more details.

ARP

Address Resolution Protocol is used in translating the hardware address (e.g., MAC address) of a computer from its IP address.

ARPU

Average revenue per user is a metric used in subscriber-based service businesses such as cable television.

ASIC

Application specific integrated circuit is an IC or an electronic chip that was customized (usually to reduce cost) for a special purpose or application and not a general-purpose IC.

aspect ratio

A display monitor's width divided by the height. For example, a standard television aspect ratio is 4:3 (or 1.33:1), and a high definition television aspect ratio is 16:9 (or 1.78:1).

ATIS

Alliance for Telecommunications Industry Solutions (www.atis.org) works on standards for the communications and related information technologies industry worldwide. See Chapter 7 for more details.

ATM

Asynchronous Transfer Mode is a high bandwidth, switching and transmission system integrating multiple data types (voice, video, and data). ATM uses a fixed-size packet called a *cell*, which is 53 bytes long with 48 bytes of payload.

ATSC

The Advanced Television Systems Committee (http://www.atsc.org) is an international, non-profit membership organization developing voluntary standards for advanced television systems.

A/V

Audio and video.

AVC

Advanced Video Coding is a digital video codec that is commonly considered one of the advanced compression formats. It was developed jointly by the ITU-T Video Coding Experts Group and the ISO/IEC MPEG (Moving Pictures Expert Group). Because of this joint development, the codec is also referred to as JVT (Joint Development Team), as well as H.264, MPEG-4 part 10.

 B

B-frame
Also known as a bidirectional frame; part of the MPEG compression algorithm. B-frames are created from parts of I- or P-frames that occurred earlier in the sequence or will occur in the future.

baby bells
See RBOC.

bandwidth
A range within a frequency spectrum (in units of cycles per second); or a range for digital systems to data rates (in units of bits per second).

bit
A single digit (base 2 numeric system) used in computers or digital systems.

bitmap
A two-dimensional array of pixels elements that form a digital image (e.g., 640×480).

bitrate
The number of bits transmitted or processed over time. For example, *bps transferred* refers to the number of bits per second that are transferred from one point to another.

bits per pixel (bpp)
The number of bits used to represent a pixel's color and/or brightness in a graphics (bitmap) or video (frame) image. Also referred to as *color depth*. Common color depths are 8 bpp, 16 bpp, and 32 bpp.

bitstream

A series of bits that represent data that is intended to be processed over time. Examples of bitstreams would include encoded digital movies and EPG (electronic program guide) data.

BitTorrent

A file sharing protocol widely used in peer-to-peer (P2P) networks and applications.

broadband

A data service with data rates exceeding traditional telephone (e.g., POTS) data service. The two dominant broadband service providers are cable operators and telephone operators.

broadcast flag

A proposed bit that was to be embedded into broadcast digital television bitstreams indicating that the content was not to be copied or output without copy protection management measures in place.

bridge device

A network bridge that connects multiple network segments together. The bridging function takes place at the data link layer within the OSI model.

byte

A commonly used storage element in computers or digital systems. Eight bits form one byte.

 C

CA

The Certificate Authority signs and maintains digital certificates to support a public key infrastructure.

CableCARD

A separable security module used to decrypt premium cable programming. The CableCARD is inserted into a DTV or STB.

CableLabs

A non-profit research and development consortium dedicated to enhancing the cable companies' ability to distribute services over cable networks.

cable modem

A broadband device designed to connect to the Internet via a cable service. It interfaces to a Cable Modem Termination System (CMTS) via RF carriers.

CAS

A Conditional Access System protects digital media by encrypting it and allowing only authorized users to view it. See Chapter 6 for more details.

CAT5

A Category 5 standard cable is an unshielded twisted-pair cable type commonly used for Ethernet distribution.

CATV

Community Access Television, commonly referred to as Cable TV, refers to video programming transmitted via RF signals to receivers.

CBR

Constant bitrate is a form of video encoding where the number of bits per second is constant over time regardless of the content being encoded. Refer to Chapter 4 for more details.

CCI

Copy control information, used by DTCP and CableCARDs to convey rights to make copies and other information associated with protected digital content.

CCIR

Comite Consultatif International en Radiodiffusion is an international committee focused on radio technology, which eventually merged with other organizations forming the ITU (International Telecommunication Union).

CCIR 601

A CCIR standard for encoding interlaced analog video into a digital format. It includes support for NTSC (525 lines) and PAL (625 lines) systems with 720 pixels per line. This standard has been renamed ITU-R BT.601.

CCIR 656

CCIR 656 (also known as ITU656 and BT.656) standard defines a process for transferring uncompressed standard definition digital video (NTSC or PAL).

CCITT

Consultative Committee on International Telegraphy and Telephony, now known as the ITU-T.

CE

Consumer electronics devices such as televisions, DVD players, and set-top boxes.

CEA

The Consumer Electronics Association (www.ce.org) is an organization supporting the consumer electronics industry in the United States.

CEMA

The Consumer Electronics Manufacturing Association (www.cema.org) is now known as the CEA.

CF

Compact Flash is a non-volatile (flash) memory device packaged in a removable enclosure. CF is popular in portable devices (i.e., digital cameras) that easily interface with computers. CF has also been deployed in high-end set-top boxes.

CGMS-A

The Copy Generation Management System is used to prevent recording by VCRs of analog outputs from an STB.

channel

A channel of programming containing audio and video; a slot of frequency within an RF spectrum. In a digital broadcast system (e.g., digital cable), multiple programming channels can fit into one frequency channel.

chrominance
Chrominance and luminance are the components within a video signal (e.g., television). Chrominance defines the color within the video.

CIF
Common Intermediate Format standardizes the number of pixels in a picture or video frame: NTSC = 352×240, PAL = 352×288.

cipher
The process of applying an encryption or decryption algorithm used in protecting digital data.

ciphertext
The resulting data after being encrypted by a cipher.

cleartext
Also known as plaintext; the data without encryption being applied, commonly known as "in the clear" data.

CLEC
A Competitive Local Exchange Carrier is a telephone company that was created after the breakup of AT&T. CLECs compete with ILECs for consumers' phone business.

CM
See cable modem.

CMTS
A Cable Modem Termination System is a piece of equipment located in a cable plant headend. A CMTS provides broadband service to cable customers by handling IP packets over a cable network.

CODEC
Coder/decoder. A codec can be implemented in hardware or software and can encode or decode media (audio and video) according to a particular algorithm. Typically refers to media compression algorithms such as MPEG.

composite video

An analog video signal consisting of the three video components: Y (luminance), and UV (two orthogonal phases of a color carrier called chrominance).

content aggregators

Content aggregators securely distribute content (e.g., movies, network programming, etc.) safely and securely to consumers.

content owners

The companies that create or own rights to content. Examples include movie studios (e.g., Disney, Warner Brothers, Universal Studios, etc.), cable channels (e.g., ESPN, CNN, etc.), and network broadcasters (e.g., CBS, NBC, ABC, FOX, etc.).

CPPM

Content Protection for Prerecorded Media was developed by the 4C and provides copy protection of content destined for prerecorded media.

CPRM

Content Protection for Recordable Media was developed by the 4C and provides copy protection of content destined for recordable media.

CPTWG

The Copy Protection Technical Working Group (http://www.cptwg.org) is an industry panel that recommends copy protection techniques.

CRL

The Certificate Revocation List is a list of devices that have had their digital certificates revoked by a certificate authority, indicating they may no longer be trusted to keep content secure.

CRT

Cathode ray tube is a type of display device used in televisions and computer monitors.

CSS

Content scrambling system is used in DVDs, which requires descrambling within the player.

D

DASE

DTV Application Software Environment is an ATSC standard that defines a software layer that enables application development for common ATSC receivers.

datagram

Internet Protocol (IP) defines the transmission of blocks of data between a source and destination. These blocks of data are called datagrams.

DAVIC

Digital Audio Visual Industry Council (http://www.davic.org) is a global organization focused on end-to-end interoperability of broadcast interactive digital information and multimedia communication.

DBS

Direct broadcasting satellite is satellite broadcasting of video directly into consumers' homes.

DCAS

Downloadable Conditional Access System is a CAS that can be modified or renewed via a software download.

DCCP

Datagram Congestion Control Protocol (RFC 4340) is a message-oriented transport layer protocol that enables the discovery of available network capacity on a particular network path.

DCT

The discrete cosine transform is a mathematical transformation operation that is used in the MPEG compression algorithms, both MPEG-1 and MPEG-2, as well as the JPEG image compression algorithm. DCT converts the values of an 8×8 square of pixels into 64 other numbers representing the spatial frequency components of the square.

DDR–SDRAM

Double Data Rate–Synchronous Dynamic Random Access Memory is a type of memory (ICs) that provides faster data rates than conventional SDRAM memory by utilizing both edges of the clock.

decryption

The process of taking encrypted data (i.e., ciphertext) and applying the inverse function of encryption to it. The result of decryption is data that is unencrypted or "in the clear."

demux

The process of selecting a specific bitstream with various elements and routing that data to its desired destinations (e.g., audio and video decoders).

DES

The Data Encryption Standard is a cipher widely used in encrypting and decrypting data. The algorithm uses a relatively short key length (56 bits) and is considered less secure than newer encryption technologies.

DHCP

The Dynamic Host Configuration Protocol (RFC 2131) provides a framework for passing configuration information to hosts on a TCP/IP network.

diffserv

Differentiated services is an approach in providing quality of service within an IP-based network. Refer to Chapter 3 for more details on diffserv.

digital encoder

Takes analog audio and video input and digitally compresses it into a digital bitstream.

DLNA

Digital Living Network Alliance (http://www.dlna.org/home) is a global organization focused on delivering an interoperability set of design guidelines. Refer to Chapter 7 for more details.

DMIF

Delivery Multimedia Integration Framework.

DNS

Domain Name System (RFC 1034 and RFC 1035) provides the translation of domain names (or a computer's host name) to an actual IP address of a host server. DNS is a worldwide keyword redirection service residing on DNS servers. These servers enable someone to type in the name of a desired web site (e.g., www.ietf.org) and the DNS server will translate that request into an actual IP address.

DOCSIS

Data Over Cable Service Interface Specification is a cable modem standard developed by CableLabs that provides high-speed data or broadband services over existing cable networks. CableLabs has released DOCSIS versions 1.0, 1.1, and 2.0. DOCSIS 3.0 is currently being developed.

Dolby

Dolby Laboratories, Inc., specializes in digital audio compression algorithms and codecs. Other Dolby products include AC-3 or Dolby Digital, Dolby Prologic, and Dolby Digital Plus.

down-mix

Down-mixing occurs when a true surround-sound audio format (e.g., 5.1 channels) is down-mixed to two (stereo) channels left and right.

driver

A low level software driver accesses hardware and provides an interface (API) to higher level software to enable control of the hardware.

DRM

A digital rights management system makes it possible for a content aggregator or a distributor to deliver digital content to subscribers while protecting the rights of the content owners. DRM systems employ various digital encryption technologies to ensure the content is protected while enabling subscribers to view and enjoy content but not allow unauthorized copies.

DSL

Digital subscriber line is a series of technologies enabling telephone companies to distribute broadband data over existing twisted-pair telephone lines.

DSL Forum

A worldwide consortium (http://www.dslforum.org) dedicated to enhancing the telephone companies' ability to distribute services over telephone networks with DSL technology.

DSP

A digital signal processor is a specialized microprocessor designed to implement digital signal processing algorithms in real-time.

DSS

Digital satellite system is a broadcast satellite television service (i.e., DirecTV, Dish) that delivers an all-digital broadcast service to consumers' homes.

DTCP

The Digital Transmission Content Protection system is used to encrypt digital content across digital connections such as Firewire.

DTH

Direct to home refers to satellite broadcast of video directly into consumer homes.

DTLA

The Digital Transmission Licensing Administrator is the licensing authority for DTCP.

DTS

Digital Theater Systems, by DTS, Inc., is an advanced multichannel digital audio format that competes with Dolby Digital.

DTV

Digital television is a system that encodes analog audio and video into one of the compressed digital formats (MPEG-2, AVC, and VC-1) and broadcasts it to consumers' homes.

DVB

Digital Video Broadcasting is a European standards body that has developed a series of specifications targeting digital broadcasting.

DVB-IPI

A DVB specification that describes how DVB-formatted audio and video services are delivered over IP networks.

DVB-S

DVB-Satellite—DVB services delivered via satellite.

DVB SD&S

DVB Service Discovery and Selection is the mechanism that provides information about services and how they can be accessed over DVB-IP networks.

DVB-STP

DVB SD&S Transport Protocol is used to transport the DVB SD&S records.

DVB-T

DVB-Terrestrial—DVB services delivered over the air, or terrestrial broadcast.

DVD

Digital video disc or digital versatile disc.

DVR

A digital video recorder is a set-top box that has an embedded hard disk drive for storing and playing back recorded content. DVRs are a modern, digital version of the VCR.

 E

ECM

Entitlement Control Messages are delivered by the CAS/DRM system (typically in-band) to communicate key information to client devices.

ECMA

European Computer Manufacturers Association (http://www.ecma-international.org).

EEPROM

An electrically erasable programmable read-only memory device is a non-volatile memory device used in computers and set-top boxes to store information that does not get erased if the power is removed.

EFF

Electronic Frontier Foundation (http://www.eff.org), a non-profit consumer advocacy group for free-speech rights in the digital realm.

EMM

Entitlement Management Messages are delivered by a CAS/DRM system (typically out of band) to deliver entitlement information to client devices.

encoder

A media encoder (MPEG-2, AVC or VC-1) takes analog video in, digitizes it, and compresses it, outputting a digital bitstream that when played back represents the original analog video.

EPG

An electronic program guide is an onscreen listing of programming on a broadcast television service. Information displayed from an EPG includes channel number, broadcast channel name, event names, event start and stop times, event descriptions, and event ratings.

EPON

Ethernet passive optical networks are an access network technology that provides a method of deploying optical fiber lines between a carrier's network and a consumer's home. Passive technology does not require power to modify the signals.

error correction

Plays a prominent role in digital broadcast services. Detects errors in the incoming data due to the transmission of the content to the consumer's home, and attempts to recover the original data and therefore avoid a loss of audio or video packets.

ES

An elementary stream is a single digitally encoded audio or video track.

Ethernet

Ethernet (IEEE 802.3 standard) is widely used today in networking computers and other networked devices together. Today, Ethernet is commonly used with CAT5 cabling and allows for 10/100 Mbps speeds.

EULA

End User License Agreement.

 F

FDDI

Fiber Distributed Data Interface is a fiber-optic interface standard that provides high-speed data transfers while servicing thousands of users. The FDDI protocol is based on the token ring protocol. A FDDI network contains two token rings: a primary and a backup; each ring can support up to 100 Mbps.

FEC

Forward Error Correction is an error correction technique that enables a digital receiver to correct errors as the data is received without having to wait for any other data.

FFT

Fast Fourier Transform is an efficient algorithm in computing the discrete Fourier transform that is heavily used in digital signal processing, including multimedia encoding and decoding. See also DCT.

filter

Implemented in both hardware and software and removes unwanted components within signals.

Firewire

Also known as IEEE 1394, this serial bus interface standard was designed to transfer data at a high speed between computers and consumer electronics devices. Firewire also has an isochronous channel for transferring real-time data such as audio and video.

flash memory

A non-volatile memory device commonly used in computers and set-top boxes that provides a relatively convenient method to store and erase data electrically.

FPA

A front panel assembly consists of the plastic faceplate with buttons and indicators on a set-top box. Some FPAs include electronics while others are passive.

frame

A single complete image. A series of frames constitute a video sequence or a piece of video.

frame relay

A technique used in computer networking that transfers frames of data along various paths to its destination in the most efficient manner.

FTP

File Transfer Protocol (RFC 0959) is the commonly used protocol in transferring files between computers over a network.

FTTC

Fiber-to-the-curb occurs when a network operator lays high-speed fiber-optic cable to a location (e.g., neighborhood) that can service multiple customers with voice, broadband data, and video services. The fiber then gets transitioned to another access technology for entry into consumer homes (e.g., twisted pair or coax cable).

FTTH

Fiber-to-the-home (also known as fiber to the premises) is high-speed fiber-optic cable laid directly to a consumer's home by a network operator for the purpose of offering voice, broadband data, and video services.

FTTP

Fiber-to-the-premises. See FTTH.

G

gateway

A consumer electronics device residing in the home. It is a network node that connects to other networks and can provide network bridging, routing, and protocol support. An example of a gateway would be a DSL gateway in the home that would include a broadband DSL modem to connect to the service provider's network and various networking interfaces for connecting network devices to the home network (e.g., Ethernet ports, WiFi).

Gbps

Giga bits per second, or billions (10^9) of bits per second.

Gigabyte (GB)

One gigabyte (GB) equals 1,073,741,824 bytes, or 2^{30} bytes.

GigE

Gigabit Ethernet is an Ethernet technology (IEEE 802.3-2002) that enables transferring data at a rate of 1 Gbps.

GOP

Group of pictures—When video is digitally compressed (i.e., MPEG encoded), the input video sequence is partitioned into GOPs, where each GOP consists of an arrangement of an I-frame, P-frames, and B-frames.

GPON

A gigabit passive optical network is a fiber-optic network architecture that provides a very high-bandwidth network connection to the home.

GUI

A graphical user interface is a software application running on a digital set-top box that renders graphics to the television that are intended for a consumer to use while managing and controlling it.

guide

An onscreen user interface application showing the available programming along with additional information. See EPG.

H

H.264

Another name for AVC, MPEG-4 part 10, and JVT. H.264; an advanced compression technique.

HANA

The High-definition Audio-video Network Alliance (http://www. hanaalliance.org) is an industry collaboration that ensures interoperability of digital media devices connected across a home network.

HAVi

Home Audio Video interoperability (http://www.havi.org) is an open standard that allows digital consumer electronics and home appliances to communicate and interoperate with each other over Firewire (IEEE 1394).

HDCP

The High-bandwidth Digital Copy Protection system is used to encrypt uncompressed content across the DVI and HDMI display interfaces.

HDD

A hard disk drive is a relatively large, nonvolatile storage device that stores data on rotating, magnetic platters.

HDMI

The High Definition Multimedia Interface is a consumer electronics–friendly version of the DVI digital display interface.

HDTV

High definition television provides a greater viewing resolution over that of standard definition television (SDTV). HDTV supports up to 1080 horizontal lines of 1920 pixels.

HPNA

Home Phoneline Networking Alliance (http://www.homepna.org), also known as Home PNA, is a digital home networking technology over traditional telephone lines found in consumers' homes.

HTML

HyperText Markup Language is a standard used to create web pages that is rendered by client devices (e.g., home computers or set-top boxes). HTML 4.01 was published in December 1999 as a W3C recommendation.

HTTP

The HyperText Transfer Protocol (version 1.1) is used to transfer data over the World Wide Web (WWW) as defined in RFC 2616.

HTTPS

HyperText Transfer Protocol over SSL combines HTTP with SSL (Secure Sockets Layer) encryption or TLS (Transport Layer Security).

 I

IC

An integrated circuit is an electronic circuit packaged and manufactured in a semiconductor material such as silicon.

IDCT

The Inverse Discrete Cosine Transform (similar to DCT) is a mathematical transformation operation that is used in multimedia compression algorithms.

IEC

The International Electrotechnical Commission (part of the ISO) (http://www.iec.ch) is an international standards body working on specifications for electrical and electronic related technologies.

IEEE

The Institute of Electrical and Electronics Engineers (http://www.ieee.org) is an international, non-profit organization dedicated to the advancement of technology.

IEEE 1394

See Firewire.

I-frame

Also known as I Picture or Intra frame, an MPEG encoded independently from other frames whose resulting series of bits can be used to
re-create the frame in its entirety. I-frames serve as anchor points in
the bitstream. The other two types of frames are Predictive (P-frames)
and Bidirectional (B-frames).

IGMP

The Internet Group Management Protocol (RFC 3376) is used for IP
multicasting within an IP network. See Chapter 3 for more details.

ILEC

An Incumbent Local Exchange Carrier is one of the "baby Bell" telephone companies that at one time was part of AT&T. They compete
with CLECs.

interlace scan

An interlace scan occurs when a single frame of video is created by
drawing the even horizontal lines first, then the odd lines, in rapid suc-
cession. The set of odd and even lines are also odd and even fields.

Interrupt Service Routine (ISR)

A low level software module that gets executed when triggered by an
event or interrupt. ISRs are often triggered by hardware signals but
software can also create interrupts.

intserv

Integrated services is an approach in providing quality of service
within an IP-based network. Refer to Chapter 3 for more details.

IP

Internet Protocol is the networking protocol used by computers on the
Internet. See Chapter 3 for more details.

IPv4

Internet Protocol version 4 (RFC 791) was the first widely used version
of IP on the Internet.

IPv6

Internet Protocol version 6 (RFC 2460) is the next version of IP and provides more addresses for networked devices.

IPG

Interactive program guide. See electronic program guide (EPG).

IP-STB

An Internet Protocol set-top box is a digital receiver or decoder that receives multimedia content over IP-based networks.

IPTV

Internet Protocol television is a digital television service transmitted over an IP network.

ISDN

An Integrated Service Digital Network is a switched digital telephone network that supports voice, data, and video services.

ISMA

The Internet Streaming Media Alliance (http://www.isma.tv) is a standards body focused on streaming rich media content (e.g., audio and video) over Internet protocols.

ISO

The International Organization for Standardization (http://www.iso.org) is the world's largest developer of standards.

ITU

The International Telecommunication Union (http://www.itu.org) is an international organization within the United Nations System that coordinates global telecom networks and services.

J

Java

A technology developed by Sun Microsystems that enables software to be independent of hardware architectures. Java is used in MHP and OCAP middleware.

jitter

As it relates to network traffic is the variation in arrival times of successive data packets.

JPEG

Joint Photographic Experts Group (http://www.jpeg.org) is a lossy compression format used for digital images; most digital cameras store photos in the JPEG format.

JVT

Joint video team. See AVC.

 K

KB

Kilobytes, one kilobyte equals 1024 bytes, or 2^{10} bytes.

Kbps

Kilobits per second, or thousands (10^3) of bits per second.

KHz

Kilohertz is a measurement of frequency. One KHz equals one thousand (10^3) samples per second.

L

LAN

A local area network is a computer network residing in a small and immediate area, such as a home or small office.

LFE

Low frequency enhancement is a speaker; also known as a subwoofer.

Line 21

Refers to a line of analog video in the vertical blanking interval. Closed captioning data is transmitted within line 21 using the EIA-608 specification. Closed captioning is a technology for televisions that assists hearing-impaired people by rendering text translations of the audio onto the television's screen.

link layer

The data link layer is layer 2 in the OSI reference model and defines the formatting of data to enable it to move through the network. See Chapter 3 for more details.

luminance

Chrominance and luminance are the components within a video signal (e.g., television). Luminance defines the intensity or brightness within the video.

 # M

MAC

Media Access Control is part of the data link layer (OSI reference model) that manages access to the physical media. Client devices such as STBs often have unique MAC addresses.

macroblock

Utilized in the MPEG-2 video compression format. A macroblock is a 16×16 pixel square (comprised of four 8×8 pixel blocks from the DCT stage). See Chapter 4 for more details.

Macrovision

A private company that has created content protection technology. Macrovision analog video copy protection system alters analog video coming out of a set-top box so VCRs are unable to create a copy of the original video.

MB

Megabyte—1 megabyte equals 1,048,576 bytes, or 2^{20} bytes.

Mbps

Megabits per second, or millions (10^6) of bits per second.

memory

Various types of memory (storage) devices (i.e., ICs) are utilized in computers and set-top boxes for storing data. The most commonly used memory devices today are DDR memory (volatile memory) and flash memory (non-volatile memory).

metadata

Descriptive information about digital bitstreams, such as data describing the programming within a digital television signal.

MHz

Megahertz is a measurement of frequency. One MHz equals one million (10^6) samples per second.

middleware

A software module that resides within a software stack and has software layers sitting on top and below it—typically UI software above and hardware drivers below. See Chapter 5 for more details.

modem

Modulator-demodulator—translates access network modulation protocols into consumer-usable protocols—for example, the cable broadband DOCSIS network into Ethernet.

modulation

The process of converting an electrical signal onto a carrier signal. The three key parameters in modulation are amplitude, phase, and frequency. A modulator device modulates a signal onto a specific carrier. A demodulator receives a carrier and converts it into a signal.

mosquitoes

Small, dynamic shadows sometimes seen around edges in digital video due to compression artifacts.

motion vector

Used in digital compression. In a group of pictures, the compression algorithm tracks changes and uses motion vectors to represent small movements of objects between frames. See Chapter 4 for more details.

MP3

An audio compression format (MPEG-1 layer 3) that has become popular with portable media players such as the Apple iPod.

MP@HL

MPEG-2 Main Profile and High Level, used for high definition digital television. See Chapter 4 for more details.

MP@ML

MPEG-2 Main Profile and Main Level, used for standard definition digital television. See Chapter 4 for more details.

MPAA

Motion Picture Association of America.

MPEG

The Moving Pictures Expert Group is a working group of ISO/IEC that develops audio and video compression standards.

MPEG-2

MPEG's Video, Audio, and System specification, Version 2. See Chapter 4 for more details.

MPEG-4

MPEG's Video, Audio, and System specification, Version 4. See Chapter 4 for more details.

MPEG-4 JVT

MPEG's Video, Audio, and System specification, Joint Video Team version. See Chapter 4 for more details.

MPEG-21

MPEG's multimedia framework and rights expression language standardization effort.

MPTS

A Multi-Program Transport Stream is an MPEG-2 transport stream or bitstream that contains multiple programs or channels of content multiplexed together.

mTFTP

Multicast Trivial File Transfer Protocol (RFC 1350) defines how file transfers can take place over a multicast network.

multicast

A networking technique that transmits data or messages from a single source to multiple destinations simultaneously.

multimedia

The integration of several media types: text, video, audio, graphics, voice, and data. Multimedia applications can be targeted for computers or televisions (via digital set-top boxes).

multiplexing

Takes multiple input bitstreams and interleaves them into a single output bitstream.

MVPD

Multi-channel Video Program Distributors include cable companies, telephone companies, and DTH service providers.

N

NAB

The National Association of Broadcasters (http://www.nab.org) is a trade association representing radio and television broadcasters.

NCTA

The National Cable and Telecommunications Association (http://www.ncta.com) is a trade association representing the cable television industry in the US.

nDVR

Network Digital Video Recorder is a DVR service in which the content is stored in the service provider's network instead of the client device.

net neutrality

The proposition that broadband service providers should not be allowed to block access to or charge different rates for using high bandwidth-consuming websites.

NTSC

National Television System Committee, also used in reference to the current standard definition analog television specification used in North America.

NTSC encoder

Encodes a digital television signal into an analog NTSC television signal.

NVOD

Near Video On Demand is a video on-demand service in which the user must wait a few minutes to see the content instead of viewing it instantaneously.

O

OCAP

Open Cable Application Platform is a Java-based middleware defined for the cable industry by CableLabs.

OEM

An original equipment manufacturer is a company that builds or manufactures products.

OOB

Out-of-band signals are sent on a channel separate from the in-band channel. The OOB channel typically carries command and control messages while the in-band channel contains the multimedia content.

OS

Operating system—the core software controlling a PC or STB.

OSI reference model

The Open Systems Interconnection reference model describes networking software as a stack of component layers, in which each layer communicates exclusively with the layers above and below it.

 P

packet

A group of bits containing a payload of data intended for a particular destination address. In IP, bitstreams are broken up into a series of packets for delivery across networks.

PAL

Phase Alternating Line is a format of analog television used in Europe and Asia.

PAT

Program allocation table is a component of the MPEG-2 system layer specification that lists the programs contained within a multi-program transport stream (MPTS).

PC

Personal computer.

PCM

Pulse code modulation is a digital representation of an analog signal that is sampled periodically.

peer-to-peer

A method of distributing media files from personal computer to personal computer over the Internet.

PES

Packetized Elementary Stream is the MPEG-2 system layer specification that defines how elementary bitstreams are broken up into packets and form a PES.

P-frame

Also known as P picture or Predictive frame, is part of the MPEG compression algorithm. A P-frame is constructed from parts of a previous I-frame, within a sequence of frames.

physical layer

Layer 1 in the OSI reference model; defines the physical medium over which communications will take place.

PID

Program identifier. Each elementary stream in an MPEG-2 transport stream has unique PID identifying packets that carry the stream.

PIG

Picture In Graphics is a technique used in GUIs whereby a scaled version of the video is contained within graphical elements.

PIP

In Picture In Picture, two video programs are showed simultaneously, one within the other.

pixel

A tiny square representing a single color and brightness. A digital image is made up of millions of individual pixels.

pixilation

Blockiness, sometimes seen in digital video due to compression artifacts.

PKE

Public key encryption is the use of asymmetric public-private encryption key pairs to encrypt messages and create digital signatures.

PKI

Public key infrastructure is the ecosystem of chains of digital certificates and trusted certificate authorities to support use of PKE.

PMT

The program map table is a table within the MPEG-2 transport stream that identifies which PIDs belong to which programs in the MPTS.

PON

Passive optical network. See EPON or GPON.

POTS

Plain old telephone services are the traditional landline telephone services.

PPV

Pay-per-view is a pay video service.

progressive scan

A technique in which a single frame of video is formed by rapidly drawing successive horizontal lines of the frame. See also interlace scan.

PSIP

Program and System Information Protocol is part of the high definition television broadcast standard that defines how information describing the various programs being broadcast such as channel call sign and program title.

PTS

The presentation time stamp tells a decoder when a frame of digital audio or video is to be presented to the user.

PVR

Personal video recorder is another name for a DVR.

 Q

QAM

Quadrature amplitude modulation is an RF modulation scheme used in cable to transmit digital signals over coax.

QCIF

Quarter Common Intermediate Format is a small video format consisting of 176×144 pixels.

QoS

Quality of Service is an important measure of guaranteed bandwidth sufficient to sustain digital video transmission without lost or delayed packets, which would result in decreased quality of the signal.

quadruple play

The ability to offer video, data, voice, and wireless services from a single service provider.

quantization

The process of converting continuous signals to discrete ones, typically translating all possible signal levels to a finite set from 0 to a power of 2.

 R

RAM

Random Access Memory is the primary memory component of PCs and STBs.

RBOC

A Regional Bell Operating Company is one of the original companies created from the breakup of AT&T.

REL

A rights expression language is a component of a DRM system that is used to define the various rights and business models for using content.

resolution

The number of pixels, either horizontally, vertically, or the product of the two, contained in a digital image.

RF

Radio frequency can refer to frequencies within a spectrum or RF video, which constitutes both analog and video signals modulated onto an RF carrier (e.g., channels 3 or 4).

RFC

Requests For Comments are a series of numbered Internet informational documents and standards.

RGB

Red, green, blue—a three-component color-space for pixels.

RIAA

Recording Industry Association of America is a trade group representing the US recording industry.

RLE

Run length encoding is a technique used in data compression.

ROM

Read Only Memory is used in PCs and consumer electronics to store core software elements that do not change for the lifetime of the product.

router

A network device that routes packets to devices or to other networks based on the destination address of the packets.

RSVP

The Resource Reservation Protocol (RFC 2205) is used to request bandwidth resources along a network path to ensure quality of service.

RTCP

The Real-time Transport Control Protocol (RFC 3605) defines the out-of-band control and information protocols for RTP.

RTP

The Real-time Transport Protocol (RFC 3550) provides a framework for transporting real-time data across IP networks.

RTSP

The Real-Time Stream Protocol (RFC 2326) provides a framework for streaming and control of media data across IP networks.

 S

sample rate

The rate at which an analog signal is sampled in time when being converted to digital.

SAP

Secondary Audio Program is a second audio signal transmitted along with the primary audio and is typically used for a foreign language translation of the program.

SAP

Session Announcement Protocol (RFC 2974) is a framework for broadcasting multicast session information described in SDP.

SC

A smart card (chip card, or ICC integrated circuit card) contains an embedded secure microprocessor with non-volatile memory. An SC is similar in size to a credit card and is often used for secure functions. Smart cards have been utilized by CAS systems for decrypting video services.

scan line

A single horizontal line of an analog television image.

SCTE

The Society of Cable Telecommunications Engineers (http://www.scte .org) is a non-profit professional association and standards body for the cable telecommunications industry.

SD memory

Secure Digital is a flash-based memory device packaged in a removable enclosure. SD is popular in portable devices (i.e., digital cameras) that easily interface with computers.

SDP

Session Description Protocol (RFC 2327) is a framework for describing media sessions (components, bitrates, formats, etc).

SDTV

Standard definition television can refer to either analog or digital television with a resolution of 480 horizontal lines of active video.

SDV

In switched digital video, a program is transmitted to a home only when requested, in contrast to broadcast video, which is delivered to all homes regardless of whether anyone is watching.

SECAM

Sequentiel Couleur Avec Memoire is an analog television format used in France, the former Soviet Union, and parts of Africa.

SIP

Session Initiation Protocol defines a framework for initiating, controlling, and ending interactive multimedia sessions, such as VoIP and video conferencing sessions across the Internet.

smart card

See SC.

SMPTE

The Society of Motion Picture and Television Engineers (http:// www.smpte.org) is a technical standards body for the motion picture industry.

SNMP

The Simple Network Management Protocol (RFC 3411-3418) is a layer 7 protocol used to manage and control network devices remotely.

S/P DIF

Sony Philips Digital Interface Format (also known as IEC 958 type II) is used for carrying audio information: PCM stereo and compressed digital audio streams (e.g., AC-3).

SPTS

Single Program Transport Stream is an MPEG-2 transport stream multiplex containing a single program. A program could consist of multiple audio, video, and data elementary streams.

SRTP

Secure Real-time Transport Protocol (RFC 3711) is a profile of RTP that encrypts the data streams and secures control messages.

SSH

The Secure Shell is a network protocol used to create a secure communication channel between network devices.

SSL

The Secure Socket Layer is a network protocol used to create a secure communication channel between network devices, typically for web sessions using HTTPS.

STB

A set-top box is a device that sits on top of a user's television set and presents audio and video to the TV.

S-video

Also known as separate video and S-VHS, an electrical interface that carries the video information on two separate signals: Y (luminance) and C (chrominance).

SVOD

Subscription Video on Demand is a VOD service for which the user pays for a series of on-demand content as opposed to paying for each title individually.

T

TCP

The Transmission Control Protocol is a fundamental element of IP that defines a reliable communication channel between networked devices via the ordered exchange of data packets, and confirmation of successful reception of packets. See also UDP.

Teletext

A data service that delivers text messages over broadcast television signals, used primarily in Europe.

terrestrial

Refers to television services broadcast from land-based radio towers, as opposed to satellite or cable.

TFTP

Trivial File Transfer Protocol (RFC 1350) is a lightweight version of FTP.

TiVo

The company that created the first DVR and associated service.

transcode

The process that converts from one compression format to another, such as from MPEG-2 to MPEG-4.

trick-play

The non-real-time playback of various speeds of video content, such as pause, fast-forward, slow-motion, and reverse.

triple play

The ability to offer video, data, and voice services from a single service provider.

U

UDP

The User Datagram Protocol is a fundamental element of IP that defines a best-effort communication channel between networked devices via the exchange of data packets without confirmation of successful reception of packets. See also TCP.

UI

User interface is the software element within a device with which the user interacts. Also see GUI.

unicast

The transmission of data packets across a network from a single source to a single destination.

upfronts

Television advertising purchased up front for an entire season before it starts.

UPnP

Universal Plug and Play is a set of network protocols for connecting consumer devices in home networks. The protocol list is created and maintained by the members of UPnP Forum (http://www.upnp.org).

 # V

VBI

Vertical Blanking Interval is the mechanism of the analog NTSC video signal indicating the start of a new video field and is also used to transport information such as closed captioning data.

VBR

Variable bitrate is a form of video encoding whereby the number of bits per second varies over time depending on the content, resulting in higher quality compression over CBR.

VBV

Video Buffer Verifier is used in MPEG-2 compression to model a buffer within the decoder where bits are stored until they are required for decoding.

VC-1

Microsoft's advanced video compression scheme that is standardized within SMPTE.

VCEG

Video Coding Experts Group is part of the ITU-T that helped develop the AVC/H.264/MPEG part 10 Advanced Compression Video codec.

VCPS

The Video Content Protection System is used to secure digital content on recordable media such as DVD+R and DVD+RW.

VCR

A video cassette recorder is an analog television recording device typically using VHS tapes.

VGA

Video graphics array is an analog video connection format primarily used for connecting personal computers to computer monitors.

VHS

Video home system is the format of magnetic tape cassettes used in VCRs for analog video recording.

VM

A virtual machine is a software module that provides a virtual execution environment that behaves like a standalone computer system but is executed by software. See Chapter 5 for more details.

VOD

Video on demand is a service from video service providers such as cable operators in which programs can be started and controlled (e.g., pause, fast-forward, rewind) instantaneously via a remote control.

VoIP

Voice over Internet Protocol is a telephony service using Internet Protocol from end to end.

VPN

A virtual private network is an extension of a secure network over the open Internet to another secure network or device.

 # W

watermark

A pattern or code introduced into a video signal to convey authorship and to thwart piracy.

widescreen

Content or televisions with an aspect ratio of 16:9.

WiFi

Wireless networking equipment and protocols based on the IEEE 802.11 standards and certified by the WiFi Alliance (http://www.wi-fi .org).

woofer

A subwoofer in a multispeaker surround sound system that reproduces only low frequency components of the audio signal.

 # X

XML

Extensible Markup Language is a general-purpose specification for creating descriptive languages for conveying data between diverse computer systems.

XrML

eXtensible Rights Markup Language is the rights expression language licensed by ContentGuard for use in MPEG-21 and other DRM systems.

Y

YUV

The brightness (Y) and two color difference (U and V) color-space used in digital video.

YPrPb

The brightness (Y) and two color difference (U and V) color-space and interface used in high definition television.

INDEX

4:3 aspect ratio, 101, 103, 280, 282
4C/5C copy protection, 236, 280
10/100Base-T, 280
16:9 aspect ratio, 101, 103, 280, 282, 319
480i video mode, 280
480p video mode, 280
720p video mode, 280
802.11x technologies, 165–168, 319. *See also* wireless (WiFi) technology
1080i video mode, 280
1080p video mode, 280

A

AAC (Advanced Audio Coding), 281
abstraction layers, 194–195
AC-3 codec, 281
access networks, 38, 47–49
active optical fiber networks, 47
ADSL (Asymmetric Digital Subscriber Line), 47, 281
advertisements
    advantages of, 259–260
    commercial, 4–5
    over-the-top services, 259
    telescoping, 28–29
advertising models, 27–29
AES (Advanced Encryption Standard), 214
AES (Audio Engineering Society), 281
airlines, 34
Akimbo service, 15
analog audio signal, 113
analog media, 104–105
analog output, 233–240
analog signals, 116
analog television, 105–124. *See also* television
    analog audio signal, 113
    audio signal, 113

color in NTSC signal, 111–112
    composite NTSC signal, 113
    digitization of, 113–124
    NTSC frame, 109–111
    NTSC scan line, 108–109
animation, 86
ANSI (American National Standard Institute), 281
API (Application Programming Interface), 281
application layer, 74–76, 79–80, 197, 281
application servers, 41, 43, 198–199
ARP (Address Resolution Protocol), 282
ARPU (average revenue per user), 19, 282
artifacts, 79, 104, 115, 133
ASIC (application specific integrated circuit), 136, 230, 231, 282
aspect ratio, 101, 103, 282
asymmetric cryptography, 220
ATIS (Alliance for Telecommunications Industry Solutions), 248, 282
ATM (Asynchronous Transfer Mode), 282
ATSC (Advanced Television Systems Committee), 153, 154, 185, 242, 282
ATSC tuner, 188
audio
    broken, 87
    compression, 144, 160, 291, 305
    mono, 113
    multichannel, 123–124
    network traffic and, 87
    secondary, 113, 313
    stereo, 106, 113
    streaming, 60, 86
audio digitization, 121–124

audio quantization, 122–123
audio sampling rate, 121–122
audio signals, 113, 114, 121–123
authentication
    described, 210
    DRM systems, 50, 218–223, 229, 236
    two-way, 50
A/V (audio/video), 282
avails, 5, 28
AVC (Advanced Video Coding), 244, 245,
    282–283

B

B2B (business-to-business) services, 36,
    61, 65, 86
B2C (business-to-consumer) services,
    61, 86
baby-bells. *See* RBOC
bandwidth
    broadband service, 17–18
    described, 283
    multicast *vs.* unicast, 85
    multimedia applications and, 86–87
    requirements for, 126–127
B-frames (bidirectional frames),
    134–141, 283
bidirectional frames (B-frames),
    134–141, 283
bidirectional networks, 4
billing system, 43
bitmaps, 283
bitrates, 8–9, 283
bits, 283
bits per frame, 137, 264–265
bits per pixel (bpp), 283
bitstreams, 78, 90, 114, 125, 215, 284
BitTorrent, 284
"black list," 236
block ciphers, 212–215
blockiness, 133
blog sources, 58
Blu-ray Disc, 157–158
bpp (bits per pixel), 283
bridge device, 284
Brightcove, 24
broadband, 284
broadband Internet access, 7–9
broadband service providers, 17–18

broadcast flag, 234–235, 284
broadcast video, 30–32, 58
broadcasts
    HDTV, 118, 152, 242
    SDTV, 45
    switched digital, 30–32
business applications, 32–34, 61
business communications, 33–34
bytes, 284

C

CA (Certificate Authority), 221–223,
    229, 284
cable access network, 49
cable companies, 2, 257–258
cable modem, 285
cable networks, 2–6, 37, 176–188, 258
cable telephony, 257–258
CableCARD, 180, 231, 247, 284
CableLabs, 285
CA/DRM software, 190, 195
CAPEX (capital expenditures), 61
carrier waves, 112–113
CAS (Conditional Access System)
    content security, 50, 215–216
    described, 285
    overview, 53–56
    references, 272–273
CAT5 (category 5 standard cable),
    162–164, 165, 285
CATV (Community Access Television), 285
CBR (Constant Bit Rate), 141–143, 285
CCI (copy control information), 237, 285
CCIR (Comite Consultatif International
    en Radiodiffusion), 116–121, 285
CCIR 601 standard, 116–121, 286
CCIR 656 standard, 286
CCITT. *See* ITU-T
CCK (Complementary Code Keying),
    166, 167
CE (consumer electronics), 286
CEA (Consumer Electronics
    Association), 242, 247, 286
CEPCA (Consumer Electronics
    Powerline Communication
    Alliance), 169
Certificate Authority (CA), 221–223,
    229, 284

certificates, 221–223
CF (Compact Flash), 286
CGMS–A (Copy Generation
   Management System–Analog),
   240, 286
channel change delays, 94–98, 263–270
channel zapping, 94–95
channels
   access control and, 217–218
   described, 286–287
   premium, 15, 224, 255
chrominance, 287
chrominance signals, 117–118, 287
CIF (Common Intermediate Format), 287
ciphers, 211–215, 229–231, 239, 287
ciphertext, 211–214, 217, 218, 287
cleartext, 211–214, 287
CLEC (Competitive Local Exchange
   Carrier), 287
client devices, 174–203
   advanced features, 200–203
   overview, 174–175
   routers/gateways, 175
   set-top boxes. See IP STBs
client-server sessions, 79–80
clock synchronization, 147–148
CMTS (Cable Modem Termination
   System), 287
coax cabling, 165, 171–172
codec, 287
coder/decoder, 287
coding redundancy, 129
color
   digital images, 101–103
   DTV, 101–103
   NTSC signal, 111–112
   RGB, 101–102, 312
   YUV, 102, 112, 320
color depth, 102, 103
color sampling, 118–119
color spaces, 101–102
Comcast, 4, 21–22, 28, 258, 277
commercial advertising, 4–5
commercial airlines, 34
composite video, 288
compression. See also DV compression
   advanced, 281
   audio, 144, 160, 291, 305

delays in, 264–266
lossless, 130
lossy, 130, 132
video, 9–10
computers. See PC
Condition Access System. See CAS
Consumer Electronics Manufacturing
   Association. See CEA
consumers
   described, 56
   getting content/products to, 2–7,
      24–25
   IPTV and, 56–60
   shift of power to, 26–27
content
   CAS-protected, 54–56
   copyright issues, 14, 68, 159, 224
   described, 38
   importance of, 260
   niche, 57
   non–real-time, 51
   on-demand, 27
   place-shifting, 26–27
   premium, 12–13, 16, 258
   pre-packaged, 39–40
   protecting, 50–52, 233–234
   real-time, 51–53
   time-shifting, 26
   tools for creating, 272
content aggregators, 25, 39–40,
   272, 288
content encoders, 42
content in the clear, 51
content owners, 288
content preparation, 42
content preparation system, 42, 43
content providers, 24–25
content reception, 42
content security, 50–56
content/headend, 38, 41–44
copy protection, 235–240. See also DRM
copyright issues, 14, 68, 159, 224
core network, 38, 40, 44–46
corporate communications, 33–34
CPPM (Content Protection for
   Prerecorded Media), 288
CPRM (Content Protection for
   Recordable Media), 238–239, 288

CPTWG (Copy Protection Technical Working Group), 288

CPUs (central processing units), 136, 178, 230

CRL (Certificate Revocation List), 222, 288

CRT (cathode ray tube), 106–107, 288

CSS (content scrambling system), 288

D

DAC (Digital to Analog), 178

DASE (DTV Application Software Environment), 289

data link layer, 74, 75, 303

Data Over Cable Service Interface Specification. *See* DOCSIS

data service, 203

datagram, 289

DAVIC (Digital Audio Visual Industry Council), 289

DBS (direct broadcasting satellite), 2–4, 260, 289

DCAS (Downloadable Conditional Access System), 230, 289

DCCP (Datagram Congestion Control Protocol), 289

DCT (Discrete Cosine Transform), 131–133, 289

DCT quantization, 131–133

DDR-SDRAM (Double Data Rate-Synchronous Dynamic Random Access Memory), 290

decoding buffer model, 148–149

decryption, 52–56, 97, 211–217, 268, 290. *See also* encryption

demod IC, 176, 188

demux, 290

DES (Data Encryption Standard), 212–214, 290

DFs (dependent frames), 265–266

DHCP (Dynamic Host Configuration Protocol), 246, 290

DHN (digital home networking), 162–174. *See also* home networks

CAT5 cable connections, 162–164, 165, 285

client devices. *See* client devices

coax cable connections, 165, 171–172

computer industry trends, 173–174

goals of, 165

host data services, 202

hybrid networks, 162–164

overview, 162–174, 186

personal computers, 173–174, 200–201

powerline communication (PLC), 164, 168–170, 172

remote control/diagnostics, 206

server functionality, 201–202

set-top boxes. *See* IP STBs

telephone connections, 164, 170–171

transmission mediums, 164–172

triple play service, 203–204, 316

video conferencing, 86, 205

wireless connections, 164, 165–168

diffserv (Differentiated Services), 89, 290

digital broadcast television, 153–154

digital cable television, 155

digital encoder, 290

digital home networking. *See* DHN

digital images, 100–105

digital media, 104–105

digital output, 233–239

digital receivers

DSP, 182–185, 186

first-generation, 176–180

hybrid, 186–188

PC-based, 185–186

second-/third-generation, 180–182

digital recording, 26–27

digital rights management. *See* DRM

digital signage, 33, 61–64

digital signage system, 61–64

digital signatures, 220–222, 230, 310

digital television. *See* DTV

digital video. *See* DV

Digital Video Broadcasting. *See* DVB

digitization, 113–124, 131

DirecTV, 2, 233, 277, 292

Dish Network, 277, 292

disk drive storage, 11, 12

display devices, 62–64

distance learning, 33

distribution, 56

distributors, 24–25

DLNA (Digital Living Network Alliance), 248–251, 290
DMA (Direct Memory Access), 182
DMIF (Delivery Multimedia Integration Framework), 291
DNS (Domain Name System), 246, 291
DOCSIS (Data Over Cable Service Interface Specification), 49, 151, 291
DOCSIS-based networks, 49
Dolby Digital, 281
Dolby Laboratories, Inc., 291
down-mixing, 291
drivers, 190–194, 291
DRM (digital rights management), 207–233. *See also* copy protection
  copyright issues, 14, 68, 159, 224
  described, 42, 195, 208, 291
  encryption methods. *See* encryption
  layer model for, 210–228
  need for security, 14–15, 208–210
  non–real-time content, 51
  overview, 51–53
  real-time content, 51–53
  references, 272–273
DRM containers, 42
DRM license server, 42, 52–53
DRM systems
  access control, 215–218
  authentication, 50, 218–223, 229, 236
  encryption, 211–215
  hardware, 229–231
  implementations, 228–233
  IP-based, 50
  layer model for, 210–228
  legal agreements, 231–232
  renewability of, 230–231
  rights management system, 224–228
  software, 229–231
DRM vendors, 232–233
DRM-protected content, 51–52
dropped packets, 77, 87–89, 96, 258
DSL (Digital Subscriber Line), 21, 47, 268, 292
DSL Forum, 251, 292
DSLAMs (Digital Subscriber Line Access Multiplexers), 41, 47, 97

DSM-CC (Digital Storage Media Command and Control), 151
DSP (digital signal processor), 182, 292
DSP digital receivers, 182–185, 186
DSS (digital satellite system), 292
DTCP (Digital Transmission Content Protection), 210, 236–238, 292
DTCP on Firewire/1394, 236–237
DTCP on IP, 237–238
DTH (direct to home), 292
DTLA (Digital Transmission Licensing Administrator), 292
DTS (Digital Theater Systems), 292
DTV (digital television), 99–160. *See also* television
  color in, 101–103
  compression. *See* DV compression
  described, 100, 292
  digital images on, 100–105
  digitization of analog television, 113–124
DTV broadcasts, 234. *See also* broadcasts
DV compression, 125–159. *See also* compression
  formats, 127–128
  improvements in, 9–10, 11
  MPEG-1 standard, 155–156
  MPEG-2 standard, 130–143
  MPEG-4 standard, 156–159
  MPEG-7 standard, 159
  MPEG-21 standard, 159
  need for, 126–127
  overview, 125–126
  removing redundancy, 129–130
DV equipment, 10–11
DV25 format, 127
DVB (Digital Video Broadcasting), 245–247, 293
DVB-IP services, 245–247
DVB-IPI specification, 94, 293
DVB-MHP (Multimedia Home Platform), 153, 196, 247
DVB-S (DVB-Satellite), 185, 293
DVB-SD&S (DVB Service Discovery and Selection), 246, 293
DVB-STP (DVB SD&S Transport Protocol), 246, 293

DVB-T (DVB-Terrestrial), 153, 185, 293
DVD burners, 234–235
DVD players, 153, 157–158
DVD video format, 152–153
DVD+R format, 239, 318
DVD-R format, 238
DVD+RW format, 239, 318
DVDs
    Blu-ray, 157–158
    burning, 234–235
    described, 293
    DRM restrictions, 209–210
    sampling rate, 118
D-VHS (digital VHS), 236
DVP-MHP (DVB Multimedia Home
    Platform), 247
DVRs (digital video recorders), 26–27,
    202, 293. *See also* PVRs

E

EchoStar, 2, 233
ECM packets, 53–55
ECMA (European Computer
    Manufacturers Association), 294
ECMs (Entitlement Control Messages),
    53, 217–218, 219, 293
EEPROM (electrically erasable
    programmable read-only
    memory), 179, 294
EFF (Electronic Frontier Foundation),
    235, 294
electronic program guide. *See* EPG
elementary stream (ES), 144, 295
EMMs (Entitlement Management
    Messages), 53, 217–218, 219, 294
encoders
    content, 42
    described, 294
    digital, 290
    NTSC, 178–179, 307
    PAL, 178–179
encoding, 137–139
encryption. *See also* decryption
    DRM systems, 211–215
    transport delays and, 268–269
encryption keys, 211–212, 216–221
enterprise video, 65–66
enterprise video systems, 65–66

Entitlement Control Messages (ECMs),
    53, 217–218, 219
Entitlement Management Messages
    (EMMs), 53, 217–218, 219, 294
entropy encoding, 139
EPG (electronic program guide),
    151–152, 178, 198–199, 270, 294
EPG portal, 60
EPON (Ethernet passive optical
    networks), 294
error correction, 294
ES (elementary stream), 144, 295
Ethernet cables, 64, 162, 245
Ethernet connectivity, 162–164,
    173, 297
Ethernet networks, 173
Ethernet standard (IEEE 802.3
    standard), 295
Ethernet switches, 47
ETSI (European Telecommunication
    Standards Institute), 169, 252
EULA (End User License Agreement),
    232, 295
Extensible Markup Language (XML),
    225–228, 319
external access, 202

F

facilities-based architecture, 38–56
facilities-based IPTV, 56
Fanning, Shawn, 209
FCC (Federal Communications
    Commission), 234–235
FDDI (Fiber Distributed Data
    Interface), 295
FEC (Forward Error Correction),
    176, 295
FFT (Fast Fourier Transform), 295
fiber to the curb (FTTC), 47, 296
fiber to the home (FTTH), 19–20,
    47, 296
fiber to the premises (FTTP), 296
filters, 295
Firewire technology, 295–296
flash memory, 179, 238, 296
FPA (front panel assembly), 296
frame relay, 296
frame types, 133–139

frames
B-frames, 134–141, 283
dependent, 265–266
described, 296
I-frames, 97–98, 133–141, 264, 300
interlaced, 107–108, 155
NTSC, 107–111, 120
P-frames, 107–108, 134–141, 186, 309
reference, 265–266
franchises, 20
frequency range, 121–122
FTP (File Transfer Protocol), 88, 296
FTTC (fiber to the curb), 47, 296
FTTC deployments, 47
FTTH (fiber to the home), 19–20, 47, 296
FTTH deployments, 47
FTTP (fiber to the premises), 296

G

gaming, 204–205
gateway device, 297
gateway/load balancer, 43
gateways, 175
GB (gigabyte), 297
Gbps (giga bits per second), 297
general purpose microprocessor, 178
GigE (Gigabit Ethernet) technology, 297
global secrets, 219–220
glossary, 279–320
Google Video Upload Program, 23
GOP (group of pictures), 136–137, 297
government communications, 34
GPON (Gigabit Passive Optical Network), 297
graphics, 86
graphics library, 195
grouping hierarchy, 136–137
GUI (graphical user interface), 230, 297
guide, 297. *See also* EPG

H

H.225 standard, 91
H.262/H.263 standards, 156
H.264 standard, 94, 157, 283, 298, 318
H.323 standard, 91, 205
HANA (High-Definition Audio-Video Network Alliance), 298

hard drive storage, 11, 12
hardware-based IPTV services, 15–16
hashes, 220–221
HAVi (Home Audio Video Interoperability), 298
HCNA (HPNA Coax Network Adapter), 171–172
HDCP (High-Bandwidth Digital Content Protection), 235–236, 298
HDCP on HDMI, 235–236
HDD (hard disk drive), 298
HDMI (High Definition Multimedia Interface), 235–236, 298
HDTV (high definition television), 298
HDTV broadcasts, 118, 152, 242
HDTV screens, 100–101, 120
headend
content captured within, 40
described, 31–32, 38
references, 273–274
headend/content, 38, 41–44
headers, 145
HFC (Hybrid Fiber Coax), 257–258
HID (Home Infrastructure Device) category, 250
high definition digital television. *See* HDTV
HND (Home Network Device) category, 250
home networks. *See also* DHN
advanced services, 203–206
described, 38, 50
mobility and, 204
network gaming, 204–205
remote control devices, 206
video conferencing, 205
Home Phoneline Networking Alliance (HPNA), 170–171, 172, 298
HomePlug Powerline Alliance, 168–169
horizontal sampling, 119–120
hospitality suites, 34
host data services, 202
HPNA (Home Phoneline Networking Alliance), 170–171, 172, 298
HTML (HyperText Markup Language), 195, 198, 299
HTTP (HyperText Transfer Protocol), 89, 246, 299

HTTPS (HyperText Transfer Protocol over SSL), 246, 299
hubs, 64
Huffman coding, 129
hybrid digital receivers, 186–188
hybrid networks, 162–164

I

IAB (Internet Architecture Board), 252
IC (integrated circuit), 175, 299
IDCT (Inverse Discrete Cosine Transform), 299
IEC (International Electrotechnical Commission), 157, 299
IEEE (Institute of Electrical and Electronics Engineers), 299
IEEE standards, 169
IETF (Internet Engineering Task Force), 89, 242–243, 252
iFILM, 24
I-frames (Intra frames), 97–98, 133–141, 264, 300
IGMP (Internet Group Management Protocol), 81–85, 96, 192, 246, 300
IIF (IPTV Interoperability Forum), 248
ILEC (Incumbent Local Exchange Carrier), 300
images
    computer-generated, 62
    digital, 100–105
    JPEG, 62
    quality of, 136
    resolution, 102, 153, 155, 237, 244
interlace scan, 300
interlaced frames, 107–108, 155
international IPTV deployments, 20–21
Internet access, 7–9, 260, 307
Internet broadband cable, 58
Internet Protocol. *See* IP
Internet standards organizations, 251–252
Internet telephony, 86
Internet television, 56–61. *See also* IPTV
    block diagram of, 56–57
    EPG portal, 60
    system architecture, 56–61

vs. facilities-based IPTV, 56
    web portal, 58, 59
Internet-based television services, 5–24
    IPTV service models, 5–6, 7
    new content providers, 5, 6, 23–24, 28, 256–257, 259
    new distributors, 5–7, 23, 24
    over-the-top service providers, 5–6, 12–18, 66–258–259
Internet-related sites, 278
intserv (Integrated Services), 89, 300
IP (Internet Protocol), 2, 70, 300
IP client devices, 174–188
IP equipment, 30, 33
IP networks, 69–98
    described, 64
    IP suite, 70–80
    multimedia over, 85–98
    multimedia over IP, 85–98
    unicast *vs.* multicast, 81–85
IP packets, 93–94
IP protocols, 51, 190–193, 195
IP stacks, 71–72, 79
IP STBs (IP set-top boxes). *See also* STBs
    CAS systems, 53–56
    content preparation, 42
    described, 64, 301
    DRM license server, 52–53
    DSP digital receivers, 182–185, 186
    examples of, 11–12
    first-generation receivers, 176–180
    hardware architectures, 175–189, 190, 230–231
    hybrid digital receivers, 186–188
    management module, 195
    manufacturers, 274–275
    operating system for, 190–193
    output signals, 64
    overview, 175–176
    PC-based digital receivers, 185–186
    second-/third-generation receivers, 180–182
    server functionality, 201–202
    software architectures, 188–200
IP suite, 70–80
IPG (interactive program guide). *See* EPG
iPod, 14, 17, 26, 204

IPTV (Internet Protocol television). *See also* Internet television
  advertising models for, 27–29
  business applications for, 32–34, 61
  client devices. *See* client devices
  delivery methods, 254–260
  described, 2, 301
  driving forces behind, 6–11
  early deployments of, 254–255
  effect on business of television, 1–34
  features of, 26, 60–61, 197, 255–256
  future of, 260–261
  international deployments, 20–21
  operational costs, 30, 33
  operational efficiency from, 30–32
  references, 271–278
  solutions vendors, 22–23
  standardization efforts, 241–252
IPTV broadcast networks, 38–39
IPTV service models, 5–6, 7
IPTV services
  hardware-based, 15–16
  PC-based, 13–15
IPTV system model, 35–68
  business projects, 61–66
  digital signage, 61–64
  enterprise video, 65–66
  facilities-based architecture, 38–56
  Internet television architecture, 56–61
  overview, 36–38
  P2P networks, 66–68
IPTV system networks, 39
IPv4 (Internet Protocol version 4), 300
IPv6 (Internet Protocol version 6), 301
IRTF (Internet Research Task Force), 252
ISDN (Integrated Service Digital Network), 301
ISMA (Internet Streaming Media Alliance), 243–245, 301
ISO (International Organization for Standardization), 73, 301
ISOC (Internet Society), 252
ISR (Interrupt Service Routine), 300
ITU (International Telecommunication Union), 156–157, 205, 252, 301
iTunes service, 13–14, 17, 27

ITU-T (ITU Telecommunication Standardization Sector), 42

J
Java, 302
jitter, 302
JPEG (Joint Photographic Experts Group), 302
JPEG format, 127
JVT (joint video team), 157. *See also* AVC

K
KB (kilobytes), 302
Kbps (kilobits per second), 302
keys. *See* encryption keys
KHz (Kilo Hertz), 302

L
LAN (local area network), 303
layer model, 71–73
legal agreements, 231–232
levels, 139–141
LFE (low frequency enhancement), 124, 303
license agreements, 231–232, 295
Line 21, 303
link layer, 303
load balancer, 43
load balancing, 44
loop lengths, 21
lossless compression, 130
lossy compression, 130, 132
low frequency enhancement (LFE), 124, 303
luminance, 303
luminance signals, 112, 113, 117–119

M
MAC (Media Access Control), 303
macroblock, 303
macroblock matching, 135–136
Macrovision, 239, 304
MB (megabyte), 304
Mbone (Multicasting backbone), 85
Mbps (megabits per second), 304
Media Center, 173–174, 200
media codecs, 196

media data, 93–94
media servers, 42–43, 275
media software, 275–276
memory
   DDR-SDRAM, 290
   described, 304
   DMA, 182
   EEPROM, 179, 294
   flash, 179, 238, 296
   non-volatile, 179–180
   RAM, 311
   ROM, 179, 312
   volatile, 179
metadata, 105, 304
MHz (Mega Hertz), 304
microprocessor, 178–180, 186, 193,
   205, 292
Microsoft Media Center PC, 16–17
Microsoft Windows Media DRM
   (MS-DRM), 233
middleware
   described, 304
   references, 276
   set-top box, 190, 195–196
   vendors for, 22–23
middleware layer, 195–196
military communications, 34
MIMO (multiple-input multiple-
   output), 167
mitigation, 270
MMU (Memory Management Unit), 193
MND (Mobile Handheld Device)
   category, 250
mobility, 204
MoCA (Multimedia over Coax Alliance),
   171–172
modem, 304
modulation, 304–305
mono audio, 113
mosquitoes, 133, 305
motion JPEG format, 127
motion vector, 305
movie studios, 2, 3, 12, 13, 288
Movielink, 17–18
Moving Picture Experts Group. *See*
   MPEG
MP3 format, 305
MP3 players, 156, 204, 305

MPAA (Motion Picture Association of
   America), 209
MPEG (Moving Picture Experts Group),
   10, 130, 305
MPEG bitstreams, 78, 139, 215, 228
MPEG-1 format, 127, 155–156
MPEG-2 decoder, 139, 176, 178, 179
MPEG-2 format, 130–155
   CBR, 141–143
   DCT, 131–133
   described, 127, 305
   entropy encoding, 139
   frame types, 133–139
   improvements to, 158–159
   levels, 139–141
   motion estimation, 133–139
   packetized elementary streams,
     145–146
   profiles, 139–141
   program streams, 146–149
   run length encoding, 139
   subsampling, 130–131
   system layer, 144–152
   transport streams, 149–152
   VBR, 141–143
   video formats based on, 152–155
MPEG-2 transport packages, 93–94
MPEG-3 format, 159
MPEG-4 format, 156–159
   advantages of, 156
   described, 128, 156, 305
   improvements to, 158–159
   ISMA and, 245
MPEG-4 JVT, 306
MPEG-5 format, 159
MPEG-6 format, 159
MPEG-7 format, 159
MPEG-21 format, 159, 227–228, 306
MP@HL (MPEG-2 Main Profile and
   High Level), 155, 305
MP@ML (MPEG-2 Main Profile and
   Main Level), 155, 305
MPTS (multiprogram transport
   stream), 149–150, 306
MS-DRM (Microsoft Windows Media
   DRM), 233
mTFTP (Multicast Trivial File Transfer
   Protocol), 88, 306

MTU (Maximum Transmission Unit), 75
multicast, 306
multicast protocol, 81–85
multicast services, 36–37
multicast streams, 37, 43, 96
multichannel audio, 123–124
multimedia, 85–98, 306
multimedia applications
    bandwidth, 86–87
    network traffic, 87
    real-time data flow, 87
multimedia over IP, 87–98
multiple digital decodes, 202–203
multiplexing
    described, 306
    PES packets, 148–149
    statistical, 142–143
multitasking support, 193
music sharing, 36, 209
MVPD (Multi-channel Video Program
    Distributors), 2, 306

N

NAB (National Association of
    Broadcasters), 307
NagraStar (NDS), 233
NAL (Network Abstraction Layer), 94
Napster, 208, 209
National Television System Committee.
    See NTSC
NCTA (National Cable and
    Telecommunications Association),
    307
nDVR (Network Digital Video
    Recorder), 307
net neutrality, 260, 307
Netflix, 27
network bandwidth. *See* bandwidth
network delays, 268–269
network equipment manufacturers,
    273–274
network gaming, 204–205
network layer, 74, 75, 76–77
network operators, 183–185, 204,
    276–277
network traffic, 87
networks
    access, 38, 47–49

active optical fiber, 47
bidirectional, 4
cable, 2–6, 37, 176–188, 258
congestion, 85
DOCSIS-based, 49
EPON, 294
Ethernet, 173
HFC, 257–258
IP. *See* IP networks
LAN, 303
P2P, 66–68
PON, 47, 294, 297
satellite, 2–6, 37, 176–188
SDV, 37–38
WAN, 40
wireless, 164, 167–168, 319
new content providers, 5, 6, 23–24, 28,
    256–259
new distributors, 5–7, 23, 24
niche content, 57
NOC (networks operations center), 64
noise, 104, 105, 170
non–real-time content, 51
non-volatile memory, 179–180
NTSC (National Television System
    Committee), 106–108, 307
NTSC encoder, 307
NTSC frames, 107–111, 120
NTSC scan line, 108–109
NTSC signal
    color in, 111–112
    composite, 113
    quantization, 114–116, 120–121
    sampling, 114–116
NTSC tuners, 185
NTSC/PAL video encoder, 178–179
NVOD (Near Video On Demand), 307
Nyquist theorem, 115, 117, 122

O

OCAP (Open Cable Application
    Platform), 196, 247, 308
ODRL (Open Digital Rights Language),
    227–228, 306
OEM (original equipment
    manufacturer), 176, 180, 194, 308
OFDM (Orthogonal Frequency-Division
    Multiplexing), 42, 166–167

OMA (Open Mobile Alliance), 228

on-demand content, 27

OOB (out-of-band) signals, 308

OpenCable CableCARD, 180, 231, 247, 284

OPERA (Open PLC European Research Alliance), 169

operating system (OS)

   described, 308

   optimization, 16

   for set-top box, 190–193

OS layer, 192–193

OSI (Open System Interconnection), 73, 308

OSI reference model, 73–80, 308

out of order encoding, 137–139

output signals, 64

over-the-top Internet television system, 56–61, 258–260

over-the-top service providers, 5–6, 11–18, 66–258–259

over-the-top services, 258, 259

over-the-top services facilitators, 16–17

P

P2P networks, 66–68

P2P publishing, 66

P2P software, 66

P2P (peer-to-peer) technology, 66–68, 209, 309

packetization, 145–146

packetized elementary streams.
   See PES

packets

   described, 308

   dropped, 77, 87–89, 96 , 258

   ECM, 53–55

   IP, 93–94

   PES, 145–148

packs, 147

PAL (Phase Alternating Line), 106, 308

PAL/NTSC video encoder, 178–179

Parker, Sean, 209

passive optical networks. *See* PONs

passwords, 202, 206

PAT (program allocation table), 151–152, 308

PC (personal computer)

   cable television over, 257

   DHN and, 173–174, 200–201

   network gaming, 204

   over-the-top services, 11–17

PC-based digital receivers, 185–186

PC-based IPTV services, 13–15

PCM (pulse code modulation), 309

Peer-to-Peer. *See* P2P

personal computer. *See* PC

PES (packetized elementary streams), 144–146, 309

PES headers, 145–146

PES packets, 145–148

P-frames (progressive frames), 107–108, 134–141, 186, 309

Phase Alternating Line. *See* PAL

phoneline technology. *See* telephone line technology

physical layer, 73–75, 309

PID (program identifier), 150, 151–152, 309

PIG (Picture in Graphics) technique, 309

PIP (Picture in Picture), 309

pixel depth, 102, 103

pixels

   color and, 101–102

   color sampling, 118

   described, 100, 309

   digital images, 100–101

   macroblocks, 135

   subsampling, 131

pixilation, 310

PKE (public key encryption), 220–223, 284, 310

PKI (public key infrastructure), 223, 310

PLC (powerline communication), 164, 168–170, 172

PMT (program map table), 151–152, 310

PON technology, 47–49

PONs (passive optical networks), 47, 294, 297

POTS (plain old telephone system), 122, 310

powerline communication (PLC), 164, 168–170, 172

powerline technology, 164, 168–170
PPV (pay-per-view), 54–56, 310
PPV purchase process, 54–56
premium channels, 15, 224, 255
premium content, 12–13, 16, 258
presentation layer, 74, 75
private keys, 220–223, 230, 236
processing power, 127
profiles, 139–141
program allocation table (PAT),
    151–152, 308
program map table (PMT), 151–152,
    310
program streams, 146–149
programs, 146–147
progressive frames (P-frames), 107–108,
    134–141, 186, 307
progressive scan, 310
protocol stacks, 70–71, 73, 88–89,
    246
PSI data, 178
PSIP (Program and System Information
    Protocol), 151–152, 310
psycho-visual redundancy, 130
PTS (presentation time stamp), 310
public key encryption (PKE), 220–223,
    284, 310
public key infrastructure (PKI), 223,
    310
PVRs (personal video recorders), 202,
    311. See also DVRs

Q

QAM (quadrature amplitude
    modulation), 49, 155, 311
QCIF (Quarter Common Intermediate
    Format), 244, 311
QoS (Quality of Service), 89, 258, 311
QPSK modulators, 49
quadruple play, 311
quantization
    audio, 122–123
    DCT, 131–133
    described, 311
    NTSC signal, 114–116, 120–121

R

radio frequency (RF), 203, 312

RAM (Random Access Memory), 311
RBOC (Regional Bell Operating
    Company), 311
real-time content, 51–53
Real-time Control Protocol (RTCP), 91,
    244, 246, 313
real-time data flow, 87
Real-time Transport Protocol (RTP),
    90–91, 94, 244, 267, 313
RealVideo 10 format, 128, 157–158
receivers. See digital receivers
redistribution control, 234–235
reference frames (RFs), 265–266
references, 271–278
REL (rights expression language),
    225–228, 312
remote control, 206
remote diagnostics, 206
removable media copy protection,
    238–239
residential gateway, 49–50
residential homes, 58
resolution
    described, 312
    digital display, 100–101
    horizontal, 120
    images, 102, 153, 155, 237, 244
    vertical, 102
RF (radio frequency), 203, 312
RFC (Requests For Comments), 312
RFC Editor, 252
RFs (reference frames), 265–266
RGB color space, 101–102, 312
RIAA (Recording Industry Association of
    America), 312
rights expression language (REL),
    225–228, 312
rights management, 224–228. See also
    DRM
ringing, 133
RLE (run length encoding), 312
ROM (Read Only Memory), 179, 312
routers, 64, 175, 312
router/switch/hub, 64
RSVP (Resource Reservation Protocol),
    89–90, 312
RTCP (Real-time Control Protocol), 91,
    244, 246, 313

RTP (Real-time Transport Protocol),
90–91, 94, 244, 267, 313
RTSP (Real-Time Streaming Protocol),
92–93, 244, 246, 313
run length encoding, 139

S

sampling
horizontal, 119–120
overview, 114–116
vertical, 119–120
sampling rates, 115, 121–122, 313
SAP (Secondary Audio Program), 313
SAP (Session Announcement Protocol),
93, 313
satellite networks, 2–6, 37, 176–188
scan lines, 106, 108–109, 110, 313
Schumpeter, Joseph Alois, 261
SCR (System Clock Reference), 147–148
SCs (smart cards), 54, 180, 231, 313
SCTE (Society of Cable
Telecommunications Engineers),
314
SD (Secure Digital) memory device, 314
SDP (Session Description Protocol), 93,
244, 314
SDTV (standard definition television),
314
SDTV broadcasts, 45
SDV (switched digital video), 37, 314
SDV networks, 37–38
SECAM (Sequentiel Couleur Avec
Memoire), 106, 314
secure broadcast video, 58
security. *See also* encryption
hardware, 231–232
need for, 208–210
passwords, 202, 206
server functionality, 201–202
servers
application, 41, 43, 198–199
digital signage system, 64
DRM license, 42, 52–53
media, 42–43
VOD, 42–43, 51–54, 81–82
session layer, 74, 75
set-top boxes. *See* IP STBs; STBs
shared secrets, 219–220

signal conditioning, 42
SIP (Session Initiation Protocol), 314
Slingbox STB, 26
smart cards (SCs), 54, 180, 231, 313
SMPTE (Society of Motion Picture and
Television Engineers), 157, 314
SNMP (Simple Network Management
Protocol), 246, 315
SoC (System on a Chip), 182–186, 188
software drivers, 193–194
software stacks, 70–72, 188–191, 196
sound. *See* audio
source, 56–57
source load, 85
S/P DIF (Sony Philips Digital Interface
Format), 315
spatial redundancy, 129
SPTS (single program transport
stream), 149–150, 315
SRMs (system renewability messages),
236
SRTP (Secure Real-time Transport
Protocol), 315
SSH (Secure Shell) protocol, 315
SSL (Secure Socket Layer) protocol, 315
standards organizations
Internet, 251–252
links to, 277–278
statistical multiplexing, 142–143
STBs (set-top boxes). *See also* IP STBs
CA/DRM software, 190
CAS systems, 53–56
described, 315
drivers, 190, 193–194
graphics library, 195–196
hardware, 188
middleware, 190, 195–196
operating system, 190
Slingbox STB, 26
web components, 190
stereo audio, 106, 113
storage requirements, 126
stream ciphers, 213–214
streaming audio, 60, 86
streaming media, 88–89
streaming video, 86
subsampling, 130–131
subscriber database, 44

super headend, 40, 41–44
S-video (separate video), 315
SVOD (Subscription Video on Demand), 315
switched digital broadcast, 30–32
switched digital video. *See* SDV
switches, 64
system tables, 151

T

TCP (Transmission Control Protocol), 76–80, 316
TCP/IP, 217
Telco access network, 38, 47–49
Telcos
    broadband service, 9
    deployments by, 19–20
    future of IPTV, 256–258
    international, 20–21
    as IPTV distributor, 18–23
    over-the-top Internet television, 58
telephone line technology, 164, 170–171
telephone operating companies. *See* Telcos
telephony service, 203
telescoping advertisements, 28–29
Teletext, 316
television
    analog. *See* analog television
    business of, 1–5
    digital. *See* DTV
    digital broadcast system, 153–154
    digital cable, 155
television content. *See* content
television service market, 24–27
television services, 5–24
temporal redundancy, 129
terrestrial, 152, 293, 316
TFTP (Trivial File Transfer Protocol), 88, 316
thick client architecture, 197–200
thin client architecture, 197–200
timestamps, 90–91
TiVo service
    described, 15, 316
    time-shifting capabilities, 26–27
    video blogs, 24
transcode, 316

transport delays, 266–268
transport IC, 176–180
transport layer, 74, 75, 77–79
transport streams, 94, 149–152, 236, 246
trick-play, 316
triple play service, 203–204, 316
tuners, 176, 180, 185, 188, 202, 203

U

UDP (User Datagram Protocol), 76–80, 267, 317
UDP/IP, 217
UI (user interface), 317
unicast, 58, 317
unicast protocol, 81–85
unicast services, 36–37
unicast streams, 43, 64
UPA (Universal Powerline Association), 169
upfronts, 317
UPnP (Universal Plug and Play), 242, 249, 317
user interface (UI), 60–61, 71, 317

V

VBI (Vertical Blanking Interval), 110–111, 240, 317
VBR (variable bitrate), 141–143, 317
VBV (Video Buffer Verifier), 318
VC-1, 318
VC-1 format, 128, 157–158
VCEG (Video Coding Experts Group), 318
VCL (Video Coding Layer), 94
VCO (video central offices), 40–41
VCPS (Video Content Protection System), 238–239, 318
VCR (video cassette recorder), 209, 234, 239–240, 318
VDSL (very high bit-rate DSL), 47
vertical sampling, 119–120
VGA (video graphics array), 318
VHO (video hub offices), 40
VHO block diagram, 45–46
VHO capacity, 44
VHO sites, 40
VHS (video home system), 318

VHS recorders, 236, 318
VHS tapes, 209–210, 318
video. *See also* DV
  broadcast, 30–32, 58
  composite, 288
  enterprise, 65–66
  network traffic and, 87
  streaming, 86
  S-video, 315
video blogs, 23–24
video central offices (VCO), 40–41
video compression, 9–10. *See also*
  compression
video conferencing, 86, 205
Video Content Protection System
  (VCPS), 238–239
video gateway, 202
video hub offices. *See* VHO
video iPod, 17, 26
video on demand (VOD) services, 13, 81,
  307, 315, 318
video service, 203–204
video streaming protocols, 87–93
VideoGuard system, 233
Viiv Technology, 173–174
virtual machine (VM), 196, 318
VLC (variable length coding), 139
VM (virtual machine), 196, 318
VOD (video on demand), 37, 318
VOD content, 58
VOD movies, 37, 52, 81–83
VOD servers, 42–43, 51–54, 81–82
VoIP (Voice over Internet Protocol), 122,
  257, 319
volatile memory, 179
VPN (virtual private network), 319

W

W3C (World Wide Web Consortium),
  251

WAN (wide area network), 40
watermarks, 240, 319
wavelet/fractal format, 127
web browsers
  application layer, 79
  embedded, 197–198
  IP STBs and, 195
web components, 190
websites, 58, 278
widescreen, 319
Widevine Virtual SmartCard, 233
WiFi. *See* wireless (WiFi) technology
Windows Media format, 128
Windows XP Media Center, 173–174,
  200
wireless devices, 64, 165–168
wireless networks, 164, 167–168, 319
wireless (WiFi) technology, 164,
  165–168, 319
WMV9 technology, 157
woofer, 319

X

X.509 format, 222
XML (Extensible Markup Language),
  225–228, 319
XOR operations, 214
XrML (eXtensible Rights Markup
  Language), 210, 225–227,
  320
XTV service, 15

Y

YouTube, 24, 261
YPrPb, 320
YUV color space, 102, 112, 320